# Raised In Pimp City

# Book Credits

Because nothing phenomenal is done by one individual alone.

Danica Taylor Law: Inspiration and direction

Dr. Jamie Gates: Book review and mentorship

Dr. Mychal Odom: Book review and mentorship

Demetrius Harrison: Cover art & interior illustrations

Devon Bakaly: Editor

Chris Gorrie: Formatting

Published by Ariginal One Publishing

This book and my life's work is dedicated to four very important people in my life growing up: Lawrence Smith, Richard Wilson, William Waggoner, and Kenny McKnight. They all lost their lives before they were able to make it out of the trap. They were more than best friends to me, they were my brothers. Now, they are the reason that I push so hard to prevent others from falling victim to the streets.

I will love them, always.

This book is also dedicated to all of the other people that have been wrapped up in this game. I love you, and I understand. Please know that you can make it out and thrive.
You are not stuck.

I would also like to give very special thanks to Danica Taylor Law. Without your encouragement and guidance, this book wouldn't exist.

# Table of Contents

# Foreword

The first time I got wind of Armand was about two years ago, when someone shared a "Take'em 2 Chuuch" episode with me. I was in awe. You see, the year before that, as I tried to step into finding out who I was outside of the game; as I started sharing my experiences and truths, and as I dug into my healing and understanding that this issue was so much deeper than what the world was trying to make it, as I tried to understand how to share my truth in a movement and environment that wasn't very accepting of what I felt my truth was, I became fearful of continuing to speak my truth so boldly and stepping out of the victim role. The whole world around me was telling me to hate my ex-folks, the whole world was telling me I was a victim, the whole world was holding my narrative and I began to feel more trapped than I did when I was in the game. Then, I saw Armand's video. Immediately I felt a wave of hope come over me—I felt like it was safe for me to share my truth *completely*. Instantly, I became empowered, knowing that I wasn't crazy for feeling like I had exercised my choice to become deeply involved in the game. I didn't feel shame for the friendships I still held with my ex-wifeys and ex-folks anymore. I didn't feel so alone.

The healing you have brought to me personally, as a "survivor of human trafficking" has been immense and more powerful than any other healing aspects of my journey. I realized very quickly, unfortunately, that when our narratives don't fit certain boxes or perspectives in this "anti trafficking movement," we are no longer valued or respected and our insight is no longer top priority. Armand helped give me courage and validated that those closed minds don't dictate my progress, capability, or importance. Armand has shown me the importance of forgiveness. He represents so many men in my life that have hurt me, torn me down, and tried to destroy me, while simultaneously also helping me to decipher all those men, showing me a way into understanding their stories, a way to forgive them by seeing their pain. Armand's pain, which he has so openly shared with the world, has helped me understand those who have hurt me. By being accountable for past actions, by living every single day to make up for the pain that was caused, by living each day to prevent even one young person from feeling the loss and pain we have all been subjected to, Armand has shown me the path to true healing.

To those allies who are reading this: please know that these words and these emotions are valid, necessary, and needed to open the gates of change in the community. Please know that whatever your personal feelings are towards this man (and others you identify to be like him), they have to be put aside at least momentarily so you can read the following pages with an open heart and an open mind. If you consider yourself an ally in ending this issue of domestic sex trafficking, you *must* embrace this dive into a full scope of understanding. When you begin to understand the things in this book, you will begin to understand the depth of this issue—which will open the door for all of us to fully figure out how to start healing and working towards ending this epidemic of exploitation.

To those who have no idea what this game is: thank you for wanting to understand. Thank you for taking time to read this man's personal journey, and for recognizing him—and so many others—as human and understanding that this issue goes deeper into humanity than we could ever imagine. We are all responsible to take time to understand stories like this.

To those who are still in the game, or want to be in the game: I see you and value you and know that your journey is unique. I need you to know you're not alone. Read this book, and let it be a gateway into your healing and consider giving yourself the opportunity at the life you deserve. Read this and know you are never too far gone, to get back to where you truly want to be. Read this and know that your life has value beyond this game, beyond the streets, beyond the hustle, and know that even though we weren't dealt the most positive hand, this book is the hope for us all that there is always the possibility of transformation, breaking cycles, and powering through obstacles to come out as forces to be reckoned with on the other side.

*Raised in Pimp City* gives a one of a kind dive into the deeply rooted and vulnerable realities of what we think we know of "the game." This book also gives the hope that there is an opportunity to continue fighting the devastating way of life we have become accustomed too. Armand, you give hope—which is exactly what our community needs most.

Your sis always,

Jaimee Johnson
CEO of Sisters Of The Streets

# Armand King

As you read this book you will learn about several individuals and real life experiences that have helped to mold me into the person I am now. Far from being finished in my growth and development, I feel that it is important to take you from the beginning; to guide you through the set of circumstances that led me to compose this book. Let me start by introducing you to a group of high school friends growing up in the mid-nineties, which was the beginning of San Diego's pimp and prostitution explosion. These are real individuals and their stories are true. They are some of my best friends and it would be an injustice to tell my story without including some of theirs.

My experience comes from over 20 years of being directly involved in the world of Pimping, Prostitution, and gangs. Most of those years I was on the side of those involved in the gang activities and pimping—since 2012 I've been on the side of helping to end these activities. I was brought up in a two-parent home until I was about eleven years old. My home life was chaotic and verbally abusive throughout my entire young life. My family was living in poverty, but I wasn't really aware of that for much of my youth. Both my mother and father were firm believers in working for themselves and entered into numerous entrepreneurial ventures. My mother was a seamstress and worked from home; my father would sell cleaning products, and any other legal product he could buy into and feel good about. Eventually, he bought a restaurant from a friend who was going out of business. I continuously learned and observed everything that they were doing. My father had a mantra: "Love your own and do for self." He would repeat this to me regularly. My father would always talk the talk, but not walk the walk. My father had a serious infidelity problem and couldn't seem to stop having extra-marital affairs with different women. After the third affair was discovered, my mother stopped counting. The arguing and fighting between my mother and father were a regular occurrence. Night after night, my sister and I would sit in our room and listen as our parents would yell at the top of their lungs at each other. At some points it would become physical but nothing too crazy. My father wasn't the physical type. At some point my mom would become physical and took swings at my father, but he maintained restraint and would not hit her back. Instead, he would break pictures, smash furniture, and destroy what he could to express his anger. I would often wake up in the middle of the night to arguments or intense conversations that no kid should witness.

When I was eleven years old, my mother finally had enough and kicked my father out of the house. I'm not certain at what point after the official separation that it started, but my mom began to fall off of her motherly duties. One day, as I routinely reached into my mother's coat pocket in search of a stray dollar, I felt something strange, something different. I immediately pulled it out—I did not recognize it, but it was something that would ruin the great bond my mother and I had for a long time to come. In this period of my young life nearly every interaction with my mother was full of high emotions, heated tempers, and drama. I could tell I that I was losing my mother and it hurt.

For the next six months my mother and father were separated. Throughout that time my father would terrorize our household by breaking in and stealing everything we owned and destroying my mother's clothes. One night I was awakened by noises coming from my mother's room. I knew that my mother was out and was curious about who possibly was up fumbling around in her room. "Is this my Dad again?" I thought to myself. Not being able to hold my curiosity back I proceeded to enter my Mother's sewing room where my fears were confirmed. "What are you doing here?" I yelled at my Dad. Without a second thought my father reached down, picked me up and proceeded to throw me to the ground causing me to hit my head and momentarily lose consciousness.

About a year after my parents had separated, I started junior high school. My Junior High was located in a heavy gang-infested area. It was around this time that I began to admire the gangsters. There was no mystery what I admired about them and why I was drawn to them. All of the "cool kids" were gangsters. All of the pretty girls liked them. My older cousins that I looked up to were all in gangs. I was constantly around people that were the epitome of the gangster music I had grown to love and idolize. I saw these people as a much-needed security blanket; they were able to provide me with some form of structure and identity.

Upon arriving home from school one day, I noticed a huge lock box on our doorknob with an eviction notice. Over the next two years, my mother, my 13-year-old learning-disabled sister, and two female cousins (11 and 2 years old at the time), were homeless. Sleeping at whatever friends' house that my mom could find. My mother had to not only deal with taking care of her own two children, but she had also taken on the responsibility of caring for her sister's children. My Aunt, who was constantly stuck in a toxic street lifestyle, was in no condition to care for her own children. During this time of transition we would sleep on my mom's friends' living room floors or any other available areas of their homes. We lived in three different homes over the next two years. The first was a friend of my mom's, the second was a distant family member, and the third was a male friend of both my mother and dad. By the time I reached the third location I had given up on thinking that we were going to ever get our own place. My sister and cousins were always hungry and often left alone. At times, I remember stealing food from Jack in the Box's drive thru window as it was passed from the cashier to the customer so I could take it back to my family. By the age of thirteen, I had already come to realize that I had to take care of my family in any way that I could. A typical day for the girls was sitting around whatever house we were staying in and entertaining each other with games and television while I spent my time wandering around the neighborhood, smoking weed and looking for things to get into. I eventually discovered a vacant apartment in the building that I was staying in—I broke in and made it into my private refuge. That is where I would stash my marijuana paraphernalia and playboy magazines.

From age twelve to fourteen, being a blood from the neighborhood gang was all that I could see myself doing. Being a young black male growing up in Southeast San Diego, there were few alternatives to occupy time or mind. I wanted to be a blood because my surroundings were blood territory. If I had grown up in a Crip neighborhood, I would've wanted to be a Crip. The choice had nothing to do with a preference of one over the other, it only had to do with the area that you grew up in and the friends that you were around. Throughout my entire three years attending Junior High school my grades were never higher than a D. I ran around the school without correction or intervention. Every year I was passed onto the next grade level regardless of how horrible my grades were. I never attended summer school or even attempted to fix my grades, and the school didn't care. Never once did a teacher intervene and try to help me. Never was I asked, "Is everything was ok at home? Did I eat today? Why was I so disturbed?" At one point I was kicked out of two of my class periods and had to sit in timeout in the counselor's office, and yet and still there was no outreach. It was as if they just wanted me to hurry up and get out of their hair. One day in the beginning of 9th grade, the school got their wish when I was involved in a gang fight with a rival Filipino crip. This fight got me expelled and I was out of school for nearly a year.

Within that year, my mother was finally on her feet and our family moved out of the hood and into an apartment in a rural part of the city. I was completely out of place in this new, primarily white, high school. Still dressing in gang attire, I stood out like a sore thumb. Although my family was no longer homeless, we were still extremely poor. I quickly began selling pre-rolled marijuana joints at school to make money. I was a natural hustler. Selling marijuana was something I had grown up watching family members do for as long as I could remember. My aunt and uncle—two of the biggest influences in my life—were two of the biggest suppliers in Linda Vista and had taught me the ropes without even knowing they were doing it. It was not hard at all for me to pick up what seemed like the family business and run with it. I turned all of the money over to my mom, never telling her where I got it. She never asked. She figured if she didn't know she wouldn't feel guilty.

Within a month of attending this new school in this strange environment I became acquainted with a new friend, Roy. He was another black male who was street savvy. Roy was a little different than the other kids I was used to hanging around. He dressed like a preppy, Ivy League kid from the suburbs. Polo, Nautica, Tommy Hilfiger, and Eddie Bauer were the style and Roy made sure I knew that. Although Roy grew up in the same neighborhood as me, he saw being a gangster as "old school" and negative. To Roy, being a pretty boy and a lady's man was a better way of life. You could have fun and not have to worry about dying or going to jail—a mentality that I quickly absorbed. In reality, I really was a good kid who did not want to have all of the drama that came along with gangbanging. By the age of 14, I had already lost a handful of friends to gang homicides and had watched my older cousins go in and out of prison.

Roy quickly became my best friend. He introduced me to his own circle of friends: Richard, Lawrence, Kenny, Will, Asa, Chris, and Demitrius. All young black males around the same age and in the same grade. This was the beginning of a bond that would only be broken through death; a bond that became the driving force behind the man I am today.

Now, at 37 years old, I am currently the co-founder of the aptly named non profit organization "Paving Great Futures." Paving Great Futures is a grassroots organization that was birthed out of my heart and mind when I realized that death and incarceration was continuing to plague my community. I also realized that I was playing a major part in continuing that cycle. I had up until that time continued to condone pimping, prostitution, and all types of illegal hustle. I was not helping the next generation of men and women that were looking up to me. I was duplicating myself, just like the generation of gangsters and drug dealers before had done to me and my friends. "This has got to stop" I thought. Once I realized how big my influence over the generations after me could be, I felt that it would be my responsibility for the fate of those that followed in my footsteps.

Now, fueled by my experience in the streets, I serve as a shepherd to guide others out of the prison pipeline, criminal activity, and the pimp and prostitute subculture that I know all too well. After the loss of several of my closest friends to murder, prison, and drugs I decided my entire life would be dedicated to helping anybody that I might be able to reach. I feel that my mission in life is a path set out for me by God, with my only goal to save other lives from the many pitfalls that I have witnessed and been a part of myself, growing up in underserved communities in San Diego.

Why human sex trafficking? As a young teen I grew up in an era where over half of my peers had either become directly involved with or heavily influenced by pimping and prostitution. All of my closest friends became pimps, myself included. As I grew older, I watched as lives were impacted by the biggest human sex trafficking (HST) epidemic ever in the history of America—only surpassed by the Transatlantic Slave Trade that founded this country. For close to two decades this epidemic took over the streets of America. It hit its climax and then slowly started to fade away from its prime when human sex trafficking started to become a huge topic of discussion. I have witnessed many HST survivor advocates, law enforcement officers, religious groups, and others being misinformed about this epidemic. As a result, I see a need for clarity regarding the issue of *Domestic Human Sex Trafficking*. I understood how detrimental this could be to the many people that are involved with and affected by HST. For that reason I sought to help in any way that I could—to get the right information to as many people that would listen with an open mind and heart. The more I became involved in the HST survivor advocacy field, the more I realized that my voice and perspective was not only rare, but practically nonexistent. There were no other former Pimps that were out there actively trying to help. This has to change. In order to help change a situation this enormous, there has to be as much understanding and information as possible. I had no other choice, but to become an active part of the solution.

For many years I was misguided by the streets and helped mislead others, not realizing the power of my actions. I am now trying to rewrite my past, and helping others pave a greater future.

# Human Sex Trafficking

Human Sex Trafficking and Sexual Exploitation comes in a variety of forms and styles. Far too often I hear the subject of human sex trafficking spoken about as if all of the various types fit neatly under one umbrella, to be looked at as the same issue and problem. I, on the other hand, know that each variant is a uniquely different classification of HST. I would be doing you a disservice if I claimed to be an expert on Human Sex Trafficking as a whole, since it is an incredibly complex construct. Let me clarify what I am claiming to be an expert in, because as I mentioned before even domestic human sex trafficking can be many different things. It's important to keep in mind that "domestic" means the trafficking was done here in the US. For example Familia Trafficking, LGBTQ Trafficking, Child Trafficking, Forced Sex Trafficking, Brothels, and Massage Parlors are all different forms of trafficking that are found here in the US. I am not an expert on any of these forms of trafficking or sex work—I am aware of their existence, but that is the extent of my knowledge on those subjects. My sole expertise is what I would label "Urban Domestic Sex Trafficking" and "Black Street Gangs." To make myself very clear, I am an expert in the subculture of pimping and prostitution here in America. This form of sex trafficking is usually birthed out of the many impoverished communities throughout the U.S. This form usually pertains to minority men that facilitate, and woman (of varying demographics) that become prostitutes.

At the age of 16, I was indoctrinated into the culture of pimping and prostitution. It has been over two decades since my entry into this subculture, and in that time I've met and befriended hundreds of pimps and prostitutes from all over the United States. Now in the professional world, as the COO of paving great futures I am still heavily connected to the streets and intentionally keep the pulse on what is currently happening within the subculture of pimping and prostitution. Recently, I've heard negative comments about how I am still actively engaging with people in the game. My thoughts on that matter is that I have to be with and around the people that I am trying to help out of these dangerous lifestyles in order to reach them. It is also imperative that I stay current on the trends, language, and methodology so that my knowledge can remain current and relevant to the times. In these rapidly changing times, if you do not stay current your knowledge, you may quickly become irrelevant and outdated. Unfortunately, I have seen this happen with many people within the sex trafficking advocacy community.

In my opinion, pimping and prostitution and human sex trafficking are two different things. If someone would've asked me if I was involved in sex trafficking ten years ago I would have adamantly said, "No." I would've described sex trafficking as a foreign issue with girls being held captive. I would have thought about the movie "Taken." The term Human Sex Trafficking is only about five years old for me. When I was active in the game, I knew what we were involved in as "Pimpin and Hoin." Even today, when I ask an individual involved in the game about human sex trafficking they have no idea what that is—or that what they are doing can legally be described as such. The awareness of human sex trafficking is becoming known to the urban street pimp because more people are being charged with sex trafficking, as opposed to the usual pimping and pandering charge of the past.

The difference between pimping and trafficking comes down to one major factor: *the use of force*. The short definition of sex trafficking is, "the use of force, fraud, or coercion to get someone to sell sex in exchange for something of value." When I first became aware of this definition I disagreed. The game that I was familiar with was anti-force, and anti-fraud. That "coercion" piece is where the line becomes thin between trafficking and the traditional pimping that I am an expert in. I will discuss this in detail later on in this book.

# My Heart & Intentions

Wholeheartedly, let me express that yes, pimping is wrong. The manipulation of and encouraging someone to sell their body is wrong. I recognize pimping is horrific and a completely negative way of life. I will continually mention this throughout this book because I want that to be extremely clear. I truly do not want to be perceived as trying to gain sympathy for the exploitation that leads to pimping or minimizing the damage that is caused by pimping. There's a certain level of power, privilege, and culpability involved in pimping that can't be denied. I want to make sure that every reader understands that before we dig in any further.

As you read through this book I humbly ask for you to open up your mind and your heart. My intentions are not for you to become sympathetic towards those victimized into pimping. I really want you to understand not only me myself personally but the thousands of people that I know that come from my same background and social demographics across America. As you read please know that I acknowledge that a sympathetic ear towards those victimized into pimping comes from more than just telling the longer, more complicated history of exploitation in black, brown, and marginalized communities. From telling stories of how racist and class-biased social structures demean and diminish and leave few options, to pointing out the cost of social sin and cycles of dysfunction that play out in the lives of particular individuals— sometimes across generations—I really want you to know that I, Armand King, am taking complete ownership of my actions as a man who has victimized people; I have led men and women into becoming pimps and prostitutes. Even women that I did not directly turn out, I did influence to get into the game. My actions were wrong and by no means justified. I recognize my sinful past, and I am completely owning up to it. As you will read later, my life has completely turned around and I live out every waking moment striving to not only right my wrongs, but to help others from going down the path that my peers and I once traveled.

This is more than a book to me. This is not simply a dictation of historical facts of my personal opinion based research. This entire book has been a spiritual journey for me. Not only am I confessing to things that I previously thought would never come out, but by going through this writing process I am tapping into thoughts that I never even recognized within myself. There are areas of the game that I never bothered addressing or understanding that I have now dissected. Before writing this book I already understood that the lifestyle I grew accustomed to was wrong, but through this deeper reflection I have been brought to my knees in repentance. I don't know where my karma meter stands but I will spend the rest of my life striving to make my good deeds outweigh the evil deeds of my past.

One of the purposes of this book is for you to see what it was like for me to merge into the lifestyle of pimping so that you can have a deeper understanding. With that being said, to any survivors of the game, and human sex trafficking: please accept my deepest apology for anything that I have done in this game and anything that I may say that offends you. It is not my intention to hurt or trigger. You have my utmost respect and admiration for still standing tall. To anyone that I have personally influenced into the game: please understand that I was lost in my youth and did not understand the damage that I was inflicting on you.

## The Evolution of Pimping and Prostitution

Evidence of prostitution is found as far back as the Bible. It is said to be the world's oldest profession. We don't know the exact moment when a man realized he could make a profit off of prostitution or exploitation, but we do know that some form of human trafficking—sex and labor—has taken place in almost every region of the world as far back as documentation can tell us.

In my opinion, pimping in the United States, although overlooked as the source, is directly a result of the European invasion of the Americas and the West Indies. The indigenous people of this region were often bought and sold amongst the

European invaders for the sole purpose of sexual service. This behavior and business model only increased with the enslavement of the African people, being trafficked to the new world for physical servitude. There were slave camps established with the sole purpose of breeding women as products of sexual service. There are many written documents of these activities taking place during and post-abolition of the American slave trade. One of the sources of this information is from the author and historian Robert William Fogle in his book, *Time on the Cross*. Along with slave breeding and trading for sex amongst European slave owners, systems like Plaçage of French and Spanish slave colonies only furthered the launch of the domestic sex trade. These activities were the foundation of pimping and trafficking that we see today.

In the past century we have watched pimping and pandering fluctuate in popularity and style in urban communities within the United States. Throughout the early thirties and forties pimping started to become more socially acceptable in the black communities. Being a prostitute or having a prostitute was viewed as a social profession. This was not only the case in black communities, but in white communities as well. The Mafia would run and utilize brothels and gambling spots where the Johns/Tricks would come and enjoy a drink and a sexual escapade with a working girl. These "Johns" were frequently politicians and law enforcement officers, along with the common working man. This business continued to expand in the United States and in the urban communities. In 1967 New York eliminated massage parlor license requirements, which was an invisible permission slip that allowed them to turn into brothels. Nevada started to regulate the already existing prostitution houses that they had in existence during the 1970's. In 1971, The Mustang Ranch established itself as the first legal brothel in Nevada. Prostitution at this time was not on the decline, if anything it was becoming more acceptable in the male-dominated business world, yet remained underground at the same time.

Meanwhile, pimping and prostitution was on a major rise in the urban communities. Not just as a business, but as a brand, idea, and image of success. The seventies had the biggest impact on the urban pimp culture, by far. This was the time when pimps became the inner-city superhero. They were admired by children, women, and men. The style of a pimp's clothes, cars, and women started to become a sought after look. Pimps of this time would wear extravagant hats and clothing. Furs, matching clothing from hat to shoes, and the bigger and brighter the better was the common theme with cars and clothes. Expensive brands were sought after to show their style and level of success. Hair was a badge of honor and was usually done up in fancy slick styles. The pimps of that time would often have their women wear similarly matching clothes, especially when going out to events or on special occasions. Other men in the neighborhood would admire the vision of a pimp, surrounded by his women. The seventies' image of a pimp is still the current image. If you conduct a Google image search "pimp," at least the first twenty pictures will be of people dressed like pimps from the seventies. You don't see any images of brothel owners. No images of adult magazine owners. You see mostly black males, typically dressed in pimp attire dating back to the seventies. The seventies' impact on society's image of a pimp was astronomical. There is no debate that this was the biggest movement of urban community pimping and prostitution.

Urban community pimping nearly ended during the eighties and early nineties almost solely because of the introduction of crack cocaine and gang banging. However, urban pimps began to reemerge in the late nineties, led primarily by youth from the inner cities who had felt the horror of drugs and gang life and knew that this was not a prosperous lifestyle for them. Gangs and drugs meant death or jail. Left without mentors, guidance, and stuck in impoverished communities, these young males reached back and brought the seventies pimp era back to life—this time with a new millennial twist. Instead of the extra glamorous, flamboyant look of the seventies, these young men could be found in tennis shoes and white t-shirts. This change in apparel is primarily based on the current influence of the Hip Hop culture and "street" look. The classier, new urban pimp would wear dressier attire: European designer brands, dress suits, derbies or brim hats, snakeskin or alligator shoes, and furs. The late nineties through the early 2000s had been the rebirth of the seventies for pimping and prostitution. Both males and females found identities in this reborn era. For over a decade, getting caught by law enforcement through pimping and prostitution seemed much harder than selling drugs, while making money off it it seemed much easier.

I believe that this era of pimping was even bigger than the one of the seventies. Although the style of the seventies and rules of conduct came from that era, the actual mainstream explosion was nowhere near what came in the late nineties and 2000s. I personally witnessed entire communities of young males and females move towards some level of commercial sex. If a girl wasn't a prostitute walking the blade, she was an exotic dancer, webcam girl, escort, or madam/pimptress. Young men, whether they were nerds in school or the cool gang member, began to pimp or became interested in trying it out. This was not the case in previous years within urban communities. With the growth of internet and many online sex sites, becoming a prostitute was easier than ever before. So easy that girls began to realize that they really didn't need a pimp. Many girls began to leave their pimps and began prostituting themselves. Sites like backpage.com and craigslist.com made it easy to sell sex for money. Posting ads became the thing to do.

With the major internet boom and oversaturation of men and women getting into the game, the game inevitably started to change. Many people realized that the pimp and prostitute life wasn't for them and made their exit around 2010. Many girls who stayed in the life had taken on more dominant roles in selling their bodies. They accepted the role of independent sales woman, also known as being a "renegade." This was once really looked down upon, primarily because the pimp subculture did not permit it. Being a renegade was against the unspoken law. Working girls and pimps would enforce this by harassing the renegades, often times talking trash, name calling, and sometimes physical harassment was the norm. Fewer and fewer women worked the blades as the internet became a fast-growing and safer means of prostitution.

As female mentality started to change, more pimps began to stop pimping. Many of those that remained were no longer in control as they once were. Oftentimes pimps were starting to take percentages of a girl's earnings. Taking percentages and making deals is totally contrary to the rules of pimping; if you were even thought to be doing this by other pimps you would be viewed as weak, not "truly" pimping, and poisoning the game. The more traditional pimp was once again becoming extinct. Another emerging development was that even traditional pimps were starting to become one-woman men—beginning to have more of a boyfriend-girlfriend relationship with their main prostitute. She remained working as a lady of leisure, taking care of the bills and his needs, no different than a spouse that makes all or most of the money for the home. By 2012, those left in traditional pimp and prostitute roles were nearly extinct.

For almost fifteen years pimping and prostitution exploded around this country with no major legal backlash. This shifted around 2012 as human trafficking became a hot-button issue. Since 2011, there have been three major federal indictments linking urban street gangs to prostitution in the city of San Diego alone, all of which had over twenty individuals, both male and female. In recent years there has been a major nationwide push on awareness and prosecution of participants of commercial sex. Although the awareness push seems to be focused in all areas, the prosecution side seems to only target urban areas and predominantly black males and the poor. Unfortunately with social media platforms like Facebook, Twitter, and Instagram, young misguided black males have recently found it to be a tool to use towards presenting themselves as a pimp. Often this is exaggerated or completely false to who they really are. All of which have become the evidence needed to indict.

# Chapter 1: Dig to the Roots

Dear Devon,

Nephew before I begin, let me start off by telling you that I love you. I'm not just saying that because that's what people are supposed to say, but because I really love you with all my heart. You remind me of myself and my friends when we were your age. The time that we have spent with each other recently has felt really good. I miss you right now. You are my little buddy. I hate the fact that you will not return my calls or texts. All I've been trying to do is be there for you. I've been trying to fill in for your Mom who isn't teaching you to stay out of the streets, but is instead enabling you to dive deeper into this lifestyle, and this culture. I've been trying to teach you the things that your Dad hasn't been teaching you because he is choosing to act like you don't exist—a feeling I know all too well.

Devon when I look at you and the life you're living out, I can see the pattern. The same damn pattern I saw with my friends and myself. I know it's cliché to say, but I've been right where you are. I fear that if things do not change in the course of your life right now, that you will end up in the continuing cycle of death and incarceration that has plagued the black community for a long time. A plague that started even before I was born.

I need you to see Devon! I need you to know! I want you to have an opportunity to make it past the traps laid out by powers bigger than both of us. This pen cannot truly capture the pain that I feel right now. The loneliness that I have in my heart sitting here at 37 years old with almost every person that I called a best friend or brother dead.

I really wish that you were sitting in front of me right now, so I could say these things directly to you. So I could tell you about the lifestyle of a hustler, gangs and pimping. I know that I've been trying to recently, but I also know that I played a role in making you think that this lifestyle was cool early on in your life. I too am growing into a man. Brought up without the proper guidance and opportunity to succeed. I am lucky to be alive. My misconceptions of what it means to be a man and a good person had me traveling down a path of destruction. Please take heed of what I am trying to teach you. The lessons and knowledge that I had to learn the hard way can help you to avoid the regret and torment that I live with daily.

I write this letter to you at this time based off of the recent information shared with me. I have been told that you were caught with the gun. I was also told about you getting jumped. When I received this information my heart was struck. I have seen this movie before. As a child raised in a culture infested with gang activity, I unfortunately know all too well where this has come from and where this can lead. Unfortunately, I was born in the 80's when the black community in San Diego was hit hard by crack cocaine. My elders were crackheads and the world around me seemed as though everything had gone mad...

# Crack Cocaine

*Crack became popular in the 1980's due to its psychopharmacological properties and it has been called the 'most addictive drug on earth.' Crack cocaine's introduction into major cities in the United States was gradual, first it appeared in large cities like Miami and Los Angeles in the early 1980's and appeared later in cities like Chicago (Curtis, 2003). The availability of street drugs prompted Congress to take action regarding drugs in America, leading to the passing of the Federal Anti-Drug Abuse Act of 1986 which was passed at the peak of the crack cocaine movement. Crack allowed for consumers to utilize a cocaine based substance at substantially lower prices than powdered cocaine substance (Blumstein & Jonsson, 2003). Smoking crack cocaine was a movement that swept across the United States and has had a great impact on American society (Curtis, 2003).*

Crack Cocaine affected almost every family that I knew in my community. As a child, I remember all of my Uncles and Aunties being heavy crack users and my older cousins selling drugs. My mother would help them every now and then when they fell on hard times. One of my Aunts had fallen so deep into her addiction that she was no longer able to take care of my cousin. My Grandmother had to step up to the plate—like many other Grandmothers in my community around that time—and ended up taking in my cousin. At that age I didn't truly understand the detriment of the crack epidemic.

It wasn't until a few years later that the effects of the epidemic were brought home to me. Around the age of 11 my crack-addicted Aunt gave birth to another child. Since my Aunt was still not in any condition to take care of any children, my mother found herself running into a crack house one night to rescue the newborn. Right around that same time, my Grandmother decided to move to the East Coast, so the cousin that she was taking care of also came to live with us. Now with both cousins living with me, I was able to witness firsthand how one drug addict in a family can quickly and directly affect everybody else.

# The End of the Crack Era

Crack cocaine led to what I like to call the "Genocide Era of urban America." The introduction of crack cocaine into the poor urban cities of America in the mid-eighties hit like a natural disaster. It destroyed numerous families, sent thousands to prison, and wrecked the lives of those who crossed its path from the mid-eighties to the early-nineties. In my opinion, the inner cities of America have yet to see another drug of its magnitude. No, it is not totally eradicated, but its popularity and disastrous effects have lessened tremendously.

During its decade plus reign, people from impoverished cities used crack cocaine as a tool. For some, it was a tool to get high and escape the realities of the ghetto. This drug was highly addictive, offering a short but intense euphoria. It is, to this date, the strongest form of cocaine. To those who weren't addicted, crack cocaine offered an employment opportunity and a means to earn a living. Not just an average living either—crack cocaine enabled many to earn wages equivalent to an upper-middle class working person. To those able to avoid addiction, crack became a way to live a better life than their normal, impoverished day-to-day existence.

Crack's introduction into the inner city affected many of the street organizations. The Bloods and Crips were formed after the downfall of the Black Panthers, primarily to protect their communities from racist attacks. This mission was detoured once crack cocaine hit the scene. From the late seventies through the eighties, crack cocaine and guns created an atmosphere of murder and money within gangs. Crack became a means to make money, and with that money came power and control. Growing up in a part of the city that was influenced by gangs was normal for me. It had been that way since I was old enough to remember. There were

6

unwritten rules and protocols that you had to adhere to. Rules like which parks you were allowed to be in and the people you were permitted to socialize with. If you didn't follow these rules, you could face physical harm and even lose your life. You don't really think about how crazy that is as a young person growing up in it. It's just life to you. The murder rate in the inner cities began to rise as gangs began to fight for profitable territory. These situations birthed rivalries that still exist today.

Although those involved in the crack epidemic used the drug as a means of escape, in reality the drug led to death and destruction. Homelessness, violence, drug-addicted children, the foster care system, and incarceration skyrocketed. President Nixon's "War on Drugs" led to a government crackdown on those possessing and selling crack cocaine. The number of black and brown individuals from the inner city began to grow enormously in the prison system. Some like to call this period the birth of mass incarceration in America. Simply being a gang member could add time onto any criminal sentence. Combine jail, murder, and poverty to the label of "gang member" and a generation that is turned away from entertaining the idea of becoming involved in gangs and crack is born.

By the mid-nineties, crack cocaine users and sellers began to diminish. Not only was selling the drug beginning to lose its appeal due to stricter laws, the drug's attraction to new users was drastically decreasing due to the fact that there were now thousands of examples of the results of using:

*Drug trafficking, the availability of crack, and the Federal Anti-Drug Abuse Act led to mandatory minimum prison sentencing of dealers which has been a controversial issue. Originally the sentencing for crack versus cocaine was 100:1, meaning the amount of crack versus the amount of powder cocaine needed to establish a mandatory minimum prison sentence (Blumstein & Jonsson, 2003). For example, possession of three grams of crack would mandate the same prison sentence as 300 grams of powder cocaine. Sentences for crack are 44% harsher than sentences for powder cocaine (Gill, 2008). Researchers indicated that the mandatory minimum prison sentencing was racially motivated and specifically targeted Blacks (Blumstein & Jonsson, 2003; Gill, 2008; Hartley & Miller, 2010). Black males, between the ages of 26 to 34, reported using crack cocaine more than any other racial and gender combination (Peters, Williams, Ross, Atkinson, & Yacoubain, 2007) and according to Hartley and Miller (2010), 85% of offenders arrested for crack cocaine were Black. Blacks made up a vast majority in most crack cases thus receiving the mandatory minimum prison sentencing more than any other ethnicity. According to Gill (2008), mandatory sentencing did not reduce the amount of drug trafficking into the United States. Instead it turned state level offenses into federal crimes, created strain on families by imprisoning violators for long periods of time, and impacted minorities "resulting in vastly different sentences for equally blameworthy offenders" (Gill, 2008, p. 55). Some states, such as North Dakota, Louisiana, Texas, and Connecticut have repealed or adapted their mandatory minimum sentencing and implemented drug court programs or drug treatment programs for offenders who received the mandatory minimums years ago (Gill, 2008).*

In my own life, several members of my family were addicted to crack. Witnessing the effects of the drug firsthand from when I was only six years old, deterred me from using or selling it. As a kid, I never physically saw the drug, but I knew that it was the reason my aunt or uncle were "crazy" as my parents would say. They never really hid the fact that my aunt or uncle were addicts. They talked openly about it, however they never really explained how they got hooked on it.

Growing up in the nineties, being a "crackhead" was a joke and something kids would say to talk down to other people. In urban communities affected by the crack epidemic, kids would use the word "crack" as an insult. "Your mom's a crackhead," and "You smoke crack," are a couple that I remember. The sad thing was that

8

a lot of these kids' mothers did "smoke crack." Many of these children were born with crack in their system. I grew up alongside many "crack babies," although I didn't realize where their problems came from when I was young. I just saw them as kids with learning and/or behavioral problems. Sometimes they were kids with no noticeable problems at all. Now, as an adult looking back I can see why many in my generation were as badly behaved as we were— why many joined gangs and became ruthless killers. Crack left parents unable to parent and their children born with a chemical imbalance in their brain.

The devastating effects of crack cocaine on the black and brown communities brewed a generation of people that would never go back to this as a means of escape—neither as a source of income, nor to use. Yes, there still remains a few isolated pockets of crack dealers and users, but nowhere near the same amount that existed during its height. With crack cocaine becoming extinct in the inner cities, many young African Americans had to figure out a new means of making money. The underlying conditions that created the crack epidemic in the first place were never corrected. The communities still were underserved, stuck in poverty, and lacking positive role models more than ever before. Many children were growing up in foster care or raised in single-parent homes, usually raised by the mother and or grandmother. Options to lead a successful life still seemed invisible. By the late nineties and early 2000's, the youth raised during the crack era were becoming young adults. Many had to take on the responsibilities of adulthood at an early age. The children of the crack era needed to be able to provide food, clothing, and shelter for themselves and their own families. Unfortunately, without proper guidance and mentors to direct these young adults to a successful path, many resorted to an illegal occupation that had thrived previous to the gang and crack epidemics. The seventies pimp game was reborn.

# The Crack in the Game

Once the seventies wrapped up, crack cocaine hit the inner city like a tornado in the Midwest. Families were destroyed in masses from coast to coast. Its effects on the pimp game were just as detrimental. There were pimps with more money than they knew what do with, and emotionally destroyed women, both of which were extremely susceptible to this new narcotic on the streets. The effects of crack hitting the streets and the introduction of "gangbanging" in the inner city was a nearly fatal blow to the game. "Gangbanging" not in the sexual sense, but the activity of an urban street gang member participating in the gang. Even the pimps that weren't addicted found it hard to maintain a prostitute that was addicted. Once drugs of that nature are introduced into the equation, the drug becomes the real pimp because it is in control. The man has to compete with the overwhelming power of the drug. Once a person is addicted to crack cocaine they no longer have the same loyalty or respect for anyone or anything that they may have had previously to their addiction. Before addiction, the pimp would be nearly 99% sure that all of a prostitute's earnings were coming back to him. Once a prostitute was addicted, the percentage became 99% sure that he wasn't receiving all of the money. The pimp was no longer first on her mind. The drug was.

From the eighties to the early nineties gangbanging and drugs (mostly crack) owned the communities. Yes, there were still pimps and prostitutes in the communities, but they were no longer as prevalent as in the seventies. The new role model was the gangster and the drug dealer. The public media began to promote and glamorize gangbanging and drug dealing as it had done with pimping in the seventies. No longer was conscious or positive hip-hop promoted. Gangster rap was primarily pushed by record executives and the music industry. By the end of the eighties, gangbanging had spread across America, taking over the inner cities' black and brown populations like an infectious disease. Thousands of people were killed due to gang violence—mostly young men.

By the mid-nineties crack had nearly faded completely out of the black community. However, gangbanging became so deeply rooted that there is still no visible finish line today, although it has steadily slowed down from what it was in the late eighties and early nineties. Both drugs and gangbanging were cracked down on by law enforcement and new laws and policies. The 1980's saw the passage of four major anti-drug bills: the Comprehensive Crime Control Act of 1984, the 1986 Anti-Drug Abuse Act, the 1988 Anti-Drug Abuse Amendment Act, and the Crime Control Act of 1990. The California three strikes law enacted in 1994, as well as California gang injunctions enacted in the 80's, created the necessary tools the judicial system needed to incarcerate gang members. The selling of crack cocaine and gang-related crimes were sending people to jail for decades at a time. American prisons began to fill up at alarming rates.

## Inner-City Gang Evolution

The word "gang" can be used and viewed in many different ways. There are biker gangs, the Italian mafia, White supremacists, Latin gangs, and rap crews that can all be referred to as a "gang." When I use "gang" in this book I am referring to mainly black urban street gangs such as Bloods and Crips.

The following is an accurate description from my experience and knowledge of both gangs that I am referring to. The Bloods are primarily, though not exclusively, an African American street gang founded in Los Angeles, California. The gang is widely known for its rivalry with the Crips. They are identified by the red color worn by their members and by particular gang symbols, including distinctive hand signs. The Crips are also a primarily African-American gang. They were founded in Los Angeles, California in 1969 mainly by Raymond Washington and Stanley Williams. What was once a single alliance between two autonomous gangs is now a loosely connected network of individual sets, often engaged in open warfare with one another. Its members traditionally wear blue clothing, a practice that has waned somewhat due to police crackdowns on gang members.

Having been born in 1981 and raised in the urban areas of San Diego, I have been overly exposed to gang life and activity. Almost all of my male cousins, all of the friends I grew up with, and myself were in some way affiliated with a gang, whether as a full-fledged gang banger, a member, or affiliated by association. Many of these individuals had solidified their gang involvement or affiliation by the time they were in Junior High School. In urban communities, most young men and women had already accepted their neighborhood as the place that they represented. This didn't mean that they were a criminal or violent, as is often depicted as a "gang member." They simply represented the area that they called home. Growing up in Southeast San Diego you cannot avoid being associated with gangs in some way. It is easy to just be a "member" of a gang. You may simply be born into it or become a member by association. You simply carry the banner of your set. Everybody around you knows that you're from that particular set and when asked, you will not hesitate to say. You will more than likely wear the distinctive colors of that particular gang, use your hands to express the gang's sign, and use the vocabulary of that gang. Like the word, Ru, Blood, Cuz, Loc, Dog, Hound, etcetera. You can do all of these things but none of them mean that you're an active, full-fledged "Gang Banger."

A gang banger is the person that is on the streets "putting in the work" for the set. Activities such as: shootings, robberies, holding weapons, drug dealing, and fighting opposing gang members on the streets for the gang. You can be a gang member and not be a criminal, but it's not likely that you're an actual gang banger and crime free. I used to think that the people who didn't get involved in gangs must have had a father in the home or had come from a wealthy background, but those ideas were false. There is no real reason that you can pinpoint as to why some individuals got deeply involved in gangs, and why others stayed completely out. There are many people that I know that come from two parent middle class homes that become gang members and there are really poor, single parent raised kids that remain gang free for their entire life. The reasons and situations vary and there is no clear cut answer that would cover every situation. However, it is true that the likeliness of a kid that grows up in the impoverished hood without a father, proper guidance and mentorship has a greater chance of becoming involved in gangs.

Since I was a kid, I've been fascinated by gang life. However, I didn't just wake up one day and say "I want to be from a gang when I grow up." It was just the culture that I grew up in. From the area around me, the clothing style, to all of the coolest music on MTV and the radio. Gangsterism was in and taking America by storm. From the tender age of twelve I wanted to become a gang member, and I became one. There was no initiation process for me. I was not jumped in or required to do any task to be accepted. I simply began hanging out with the other young men my age who were already involved. My older cousin being from the same gang was also a sort of pass for me to represent the set also. My dress code, the way I talked, the way I walked, and my personality all began to mold to fit the gang lifestyle. The only music I was interested in was West Coast gangster rap. As a youth, I craved to learn all I could about gang culture and history. The only book I remember reading as a pre-teen was *Monster* by Sanyika Shakur. *Monster* was the biography of one of the original Crip gang members, Kody Scott. Although I was a Blood, I still found it fascinating to know his history.

When I was young it seemed like every male was affiliated with a gang in some aspect. If I was to approximate the percentage of actual gang members that went to my Junior High school, I would say about 20% of the black males were active. The same would be for the Latinos and Asian males. Most of the males that joined did so between the ages 12 and 14. Every kid was at risk. The same exact conditions of poverty, family structure and environment could be the same for two brothers and one can be a full-fledged gang member and the other not.

I lost my best friend to gang murder when I was thirteen years old. When he died I was told that he had killed himself. I knew this wasn't true. Even at a young age I knew that this was another case of the police not caring to enough to investigate the murder of a "black gangster." From his death to this day, I've lost close to fifty friends to gang violence. As cool as it might have sounded to be a gang member when I was a teenager, the reality was that there were too many downsides to this way of life. Constantly having to

13

watch your back from rival gang members, and fighting others to maintain respect or to just have street credibility. Jail and death were at the top of that list. I didn't need a lecture or a documentary to explain this to me. There were examples of these consequences happening all around me on a daily basis. Watching my older cousins going in and out of jail all of my young life was starting to wear on me. Losing friends and others from the city to gang homicide was also starting to become a regular occurrence.

As I got older, I slowly pulled away from traditional gang life, but I never left my community, or stopped visiting other gang areas throughout the country. The gang-infested areas of San Diego were my home, and my friends lived in those areas throughout the country. Leaving those areas would have meant leaving all of me— including my family—behind. Although I drifted away from the gang life, I still wanted to learn about the history of gang culture. My Stepfather, Joey Colbert, was one of the original Crips in Los Angeles. He and others continued to tell me the stories that I would store up in my mind. These stories made me a true quality source of knowledge on urban street gangs. Unlike many people that claim to be experts on gang lifestyle who received their knowledge from textbooks, seminars, movies, and trainings, my knowledge and understanding is firsthand reality. With that being said, let me walk you through the past forty years of urban street gangs.

As with everything in life, there is a natural evolution. The same rule applies to gangs. In the fifties and early sixties, urban black street gangs began to form out of necessity to defend their neighborhoods from racist, white street gangs that would terrorize their communities. Many women and children from the black communities were being attacked for no reason other than that they were black and vulnerable. The young men in the communities began to create security teams to become the protectors of their neighborhoods. Two of these groups were the Bloods and Crips. Since my childhood, my uncles and other elders in the neighborhood have told me about the origination of these two major gangs. All of their accounts coincided. Some minor details may differ, but the core of their stories remain the same.

During the sixties, the Black Panther Party (BPP) began to assume the primary role as protectors of their communities. Many of the "Blood" and "Crip" community protection group members started to join the BPP, but they never truly separated themselves from their affiliation with the Blood and Crip names. The BPP was quickly spreading across the United States in the urban communities in every major city. They were a direct threat to racial injustice and inequality that had for so long been upheld by the American government. When the BPP began to gain major support from other people outside of black communities, people began taking a closer look at America's many injustices to black people; the Federal Bureau of Investigation began to look at the Black Panther Party as a threat. FBI director J. Edgar Hoover began a full-fledged attack on the BPP. He infiltrated their organization and used other forms of covert operations. Operations such as using agents to go undercover as BPP members and commit crimes in the name of BPP, falsely accusing and incarcerating members of the BPP, and murder of leadership. In 1967 the FBI initiated a program called COINTELPRO. COINTELPRO was setup to destroy the BPP or what they called "Black Nationalist Hate Groups." During this successful operation, J. Edgar Hoover and the FBI began to arrest, discredit, and even murder the black urban community leaders throughout America. The infamous raid and murder of Black Panther leader Fred Hampton was thought at first to be the sole action of the Cook County police department—it was later discovered to be guided by COINTELPRO. Many also believe that they had direct involvement in the deaths of both Dr. Martin Luther King and Malcolm X. If a black person was assumed to be a leader, they were taken out. Although I've had the honor of learning this information first hand from people that were actual Black Panthers during this time, most of these details can also be found in documentaries about the BPP or any of the surviving members' testimonials.

Coming into the seventies, we now had a generation of young black males with no leadership or guidance left with the responsibility of trying to figure out how to control and maintain their impoverished and underserved communities. The Bloods and Crips re-emerged as the communities' protectors, only this time led by a new generation. A leaderless generation. A generation that no longer even realized what they were established for in the first place. Slowly but surely they became territorial. Then, on the fatal night of June 5, 1972, Frederick "Lil Country" Garret from LA Brims was shot and killed by an unknown Westside Crip. A rivalry was born. The Brims is one of the largest Blood sets. An act of murder on one of them was viewed as an attack on all Bloods.

As the late-seventies arrived so did another unexpected attack on the black community, only this time it was in the form of a lethal substance that we call crack cocaine. Even harsher than the FBI's COINTELPRO operation, this drug came in and not only destroyed potential leaders, but took out entire families. With this substance in the hands of violent gangs, it became a means of making money—a lot of money. Communities were broken down into very distinct territories that were run by whatever gang existed in that area. Violence erupted in record numbers and gangs began to grow. Enlisting new members was a priority. Each gang wanted to have the biggest numbers and the most weapons. If your gang was not feared, it was stepped on by other gangs. This meant that people had to die. How do you strike fear in your rivals hearts and minds without violence? This was the beginning of an urban war that would last for decades.

Growing up in the black communities of the eighties there were two big issues that everyone knew and talked about: gangs and crack. As a young kid I had good parents who taught me right from wrong, the do's and don'ts of life. Then I had my older cousins who were a few years older than me and who were, in my eyes, the coolest people ever. Unfortunately, they were already engulfed in the gang life. These were the ones that I looked up to and admired. Take this admiration and mix it with the gangster rap I would listen to when my mom wasn't around and you have a budding gang banger.

Through the eighties and early nineties, gangs were not just a fad or something law enforcement could just stomp away like they did with the Black Panther Party. Urban street gangs like the Bloods and Crips had become an established piece of America, reaching coast to coast. There was no one leader, no organized structure. By the mid-nineties, being from a gang did not mean that you were initiated or "jumped in" as it's called. It didn't mean that you had to commit a crime for the gang to be a part of it either. Yes, these types of events did and do occur, but they were not the norm. Gangs had become so much a part of the culture of the communities they were in that you would become a member of that gang simply by growing up in that community, or having a family member that was already a member of the gang. You could easily become a gang member with no extra effort on your part.

In the eighties and nineties you could become a gang member by simple affiliation. If the friends that you hung out with, grew up with, lived by, or knew your whole life were from a certain gang then you were too. I remember in the sixth grade at my middle school if you were not from the certain Blood gang that ran the neighborhood, you were not cool. For example, if you were not from the neighborhood gang you would not be accepted in certain areas of the school, or certain parties. Whereas if you were a part of the gang, there was nowhere that you couldn't go. You might not have totally understood what the gang life entailed, but one thing was for sure—you wanted to be a part of that gang. With this mentality continuing over the next decade, gang neighborhoods became more than small isolated sets—they became more of a tribe.

Sometimes young men were forced to become members of their neighborhood gang by their rivals. It was not uncommon for a neighborhood gang rival to approach a person with intimidation and ask, "What set are you from?" If your reply is "nowhere," then you were asked a series of questions that were used as a way to figure out what part of town you live in. "What school do you go to?" "Where does your momma stay?" The rivals were attempting to figure out if you lived in a rival neighborhood. Once it was established that you did, you just became the enemy and your physical safety was now on the line. If you could be beat up or worse for just living on a certain block, why not actually be from that gang? At least then you'd have some sort of protection. This was a common train of thought that led many young men into the gang life.

The nineties were a time of strict gang laws and penalties. Gang members were either dying by each other's hands or being incarcerated. It was dangerous to be a gang member or affiliated with a gang. Situations that would normally result in a fist fight were now resolved with a gun. With the introduction of gang documentation, gang injunctions, sentencing enhancements for gang affiliation, and many other legislative actions taken to suppress gangs, being a gang member had not only become dangerous to your life on the streets, but was almost surely going to take away your freedom.

Once you were documented as a gang member you would be placed on a California database called CalGang. The CalGang system is funded by the state of California, and is Local Law Enforcement maintained and controlled Criminal Intelligence System that specifically targets members and criminal associates of street gangs. The CalGang system operates pursuant to the United States Code of Federal Regulations, title 28, section 23 (28 CFR 23), ad seq. as a Criminal Intelligence System. CalGang is a wide area, low cost, easy to use, securely networked, relational intelligence database, specifically targeting members of criminal street gangs, tracking their descriptions, tattoos, criminal associates, locations, vehicles, criminal histories and activities.

Gang injunctions are a type of restraining order issued by United States courts that prohibit assumed gang members from participating in certain activities. That includes being around other assumed gang members. It is based on the legal theory that gang activity constitutes a public nuisance that prevents people in the community that are not gang members from partaking in the day to day liberties of a law abiding citizen.

After generations of death and incarceration due to gang lifestyle, a new state of mind began to emerge amongst the youth in the impoverished inner cities. The new generation of young men and women that grew up watching people in their community and family die or go to jail had almost simultaneously started to think outside the Crip and Blood box. The realization that going down those traditional gang paths would be detrimental to their lives was starting to sink in. These young minds began to break away from the traditional gangs. They were no longer a part of the set. They formed small groups or cliques, establishing their own identity. Most of these cliques were of the shared mindset that being a gangster was old news and being a ladies man was the way to go. Why worry about your life being taken away by a bullet or jail cell when you could party and have sex instead?

With the end of crack cocaine as a means to make money, a new generation of young men from the inner city were in search of another way to make money. America, "The Land of Opportunity." People say, "you can be whatever you want." All of that sounds really good, but the sad reality is that if these so-called opportunities are not seen or even acknowledged as an option then they might as well be non-existent. In the inner cities during the mid-nineties, the only options for a black man seemed to be sports, rapper, drug dealer, or gangbanger. Now the process of elimination begins. Take a moment and journey with me into the mind of an adolescent black male growing up in the inner cities with these options:

1.  Sports? The odds of making it pro are slim to none, even if you have the talent and skill to begin with. That's out.

2.  Rapper/Entertainer? I can't do that! I can't rap! Everybody from my hood tries and they're all in the same condition I am.

3.  Drug dealer? What would I sell? Crack will get you ten-plus years in jail. It's not even a lucrative business anymore. Plus, I lived through the damage it did to my family.

4.  Gangbanger? Forget about it! I've lost too many friends and family to gangbanging. There's no money in it, just death or jail.

As crazy as this might seem to somebody who grew up in different circumstances, these are the thoughts that went through the minds of many male teenagers in the inner city, including myself.

The late nineties, specifically 1996-1997, was the beginning of major shifts in gang life. These years saw an explosion of the "Clique." In 1997 there were over thirty established cliques in the San Diego area, with many others on the rise. These cliques were typically totally separate from the Blood and Crip gangs that had run the communities since the seventies. Some cliques did branch off from bigger gangs. These groups were normally made up of young people that had already been so deeply rooted in the gang life that they couldn't really break away completely. Instead, they created their own identity but remained somewhat tied to the big traditional set. Being from a clique was the new trend. If you weren't from one, you and your group of friends were quickly creating one.

Unlike a gang, cliques did not follow the traditional model of a gang. They were not stuck to a particular territory (although the bulk of the members may live in a certain area). They may or may not use a distinct color to represent their affiliation. They could be from both blood and crip backgrounds and still be from the same clique. Cliques may have been formed to be dancers or party goers, sports crews, school friends, or any other found similarities. A clique, unlike a gang, is made up of a group of friends; whereas a gang can have members that may not even know each other. A clique is a group of friends that have chosen to identify themselves under a banner. This identification method stems directly from the gang culture and has obvious roots in the way the clique is branded. Cliques would usually have hand signs they would display to show what clique they represented. These behaviors were very similar to behaviors exhibited in gangs. There may even be rivalries amongst cliques—rivalries that result in fighting. Although there are many similarities between cliques and gangs, the most substantial difference would have to be that even with the rivalries and fights there are never any cliques murdering or attempting to murder rival clique members.

During this time period there was a mental and physical shift happening with young urban males. Being a gang member was no longer cool. To be a new gang member in the late nineties was almost a joke. Cliques were starting to be composed of young men from different gang affiliations. People who were traditionally rivals, Bloods and Crips, were no longer worried about what set people were from and linked up under a new banner. The clique that I co-founded in 1996 was comprised of almost every gang in San Diego. We specifically chose to wear every color associated with a gang to show that we weren't aligned with any one gang. People even began dressing different. The gangster style of Dickies, khakis, Ben Davis Clothing, Pendletons, and Chuck Taylors were out. Looking like a gangster was a thing of the past. The new look of urban America had become the "pretty boy" look. Nautica, Tommy Hilfiger, and Abercrombie & Fitch were some of the leading brands. Brands that would normally seem too expensive for youth from the hood weren't as hard to acquire as one might think. When you want something bad enough you will find a way to make it happen. Even if that meant spending all of your part time job earnings, back to school clothes money, or your girlfriend's parents' money on the newest gear. Personally I was super thankful for designer discount stores such as Ross, Marshalls, and Burlington Coat Factory for keeping me fashionable. Either way young teens from the hood were starting to wear fashion that had previously been associated with the suburbs.

Another more important physical change that came with the clique era was the loss of gun violence. Yes, cliques did end up with rivals and other crews they didn't get along with, but their arguments never escalated past a good fist fight. My clique had a main clique rival that we fought on many occasions, but at the end of the day we all lived. Times were definitely changing and gang life was in the process of evolving for the better. What is sad is that this evolution did not seem to be recognized by law enforcement or community leaders who had the capabilities to seize on the era and help put an end to the gang epidemic. I believe that if what was going on in the inner cities was recognized for what it was, by people who had money and power to make the necessary improvements and implementations of proper programing, there would have been a substantial intervention of further street gang activity. This would have set these troubled communities on a new course of prosperity and growth. Instead, the generation that was unknowingly reaching for a change was left to continue to learn on its own. Eventually some of these cliques were disassembled and fell back into the bigger gangs. The others were forced into raising themselves with lack of mentorship.

By the time the nineties were coming to a close, a large amount of these clique members had turned to pimping as their means of survival. The members of the cliques were not kids anymore. This meant that more than likely their parents were not providing for them. Quickly becoming adults with adult responsibilities, needs, and desires—all of which required money. Going back to gang banging was not an option, and selling drugs was definitely not the way to go.

As Clique members were growing into adulthood and merging into pimps a new era of gangs began with those that remained in the gang and new members that did not fall into the clique era. Rivalries were still intact. There were not any big truces. However, in the inner cities there was now a mix of pimps, gangsters, and "cliquesters." The new up and coming gang members were not as violent as the preceding generations. Many gangsters were merging into the pimp lifestyle and leaving gang banging to the wayside. Times had definitely changed. Bloods were wearing blue and Crips were wearing red. This may sound petty, but this was an extreme switch. For decades people were killed over these colors.

Since 2005, I can say that black gang evolution in San Diego has almost stagnated. Since the decade long pimp and prostitution epidemic died down, gang activity has increased, but has never gone back to the life it had in the eighties and early nineties. From San Diego, Los Angeles, Chicago, and New York, things have changed as far as the operation of the street gangs. There has been a shift from a focus on the individual from a focus on the benefit of the gang as a whole. Gang members openly care less about the bigger operation of the gang, and more about their individual well-being. Smaller groups within the big gang are out for themselves. In recent years in San Diego, a majority of the gang related homicides have been same gang against same gang. If the homicide happens to be between two people from different gangs, the incident likely occurred because of a personal problem between the two individuals and not a problem due to merely being from a rival gang. Although this does still happen, it is not the norm. Currently, people who are still affiliated with gangs are typically doing so because they don't see another option. A majority of what society would call a gang member is non-violent, doesn't care about actively gang banging, and is claiming a gang just because it's representative of the community that they grew up in. The population of people that are still shooting and actively committing gang crimes is small. In today's judicial system, and in our society, the label "gang member" is equivalent to the word "criminal." In reality the two are far from synonymous. In today's urban communities it is not uncommon for Blood gang members and Crip gang members to be friends, business partners, or share in other endeavors that previous years would have forbidden. Gang culture has definitely evolved and is continuing to evolve for the better. If these efforts were recognized and then financially supported by our local and national government we may truly see the final end of the gang epidemic.

24

27

# Fantastic Transitions

In 2004 I was released from Federal Prison where I had just served 30 months for a marijuana conspiracy charge. When I arrived home I was finally able to get together with my friends and hear the story that I could not hear over the prison phone. The story of the most tragic event to ever strike my life.

*"Parties are so lame. I mean you can't hear the girl next to you that you're trying to get at, you're too sweaty at the end of the night, and you have to compete with a bunch of square-ass dudes with no game to get the same bitches."*

An average conversation with a group of pimp friends is underway. During this time of running your mouth, you're either dominant or you shut up. You see, in the pimp game, your mouthpiece is everything. It's what makes or breaks your status in the pimp world. Rather than enter the club the group of young men would rather try and talk to girls in the parking lot. This is known as "parking lot pimping."

*"Shit, that's why we parking lot pimp and pop at the bitches coming in and coming out."*

*"For real why spend the extra dough in there? I'm trying to make my dough out there."*

One out of the group seems to stand out from the rest of the crew. His clothes are just a little bit more prestigious and his smile is just a little bit brighter. He's leaning up against his brand new luxury car that he bought from the spoils of his pimp career, as he listens to the others. At twenty-one years old he has quickly grown to be one of the most admired pimps from the city, and not just in the city of San Diego. This young pimp has already traveled throughout the United States, courting women, meeting fellow pimps, and making money in places like Florida, Arizona, Nevada, and Washington D.C. Whenever this young man spoke, everyone listened.

The group begins to "ooh" and "ahh," impressed at the crafty way their unsung leader manipulated the words of the classic expression "parking lot pimp" to mean a whole lot more and up his status. He let the admiration continue briefly before he spoke again,

*"Come on, let's slide up out of here and go downtown. This shit is bogus. Let's go bless some young hotties with our presence."*

The group agrees to leave the club parking lot. One by one they load into the two cars they arrived in. Four guys get into one car and two get into the luxury car: "Fantastic 6" and his younger prodigy. In the pimp world it was common for a younger upcoming pimp to connect with an older, more experienced pimp to learn the trade from. As far back as the 1960's and 70's, young men eager to pimp would seek out an older mentor. In some cases, the older pimp would actually recruit a young man to mentor and train. In the case of Fantastic and his prodigy, they were school friends. Fantastic was older and already admired by the young man looking up to him and becoming a pimp. This relationship blossomed even more as they grew older and Fantastic became successful in the pimp game.

After caravanning two blocks away from the night club parking lot they enter the freeway. Both cars starting their routine of rolling a blunt, and playing their choice rapper—typical for this group of friends. So typical and routine that they're comfortable. Why wouldn't they be? They were all in the city that they grew up in, driving the same streets that they've driven down hundreds of times before. They weren't gangbangers who had to be extra cautious in case their enemies showed up. So of course they failed to notice the SUV that followed them out of the parking lot and up onto the freeway. That is, until the SUV decided to make itself known.

The group of four friends were following the car driven by Fantastic as the SUV pulled up on the side of them. Matching their speed on the freeway the SUV windows began to lower, followed by a barrage of gunfire. "Bam! Bam! Bam!" The sound of bullets being discharged from the SUV attracts the groups' attention, causing the driver to hit the brakes and swerve away, barely making an exit off of the freeway. As if military trained, the SUV pulls up to the car driven by Fantastic. Fantastic and his prodigy passed a blunt between them, music blaring. They didn't notice the act of war that had just gone on behind them. And even as the SUV repeated its tactics on their car, sending bullets once again, they didn't notice until it was too late. Now both young men sat in the middle of the freeway, feeling the heat of burning bullets in their bodies. Within the next twenty-four hours, Fantastic was pronounced dead and the prodigy would live with fragments of a bullet in his back and the pain of losing his best friend in his heart and mind for the rest of his life.

The senseless killers were soon discovered by law enforcement. Their ages? Fourteen, fifteen, seventeen, and nineteen; young, lost men from the inner city with no respect for or understanding of life. They didn't even know Fantastic. All they cared about was earning credit from the gang; that was more important than a man's life. Fantastic wasn't targeted because he was a gang member, he wasn't targeted because he was a pimp. These young killers had no idea what or who anybody in the group was. What they did know is that they were young black men that they did not know. This means they must be enemies. The sad truth of it all is that so much self-hate has been brewed in black people since it was taught during slavery, that there does not need to be any reason other than that. These young misguided murderers were on a two week shooting spree. Fantastic was only one of four that were killed amongst the twelve that were shot between San Diego and Los Angeles by the group.

Growing up in the gang influenced San Diego Streets as I did it was overly familiar with losing young black men to murder, but this loss of life was very different. The death of Fantastic impacted my entire community here in San Diego. Famous rappers made songs about him and his funeral attracted hundreds of people including pimps and prostitutes from all over the country to attend and pay homage. His murder was in 2004 and to this day, nearly 15 years later, his birthday is celebrated at an event called Fantastic Day with an average of a hundred people in attendance. Fantastic was only 21 when he was murdered and had already impacted the lives of so many people. Fantastic used to tell me when we were kids that he wanted to be an accountant when he grew up and he definitely could have. He was smart, articulate, charismatic, and a natural leader. He could've done anything with his life other than pimping if he had been shown another way. Fantastic, whose birth name is Richard Leon Wilson, was more than a friend of mine. He was my brother.

# The Difference Between a Gangster and a Pimp

In the early nineties I began to hear the term "Gangsta Pimp," often used by real gang members. People would refer to themselves as this in rap songs and amongst their friends. The term "pimp" wasn't being used as it's true meaning—to be a gentleman of leisure. Instead, the word "pimp" was being used as a term of endearment in the urban communities around America. The word "pimp," as it was used in this context, didn't mean that you were selling prostitutes for money at all. Most of the time it was a word used to claim that you were a ladies' man that could get girls for yourself.

Once my friends and I began to enter into the pimp subculture here in San Diego, we quickly started to learn what was considered a "real pimp." We gained this knowledge from older pimps, documentaries such as *American Pimp* by the Hughes Brothers and *Pimps Up, Ho's Down* by Brent Owens and Fredrik Green, from Hip Hop music icons, and multiple pimps from across the country. We learned fast that there were certain rules, regulations, and standards that dictated how both pimps and prostitutes were supposed to operate. These rules and regulations were never written anywhere, nor were they regulated by any particular source. There was never any policing done to uphold people involved in the game to these rules, but from circles I have traveled in throughout this country these rules were always the same. Depending on what region of the country that you are in some of these rules may alter slightly. For example I remember being in Washington DC with my brother Fantastic and we were warned by other pimps that on the track out there, Pimps were not allowed to sweat (engage) girls on the actual street. You would have to remain on the sidewalk to talk to a girl working. The street was a No Pimp Zone. This was new to us and as far as we knew it was a rule adhered to only in that area. There were no technical repercussions to violating these laws and boundaries of the game. When I was in it I knew that there were strong possible repercussions that could range from chastisement to even death.

31

The most common and most undesired consequence to not behaving as a "real pimp" was the slander of your name. In this game your name is everything. As soon as the word gets out that you violated an unwritten rule your reputation would be tarnished and may never come back. A tarnished reputation can lead to many girls and guys in the game to not want to deal with you.

It is impossible to be a real pimp and be a gangster in my opinion. The way I was taught, a real pimp will not be involved in anything other than the pandering of women. A pimp will not sell drugs on the side, rob a bank, car jack, cash fraudulent checks, or engage in any other crime for profit—other than pimping and pandering. Yes, pimps have done these things in the past or may occasionally incorporate a different crime into their pimping, but this is an exception to the rule. Even when a pimp does these things, he usually does it in secret and so it will appear to the public that he made whatever illegal money he gained off of his pimping. At one point in my life there was a great opportunity for one of my pimp friends to make a lot of money from selling marijuana. He completed the transaction, used the money gained to purchase a new car and told people that he achieved this from his new turnout. Pimps take pride in their pimping, and shun anything outside of that lifestyle. This includes working a legitimate job. Although I have known a few pimps to resort back to working legitimate jobs, this was only when they were down on their luck when it came to the game. In all cases, as soon as they found a new prostitute they quit and went right back to pimping.

Drug dealing is probably the most shunned illegal activity of the underworld to the pimp culture where I'm from. All of the pimps I know saw drug dealers as low lifes for the fact that they are selling a product that kills people and ruins families. It's almost contradictory because oftentimes in the pimp subculture, prostitution can also destroy families. The pimp's logic is that prostitution is by choice and drug usage is based on taking advantage of people's addiction. The truth of the matter is that this self-induced logic that pimps tell themselves is not accurate. In the subculture of pimping and prostitution there are many situations where the woman is choosing to prostitute. That so-called "choice" is usually made out of them being in a bad state of mind previous to prostitution, growing up impoverished, lack of self-belief and guidance, or several other mental and emotional defects that can make a person feel that prostitution is a choice. The pimp in many situations knows this and is taking advantage of their vulnerability, which is similar to an addiction.

From being around the Blood and Crip gang culture in California for my entire life, I have found the following statements to be true. However, these facts may be different in different areas of the world; these are the truths and the reality that I grew up in. From my knowledge, a gang banger or gangster has an allegiance to his gang or set. He has a territory to represent to the outside world. A gangster allegiance isn't shown through monetary donations, recruitment, or service also known as putting in work. There is no organizational structure in black Blood and Crip street gangs. There is no rank of leadership roles. A majority of relationships of fellow gang members is based on simply growing up in the same area of town. Two individuals may not even know each other or cross each other's paths and still represent the same gang. Some individuals involved in gangs do not commit crimes or engage in activities to "benefit the gang." A majority of gang members commit crimes for individual benefit and survival. However, there are small pockets of people that do shootings and commit murder for the sole reason of putting in work for the gang. A pimp only has allegiance to himself. The traditional "real pimp" that I am familiar with will not gang bang. He is only involved in one mission, and that is to get money. He does not, and cannot worry about having enemies from other gangs when he is trying to get rich. The two activities are contradictory and do not mix.

Some black Blood and Crip street gang members have been known to sell a woman for money. It is not rare, but in the pimp and prostitute subculture where I'm from it does not make them a pimp in the streets—although it does to the law, researchers, and others outside of the culture. Nor do they do this to benefit the gang. Black Blood and Crip street gangs have no formulated structure that I

33

have ever been witness to. There are no fiscal dues to pay. If a gang member has a girl that's willing to sell her body and give him the money, that money is going to him as an individual. For his own survival and material possessions. In the streets where I'm from it's unheard of for the gang to get a piece of the action and they definitely do not share the girl. This is more than likely a temporary situation in which a gang member will remain being a gangster. One thing is for sure, he is not a pimp. That may be the legal definition, but on the street, a pimp does not gang bang and a gangster is not a pimp.

As a gangster you do not necessarily have a "Status" as a gang member. What you do have is a reputation. A reputation as the toughest guy around or people looking up to you. This status or reputation may attract girls to you in the same way that being the popular kid at school attracts girls to you. Gangsters don't usually use this appeal to pimp out girls. They use it to have sex with girls. A gang member who is prostituting a woman is just that, a gang member who is prostituting a woman. I've witnessed many pimps that were gang members and thugs (A thug can have the same attributes and characteristics as a gang member but does not belong to or claim a particular gang) stop being gang members and thugs once they became pimps. In fact, I will take it a step further and say that a majority of the pimps from Southern California that I know were gang members before they were pimps. With the deeply embedded gang culture in California, chances are that as a boy you became involved in the gang life as young as ten years old. By the time you reached an age of independence and needed to fend for yourself, you began looking for options to make a living. Pimping was one of those options. Once these young men became involved in pimping, they began to stop being gang members. There is a total mentality switch. No longer do they believe in committing senseless crime, hanging out with fellow gang members with no goals, and fighting over colors or street blocks. If it doesn't make money, it doesn't make sense. A few that transition still claim their gang name as being where they are from, but the meaning behind it has changed to more of heritage status.

Although this may seem bizarre to the people outside of the subculture of pimping, many people that were once enemies and would fight or shoot each other as gang members would stand side by side laughing and conversing with each other as pimps. Many people from a particular crew that me and friends had problems with actually became close friends. Growing up we would fight each other on sight. I've even been jumped (attacked by a group) by them. Once we started pimping, those days were gone. The subculture of true pimps does not allow for that behavior. People who were once violent thugs began to speak and practice finesse, courtesy, and a more peaceful way of living amongst each other and also their women. No pimp wants their stable in anything but peace. On occasion they do have to pit one woman against the other as a temporary tactic to achieve goals, but that is not the ideal situation. Instead of gang signs they would use their hand to exhibit the peace sign. I remember a rule of engagement when trying to pursue another pimp's prostitute on the blade was to put both hands behind your back to show that you were not physical. All of the gang members I'm familiar with on contrast resort to physical fights, threats, and even murder when their property is threatened. The "real pimps" I am speaking of believed that if you couldn't use your communication skills to gain control of a prostitute, you were weak. During the late nineties and early 2000's there was a major epidemic of young, urban males merging into the pimp lifestyle and away from the gangster lifestyle. At this point in time there was an extreme drop in gang activity and involvement, and a shift in the style of crimes being committed.

According to SANDAG's (San Diego Association of Governments) 2013 report on San Diego Gang Involvement Among San Diego Arrests conducted by their Criminal Justice Research Division you can see that pimping and prostitution was essentially the lowest percentage of arrest for gang members:

## Gang-Involved Arrestees Report Participating in both Criminal and Non-Criminal Activities

Hang out 95%                                   Theft 56%
Get high/drunk 91%                        Robbery 56%
House parties 81%                            Motor vehicle theft 47%
Getting in fights 77%                         Vandalism 54%
Cruise 74%                                         Pimp or Prostitute 21%
Graffiti/Tagging 58%                          Other 3%

There is not a racial breakdown to further identify what percentage of these arrests were black gang members. However this source does show that pimping and prostitution was at this time, one of the least likely crimes to be committed by a gang member.

Even though Pimps are not Gangbangers and gangbangers are not pimps, the occupation of pimping still brings about an element of death and violence. An element that I know all too well. In my lifetime involved in the game, I know of many pimps having been beat up and or robbed by gang members. I've lost my brother Richard, who was a nonviolent pimp, to murder, and two associates to murder who were also pimps. In this past year I've lost two of my best childhood friends who were both still in the game. One died of an overdose at 36 years of age. The other was killed while he was on the blade by a female who was in the process of taking his prostitute away from him. He was 35 years old.

According to the Organized Crime in California Annual Report to the California Legislature of 2004 produced by The California Department of Justice there was a substantial drop in gang related homicides from 1996 -2003. This was in comparison to the years previous where gang homicides were nearly doubled. In 1994 there were 880 documented gang homicides. Five years later in 1999 that number had dropped to 402. Many people may claim to know why this drop in gang activity happened. These people are outside analysts that did not grow up in these particular gang-infested areas and are making assumptions. I lived it. I can say without a doubt that the drop in gang activity was a direct result of the climb of pimping and prostitution among the inner city. Let me be clear, I am not saying that this is a good thing, but it is the reality of the world I grew up in. In order to thoroughly combat sex trafficking, those who want to help victims have to truly understand how we ended up where we are today.

# Lawrence

My friend Lawrence was served a cold hand from early in his childhood. Lawrence's mother and father were heavily involved in the crack epidemic of the eighties. His father was a dealer and his mother was a user. His mother would have said she was a "functional user," until shortly after Lawrence's sixth birthday party when his father disappeared forever. After Lawrence's mother realized that her spouse had left them to fend for themselves she was driven deeper into her addiction. She fell in so deeply that she ended up losing everything, including Lawrence. By the age of seven Lawrence had been taken by the city and placed into foster care. For the next six years Lawrence would grow up in foster homes and group homes—never staying in one place for longer than eight months. He was never fully accepted at any of his "homes" and he had lost all understanding of the concept of love. Unfortunately in a lot of group homes the children are looked at as an easy way to make money, and not young, vulnerable humans that need nurturing to grow. The homes that Lawrence lived in didn't treat him as the survivor of abuse that he was, but instead like a criminal that was incarcerated for breaking the law.

Everything changed when Lawrence landed in Roy's mother's home. Roy's mother was different than all of the other foster moms and group home staff. Lawrence felt that she genuinely cared for him and the other foster children that she cared for. After years of feeling unwanted and unloved, Lawrence finally felt at home. She would buy him clothes and not just use up his money she received from the state for him on "expenses." She made sure to help him with homework and showed an interest in his academics. Most importantly, she actually sat with him and talked to him like a human being.

In his early teen years Lawrence had found a love of martial arts. He was mostly well behaved and well liked. He would hang out with Roy and his crew who enjoyed partying and girls. I was also a member of this crew of young men. We were inseparable. Lawrence and Roy were both the same age so it was like having a brother and a live-in friend for him. However, when Lawrence entered high school at the age of fourteen, he carried himself more like a twenty-year-old man. His life experiences had forced him to mature much faster than any child should have had to mature. Even though Lawrence had found a "home" and a group of friends with Roy, something about that life just wasn't enough for him. Even with finally having a strong mother figure and support system in his life, the appeal of gang life was still strong. Not just for Lawrence but for many growing up in the inner city. It was the cool thing to do for some, for others it was for security, and many were just born into it. Even though Lawrence had me and our other friends around (that weren't directly involved with gangs) we were also still influenced by them or coming out ourselves. In his surroundings there were also friends of his that were completely involved in the gang life. Lawrence had already been through so much in life as a child, and by this time he yearned for security and to be accepted by a stronger brotherhood. Unfortunately, our crew never seemed to be enough for him.

About six months after starting high school, when most boys were worried about which girl they were going to take to homecoming, or whether or not they would make the football team, Lawrence joined the biggest street gang in San Diego. Lawrence continued to live with Roy's mother during the early years of his involvement with the gang, although he was occasionally thrown out for bad behavior. He would get in trouble at school for fighting other students, arguing with teachers, and for truancy. A couple of times he was caught by the police robbing stores.

He remained close to Roy and the rest of us, despite our constant attempts to talk him out of gangbanging. A night hanging out with us would typically involve trying to find the most exciting party with the most girls. With the gang, hanging out with girls was the last thing on their mind. A typical night with the gang would be sitting around getting high, drinking, and hanging out. Lawrence's involvement in the gang only deepened. His popularity grew within the gang as he fought to become someone to both admire and fear. He was a seasoned gangster within a short year's time. He had been involved in multiple drive-by shootings, fights with rival gang members, and had multiple weapons in his possession.

During the summer of Lawrence's sixteenth birthday, he purchased one of the nicest cars in the neighborhood. A mid-eighties burgundy T Top Cutlass. He had acquired money from working at my aunt's restaurant, selling weed, and from the state check that he was receiving. The car was an older model, but it was in good condition and was admirable. His car, coupled with his rising status in the gang, and his charming personality sparked a growing jealousy from rival gang members as well as with members of his own gang. That's why when Lawrence's sixteen-year-old body was found in the middle of the street that summer with bullet holes it was such a mystery as to who pulled the trigger.

The news of this tragic incident struck us hard. We had lost our brother, friend, and partner in the streets. Everyone in the crew responded in their own individual way, but all of us were hurt just the same. Roy was turned off from anybody who claimed the gang that Lawrence had. He believed that they were responsible for his death. Our friend Kenny, who had become the young protégé of Lawrence, had been driven into following in his footsteps and joined the gang. He took on his name and became deeply involved with the gang lifestyle. The rest of the crew pushed further into pimping, as it was the only way out for us. A few months before Lawrence was murdered, our crew had just started venturing into the pimp culture. We had always known about it, but now we were taking full steps into becoming involved. We lost Lawrence to gangs. This life-changing event further ingrained in us an already deeply-held belief: that we would never join a gang. There had to be another way of life and pimping was it.

# Chapter 2:
# Welcome to the
# Game

Devon, when Lawrence died our entire crew was shook up. This was not just another dead associate. By 16 years old I had already lost some good people that I knew to homicide, but never anybody as close as Lawrence was to me. I had never even been to a funeral before his. As I look back I remember seeing all of the gang members that I knew from the neighborhood and our family were there. It was standing room only. You see nephew, when you're a "cool kid" or a rider from your set, everybody shows up to your funeral. Many are sad that you died while others are just happy you're out the way. I told myself that I would never see another loved one in a casket again. The vision of seeing him lying there in that casket will never leave my mind. The hard, cold way his forehead felt when I kissed him. Devon, that moment will never stop haunting me. As I reflect back at how the homies and I never received counselling, a therapy session, or anything. As a matter of fact we were never even asked if we were "okay." You see in this gang shit, this street life... You're supposed to just move on and like we're constantly told that men don't cry. I remember punching you in the chest because you were crying one day. Damn, Devon...

After Lawrence's death, we knew that there was definitely no chance of us turning to gangbanging as an option. There are only two places that gang members end up: dead or in jail. Kenny was the only one of our crew that still flirted with the idea of being a gangster. The rest of us were on a clear path far away from gang activity. Even though to some people, our clique was a

42

*gang—but they don't know what it's like being a young black kid in the hood. We are all gang members and thugs to them. Devon, that's why I tell you that you have to work 10 times harder than the rest of the races in America. That's the only way that you will win.*

*Quickly after Lawrence's murder we began to intensify our use of women for money. Although at the time we didn't know what a pimp was. Not a real one. We knew the word but we had no real conception of the lifestyle we were headed into or where it came from. These things I'd be forced to learn over time...*

*In Loving Memory*
*of*
## LAWRENCE CHANCEL SMITH, JR.

Friday, September 11, 1998 - 10:00 AM
California Cremation & Burial Chapel
5880 El Cajon Boulevard
San Diego, California
Rev. David Green, Officiant

# Making the Urban "American Pimp"

What is an Urban American Pimp? He is one of many different types of pimps. As I have mentioned previously in this book, I am referring to the pimp that is usually from the black urban inner cities of America. What makes this kind of pimp? Or better yet, what would make this person want to make money off of the sexual exploitation of another person? To better explain this I am going to have to take you back in time because, as you know, everything has a beginning. The largest tree in the Redwood Forest has a root and before it was a root, it was a seed. So it is with every condition and situation of people. As a society that claims it wants to put an end to crime, hate, racism, human trafficking, and the other human behaviors we frown upon, we often fail to look at the root of the problem. We are quick to lock a person up without taking a step back and thinking about what lead the person to commit the bad act in the first place. To get rid of the weed in the garden, you must dig it up by its root. Yes, I am saying up front that "pimping" is bad when speaking of the "bad act."

## *The Root of the Sex Trafficking Problem in America*

As much as America would love to overlook and erase its dark past of the mass enslavement and holocaust of African people starting in 1525, it cannot. Naturally, nearly 400 years of the forced servitude of a people, now known as African Americans, had a devastating physical effect. Over 12.5 million Africans were kidnapped and shipped to the New World, with two million dying in the middle passage alone. What's worse than the physical portion of this American atrocity is the mental component that was instilled into the minds and hearts of the enslaved by their captors. Mental seeds were planted, took root, and still to this day harvest in the minds of the descendants of the African slaves.

Slaves were taught and trained by the slave master for hundreds of years, generation after generation, to not only hate themselves, but to have no respect for their women. During their enslavement, the slave master would publicly display male and female slaves being raped, sold, and dehumanized, decreasing their value to less than nothing. During this time there were actual slave breeding camps set up in America with enslaved women forced to have sex with men (mostly other slaves) sometimes even their own family for the sole purpose of producing more slaves. This took place well after the prohibition of the African Slave Trade in 1807 when the supply of slaves was limited. I can truly understand why a large portion of America, the "land of the free," would not be outspoken about this domestic holocaust. Nobody likes to be reminded of the dirt in their past, especially if you've never truly reconciled with it or made right your wrongs. However, like I previously stated, we cannot talk about any problem or exterminate a problem without examining or at least acknowledging its root. So when talking about human sex trafficking here in America, can we not look at the largest human sex and labor trafficking crime ever committed in U.S. history? I believe that this was the seed that was planted. That seed sprouted into a root and cultivated even further after slavery was abolished through Jim Crow laws, segregation, and the inequality of women's rights.

Before we move on, I can't help but reflect upon the words of the great leader and visionary Dr. Martin Luther King Jr. in his speech entitled "The Crisis in America's Cities," which he gave in 1967. In that speech he says:

> If the soul is left in darkness, sins will be committed. The guilty one is not he who commits the sin, but he who causes the darkness. The policy makers of the white society have caused the darkness; they created discrimination; they created slums; they perpetuate unemployment, ignorance and poverty. It is incontestable and deplorable that Negroes have committed crimes; but they are derivative crimes. They are born of the greater crimes of white society.

I advise all to read this speech, made forty-seven years ago, but continues to be more relevant than ever today.

## The 1970's

Nobody truly knows how far back prostitution or selling sex for profit dates. The earliest documented prostitutes that I know of are in the Bible. As far as the black community here in America, we can trace the record back to the end of the slavery. The exact origin for the first black man pimping out a woman is not documented

46

anywhere as far as I've been able to find. What is commonly believed amongst modern day pimps is that the selling of women for sex is a direct result of freed slaves still taking advantage of the former slave masters' lust for black women. At the time, the slave owners were able rape black slave women as they pleased. This was a regular occurrence. Sometimes the slave owners would hold black women strictly as sex slaves. Some of the slaves were often as young as 10 years old. Not only the slave owners conducted these acts but also many other working class, white males that were not nearly as wealthy. Now that the Black people were freed and without a means of financial income to feed themselves, this seemed like a great option.

  As time progressed, pimping and prostitution continued. Just as it has throughout history. As the civil rights movement came to an end many of the once underground pimps began to feel the freedom of their now acquired rights. No longer did they have to only shop in lower class stores and buy certain things. They could now spend their money as they wished and wherever they wanted. A new era of upscale fancy dressed pimps had emerged with this change in society. During this time period an underground, unwritten code of ethics and rules had also been established. No, these rules did not emerge from a particular pimp leader or council of pimps. Rules were established organically and seemed to be followed throughout the United States.

  The seventies pimping era set the stage, creating the culture and look for the Pimp Game. Movies like "The Mack," "Dolomite," and "Willie Dynamite," were produced in the early seventies and released by Hollywood media glamorizing the look and lifestyle of the "pimp." This only gave validity to the many real pimps that were in the inner cities of America. Children, including my own father, looked up to the pimps. They seemed to be the only black men that were achieving any form of success in the black community. Flashy cars, the nicest clothes, beautiful girls, and money—what young, impoverished child would not admire that, especially with the alternative being a life that is poor, weak, and struggling?

  A very important uncle in my life, and the older brother of my father, was a true pimp during the 70's. My Aunt was one of his girls but acted as more as a manager than as a prostitute. She was good with criminal activity and brought in a lot of money boosting and other con games. Both my Aunt and Uncle were taken under by drugs only to recover later in life clean, married and on to more positive ways of life. Neither one of them talked much to me about their experience in the pimp and prostitution world as I grew up, although I did know they were involved. It wasn't until I was about 17 years old when my Uncle discovered that my friends and I were involved in the game that he started talking to me and my friends about it. When those conversations took place, you could tell that he was proud that we were in the game. One time he told me and my best friend that if we were going to do it anyway, he might as well tell us how to do it right. We both left that conversation feeling uplifted. I believe that because somebody we looked up to for years had given us a stamp of approval on our new way of life, we were happy and felt accomplished.

Growing up everybody was so overwhelmed by gang activity and the crack era that there was no real conversations about pimping that I could remember. Our community had worse problems going on. It seemed like living through the Black Plague of the middle ages in Europe and comparing it to a runny nose. The detriments of crack cocaine are still being felt today. The Urban Pimping and Human Sex Trafficking reemergence in my late teen years is a direct byproduct of the gang explosion of the 90's and the crack era.

There is no doubt in my mind that a sympathetic ear toward those victimized into pimping comes from more than just telling the longer, more complicated history of exploitation in black and brown and marginalized neighborhoods. My purpose in writing this is to lay a foundational context to how this "Black Urban American Pimp" came into existence in the first place. For some of you this is information that you know all too well, but for others I believe a little reminder needs to be placed in this book. We must not forget the past. It is truly what created our present in so many ways. In the midst of these arguments and explanations, I also know that little goes as far as a good old fashion confession, and with that being said I know that it's impossible to erase my personal past wrongdoings, take back any hurt, or pain that I caused anybody in my life and more particularly the ones that I encouraged to enter into and continue a life in prostitution—from the deepest parts of my heart, I am sorry. Sorry to both the men and women that I helped to enter into a lifestyle of sin. I have truly discovered the error of my ways and actively fight daily to right my wrongs by saving the lives of those I would have at one time, destroyed. If you are a sex trafficking survivor and you are reading this book, I pray that you can accept my apology. This book has taken a lot out of me and forced me to go deep into buried places that I thought I would never revisit. In some ways, this whole book has been a kind of spiritual journey for me.

## What Makes a Prostitute

Before I begin this section I feel it is necessary that I point out that I do not want to appear as if I'm "mansplaining." I know that there is no way that I can fully speak for a woman that has entered the game on why exactly she entered the game. Especially since there is no one reason or one way that this happens. I could easily ask one of my many experienced, expert friends who have been involved in prostitution to write this section for me, but I feel that as a former pimp, I can touch on the ways that myself (and other males in the game) view the reasons a woman might become a prostitute. Also, one of the missions of this book is to help you see through the eyes and mind of a pimp in the game. There are many books out now that you can read about female survivors who tell you in their own words what led them in. As an ex-pimp, the difficulty of how this subject can be written such that it won't be perceived as just another way to control women and their stories is real. Even more recently I have had the honor of interviewing several women from different areas of the country for my podcast and documentary on their individual experiences within the game. All of these interviews are documented for public record and can be heard by anybody with access to the internet. For anyone that is interested in hearing these stories, the podcast is also called "Raised In Pimp City" and airs on all major podcast platforms including Google Play, Apple podcast, and Spotify.

There are many different factors that can lead a woman or girl into prostitution. Some of these factors are exactly the same as the factors that lead a guy into pimping for the women that come from the community that I was raised in: the aftermath of the crack era, lack of any economic opportunity, and growing up in and around the track. As I grew up, I sat in the same schools, lived in the same neighborhoods, and went to the same parties with girls that ended up becoming prostitutes while my friends and I became pimps. The same conditions that allowed my friends and I to justify pimping allowed the girls I grew up with to justify prostitution. We were all affected. This is a prime example of why I want to be careful about drawing historical and moral equivalents between pimps and prostitutes. Let me be clear, I am not talking about their experiences while in the game. I am speaking about the underlying factors that may have led them into the game in the first place. I am not talking about or attempting to excuse the dangerous power of patriarchy and the privilege that extends to men in particular, and, on the other side of the coin, the disproportionate cost to women when involved in the subculture of pimping and prostitution.

Growing up in my community, men were often looked to as leaders. Since most of my peers were not raised with fathers in the home, these male leaders were not necessarily their fathers. They were dope dealers, gangsters, or pimps. Women in my world seemed to follow the men in their life, especially the men they were romantically attracted to. For example, if the man a woman liked was a drug dealer, oftentimes the woman would be his accomplice. If the guy was a gang member, she would represent that gang. When many young men from my community began venturing into a pimp lifestyle, many women followed suit by becoming prostitutes. It was not only acceptable, but rapidly became the norm.

Although there are many similarities between the reasons a person becomes a pimp and a prostitute, there is one reason that drives women to become prostitutes that does not usually drive men to become pimps: love. Love is an emotion that we are all capable of having, sharing, and it's something we all desire for ourselves. It is not uncommon for a women seeking love to seek out the prostitution lifestyle. Oftentimes you will see a person remain a prostitute because she feels loved by her pimp. The desire to be loved is both the pathway into the lifestyle and the motivation to continue.

This is not the case with pimping, at least not in my experience. "Love" is a tool often used by the pimp to manipulate a woman into prostitution and to maintain her compliance. To those individuals who were deprived of love growing up as a child, or never taught what real love is, falling into false love and prostitution is easy. A deceptive love can drive a person in search of love into a life of turmoil, unable to remove themselves. In many situations, love can be a distracting emotion, almost hypnotic at times. Your sense of reality can be distorted. If someone falls in love with an individual who is purposefully using that love to manipulate and distract him or her, acknowledging that the love is harmful is ten times harder. Oftentimes a new prostitute that becomes involved in the lifestyle in search of love is kept distracted with this emotion for years. By the time she realizes the love was false, she's gone so far down the rabbit hole that she feels there is no other choice but to continue. Now she's even more broken, more vulnerable, and still in search of love. For many, drugs fill that void. Recently, a close friend of mine named Kelly explained:

I have made millions of dollars for pimps. I really didn't care for the money at all. I never liked things. I was paying for love and attention by men. Men that even though I knew none of them really loved or liked me, I would continue to pay and be a good hoe to them. I just hoped that one day it would be enough for them to actually love me. Or be with me only by default if I was good.

Anyone's upbringing can shape them into who they become as an adult. From a newborn into childhood you are like fresh clay. Society, family, friends, and other outside influences are the sculptors of that clay. A person's upbringing can undoubtedly factor into that person being susceptible to the life of prostitution. If you were brought up in a home that was already influenced by the pimp or prostitute lifestyle, it would then be naturally acceptable to follow down that path. I've met a few women that became prostitutes whose mothers were former prostitutes. I've also met a number of men whose father, uncle, or older brother was a current or former pimp. Furthermore, I have known a few people whose mother was a prostitute and dad was a pimp, which made the lifestyle even more acceptable. If someone has been surrounded by pimping and prostitution since before they can remember, how can he or she not think that it's okay?

Abuse in one's childhood is another major factor that can affect one's upbringing, potentially leading that person into a lifestyle of prostitution. Child abuse is detrimental to the psyche of any child and can leave scars permanently if left untreated. The majority of the females that I have come across in the prostitution lifestyle had been molested at some point in their childhood. No guy knows in advance or seeks out girls that have been abused in their childhood. Unfortunately, the odds are high when a pimp comes across a girl willing to take the path of prostitution.

Promiscuity at an early age can help create the perfect path for a young girl to venture into a lifestyle of prostitution. In the Junior High and High School years when a person begins to experiment with sex, a new burst of emotions and feelings arise. Sex can be just as dangerous as drugs without discipline or proper guidance. Many of us knew the "easy" girls in High School. Some girls gained this reputation early on in Junior High school and might have even been called a "hoe." Similarly, if you were known for being promiscuous as a boy you were often called a "pimp." The double standard in my opinion is based on American culture and beyond.

To a pimp, the more promiscuous girl is an easier target to turn out into prostitution. Sometimes promiscuity is a result of a lack of love or an abusive childhood. Those factors, combined with a seeming willingness to engage in sex, makes the girl an easy victim, particularly if she comes from a low-income family. A pimp will say things like, "If you're already having all this sex for free you might as well get paid for it," or, "Smart girls use what they got to get what they want. Dumb girls just lay on their backs and get used." There are many different ways to deliver this message to a promiscuous woman to make her accept this logic.

Another way I've witnessed females get into the game is through peer pressure. As with many bad habits and lifestyles, friends and peers can make a wrong decision much easier to make. If a girl is hanging out with other girls that are engaged in, or accepting of, prostitution, then it is much easier to accept it herself. Oftentimes the peers that have already become prostitutes will try to convince the one that isn't yet to join them in their new lifestyle. Not all girls succumbed to the pressure. The girls I've known with better upbringings or stronger self-confidence tend to not fall victim to peer pressure. The same way a girl wouldn't fall victim to all of the other many pressures that peers can put on you. I've been informed by several of my friends that are considered "lived-experience experts" (people that have personally lived through and experienced the game) that deep down inside when they were engaged in prostitution they knew what they were involved in was wrong. They've also told me that it is hard to have somebody around you that is an in-your-face example of the innocence that you've lost, especially if it's a friend that they've had for a long time. The only way to get this painful reminder out of your face is to bring your friend down to your level. It is also much easier to be convinced to be a prostitute by a friend that's already doing it than by being approached by a stranger. A friend has most likely already earned your confidence or established some grounds of trust. You probably have something in common or else you would not be friends. Peer pressure is one of the most effective means of converting somebody from a "square" life to a life of prostitution.

## The Customer

Like with any business selling a product or service, the only way to be successful is to have customers. Without a continual clientele stream it is pointless to be in business selling that particular product. The sex trade has been lucrative in the United States since its establishment, from the rich and famous to the poorest communities of this country. The rules of supply and demand make prostitution a lucrative business. No matter how the rest of the country fares financially, there have always been people ready and willing to buy sex.

Customers exist in every region, city, and state of this country. When one place isn't doing too well or customers aren't paying the price, pimps and prostitutes can move right on to the next location. The demand never ends. You can literally shut down shop in New York and relocate in California and resume business.

Who are these customers? These customers of the sex industry are typically called "Johns" or "tricks." Whether they're patrons of strip clubs, massage parlors, street corners, or an escort service, they are looked at the same. Any time you exchange money or property for sexual interaction you are a John. Johns come from all different walks of life. Their cultural backgrounds and economic situations vary—some are well educated and others have no education at all. There is no one type of John. A John may have a girlfriend or wife who would gladly sleep with him, but for his own individual reason he has a desire to pay another woman to have a sexual interaction with him.

I am not an expert on the psychology of Johns and what, if any, difference there is between men that pay for sex and those that don't. I do know that even men that don't necessarily pay for sex from prostitutes will still spend money on a girl inadvertently with the end goal being sexual intercourse. A guy will buy flowers, take a girl out to an expensive dinner or out for drinks and pay the bill. He will purchase gifts for her and pay bills that she may have. In many situations this is for no other reason but to be able to eventually have sexual intercourse with her and continue to do so. In many regards men that are spending money for the primary purpose of sex could also be considered "Johns." Some John's are really just sex addicts. Some Johns find this to be the best way to cheat on their significant other because there aren't any ties or ongoing relationships to worry about. To this day, A-list celebrities and politicians at all levels of government continually make the news with involvement in commercial sex scandals.

*Race*

Although this may change from region to region in America, the following is the breakdown on how urban street pimps and prostitutes view John's according to ethnicity: the white male John is the top of the food chain. He is the most frequent customer and the biggest spender. He is frequently a businessman, but Johns come from every profession. He is usually married and not looking to get caught so he will be extra cautious. The white male businessman will utilize all forms of the sex trade from the strip club to the inner city boulevards. With the internet now taking the number one spot of tools used to purchase sex, the white male businessman is the number one sought after customer; this type of John seems to be the safest to a pimp and a prostitute.

The white, non-businessman is also a top customer, he is also the most dangerous. He is known to be the most sadistic and most likely to rape a prostitute. The majority of the women that I know personally that were raped while in the game, were raped by white males.

Asian men are not known to be frequent buyers of street prostitutes or escorts within the US, but it does happen. They're looked at as similar to white males, with far less risk of sadistic tendencies and rape. I am not saying that Asian men are never sadistic or rape women, but it does not happen often enough for it to stand out to those in the game.

Hispanic men are known to be "big tricks" in the pimp world. These men are known to find a girl that they like and keep her on a regular basis. In some regions of America where you find groups of Hispanic migrant workers like Texas or California, they will solicit one or more girls for their group. Hispanic men are known to be tight on their wallet and not spend what they are asked by the girl.

The military is one of the biggest buyers of sex in the United States. A lot of them are deployed to different cities and states than where they are originally from. They find it easier to just pay a hooker when they want sex than to actually date a girl and hopefully, eventually have sex with her. Married military men who are sent away from their families will partake in buying sex often because they know it's not going to get back to their wives. These behaviors are accepted and encouraged in the military inside and outside of the country. A lot of foreign countries with legalized prostitution are called "happy zones" within the military. There are some ports where girls will line up to greet troops when they know they will be arriving. There's a known U.S. base in Panama where the girls line up outside of the base waiting to catch a date. While I was in the military, this base was talked about as one of the best stations to be sent to. A few of my superiors would warn us about staying away from those particular prostitutes due to sexually transmitted diseases. All forms of sex-buying occurs within the U.S. military: escort services, street prostitution, and strip clubs.

The black male trick is the least common. Dealing with a black trick changes from area to area. A majority of urban street pimps forbid their prostitutes to turn dates with black tricks. Prostitutes with no pimp at all and working as an independent agent do not date black tricks either. This is knowledge that I have acquired through decades of being in and around the pimp subculture throughout this country. It seems almost cliché that the white business man is the "best" John and the black man is "forbidden," but that is the way it is. Racism and stereotypes may have little to do with this but through my personal experience this classification is all truth.

Why is this? There are two main reasons that pimps do not allow their girls to solicit black tricks. The first is the fear that the guy may appear to be a trick but in reality is another pimp. From the traditional rules of the pimp subculture, if a prostitute gets in the car of another pimp, goes to his hotel room, or has any other interaction with him she would be considered "out of pocket." Once out of pocket, the pimp could take all of the money that the prostitute had on her. If she has no money at the time, she could be held on "pimp arrest." Pimp arrest means that she would temporarily work for the new pimp until she turned a date and made some money. Other pimps know the rules and will not purposely mislead a girl to get her out of pocket. He has girls that are working too and would not want that to happen to him.

Known renegades, or girls without a pimp, are not treated with that courtesy. Knowing a girl is without a pimp releases a pimp from feeling like he has boundaries that he cannot cross with the girl. He can pretend to be square to get her into his car or into a conversation. This would be a different situation if he knew that the prostitute had a pimp. Although this is rare, it can happen. If a pimp knows a girl is alone and without a pimp, then he knows he has more room to pressure her into paying him on a short term or long term basis. Short term being that she gives him what she has on hand at that moment or turns a few dates, and long term being that she actually chooses to come work with him for an indefinite amount of time.

## Legal Ramifications

California Penal Code 647b is the standing law regarding the buying and selling of sex. According to the California Legislative the potential punishments for both the customer and the buyer are the same. If it's the first offense, you can get your license suspended. The suspension lasts no more than 30 days. Other potential penalties are county jail time for no more than a year, or a fine of no more than $2,000. Legal ramifications and penalties for buyers of sex have been almost nonexistent, particularly compared to those for the pimps and even the women. Some argue that this is because the pimp knows when the female is being exploited and the John does not. I say that the John is fully aware of the situation he is getting himself into. He knows who and what he is soliciting and the fact that it's illegal. This is not a legitimate excuse. A majority of the time a John is caught and immediately released without any penalty. Several times in my lifetime I have witnessed vice and other officers tell the Johns, "Just go home to your wife."

Across the country, buyers of sex have often received only a slap on the wrist before being sent on their way. In Northern

California they have introduced methods like the John School to help stop sex-buyers. The John School is usually a one-day diversion class that trains the trick on the harms of buying sex—everything from STDs to the effects on the communities are covered. These schools are now located around the country and even in a few foreign countries like the UK, Canada, and South Korea. Even though these classes are paid for by the convicted trick, this is still an incredibly light punishment. Some other punishments for Johns include having to be registered as a sex offender, paying a fine, community service, and a day or two in jail. To a buyer, this is far from a diversion. Many men are right back at it the next day.

Why is our government so light on the actual buyers of sex? Much stiffer punishments are often handed down to the female victims than many of these tricks. Not to even mention the years upon years you can receive for being convicted as a pimp. Why is it so easy to be a John? If you think about it, the John is the reason why this industry exists in the first place. If no one was interested in buying, there would not be girls around to sell. No lives to be ruined chasing the carrot. In my opinion, there are not tougher penalties on buyers of sex because of two primary reasons. The first reason being that no matter how much people rally and fight for the survivors of human sex trafficking and for the end of prostitution, there is an unspoken acceptance of this business. The people that don't mind its existence just remain quiet on the subject to avoid scrutiny and judgment. We are talking about prostitution; it has been a piece of this country's existence since its founding. To this day, most U.S. cities have legalized escort services while states like Nevada have legalized prostitution.

The second reason I believe that Johns are overlooked and hardly punished is because of who they are and could potentially be. Since as far back as sex work has been documented in the U.S., the buyers have not only been the common blue-collar man, but have also been politicians, law enforcement, celebrities, and the enormously wealthy. This is still the case in the twenty-first century. Over the past twenty years politicians, lawmakers, rich, and famous men have been caught or admitted to buying sex. The industry might have become more sophisticated, but the clientele has not changed one bit. Of course this country couldn't be harsher on the people buying and supporting the sex industry. If they did, it might cripple Congress and Hollywood. I may be exaggerating a little bit, but hopefully you can get my point. Johns are really the core group of people that are keeping the human sex trafficking industry going. If there is no buyer there is no business. Both pimp and prostitute will find other things to do with their energy. If and when this government really wants to end domestic sex trafficking, it will start giving John's just as much jail time as it does pimps. When that happens, we will all witness the sex trafficking business in America crumble.

As a black man growing up in a primarily black, Filipino, and Mexican community, I never knew of anybody buying sex. In my community and peer group it was not okay to be a trick. You would be talked about for spending any money on a girl—even dating—when it came to my friends and associates. Far before we were pimping, being a "trick" was treated like a curse word. By 13 years old you were looked up to for being able to get girls to give you money. Before we ventured into pimping at 16 years old we would pride ourselves on being "juicers." A juicer was a person who was able to get money and material possessions from a girl. Tricking your money on a girl was forbidden by my peers. I didn't even know family members who were buyers. If anything, most of my Uncles and older male relatives were living off of women for a majority of their life. Although they were not "pimping" they certainly weren't buying.

# Types of Pimps

*Romeo Pimps*

The "Romeo Pimp" is usually the guy with a talent for communication. He's a charmer and usually good looking. He knows how to use his charm and finesse to get women to do what he needs. Violence is not his choice of behavior, although he can and will resort to it if he thinks it's necessary. Women love being around this type of pimp and you will oftentimes find him with the biggest stables. Many Romeo Pimps talk really soft and utilize extreme finesse. They like to dress in expensive, flashy clothes—fashion is a priority for them. To people outside of the pimp subculture these guys are often mistaken as homosexual because of their expression of feminine gestures and characteristics. Gestures with their hands can often times resemble that of a female as well as the soft tone in which many of them speak. My friend cared a lot about the outfits he wore, his jewelry and "remaining pretty" at all times as he would say. Regular manicures, long nails, and long hair were regular trends. Some of the hairstyles were comparable to female hairstyles.

## Guerilla Pimps

The "Guerilla Pimp" or "No-Nonsense Pimp" is known for using physical force as a means of discipline. A lot of people think that a Guerilla Pimp uses physical means to force a girl into prostitution in the first place. Any guy that physically forces a girl to prostitute is not a Guerilla Pimp or a pimp at all. A Guerilla Pimp will however, use physical force and threats to maintain his control over his prostitutes. Physical discipline is the "go-to" method for correction for what he feels is bad behavior or out-of-pocket behavior for his prostitute. A Guerilla Pimp can be a Businessman, Romeo Pimp, or a Hefner-style Pimp. The only behavior trait that gives him the "Guerilla" handle is his extensive use of physical abuse. Although I grew up around many different pimps with various styles of pimping, I have only known one that seemed to enjoy beating his prostitute. I can recall being in the same house with him one day as he disciplined his girl in an adjacent room. The viciousness of the beating was so bad that I had to leave the house. Listening to the girl cry and him yell just reminded me of growing up, and the constant arguing of my own parents. I wished that he would have stopped hitting her, but she had violated the rules of the game; at the time, we had brainwashed ourselves into believing that this was right. Yes, looking back I wish I was man enough to stop the attack all together, but unfortunately I was a young dumb 20 year old boy who had been told that this sick behavior was justified.

This particular Pimp friend was never really a happy person. He had grown up an abused child himself and had only a 7th grade education. After being labeled dyslexic as a young child, he had given up on life before he was even a teen. Being a gangster, and then later a pimp, was the only thing he believed that he could do in life. He showed signs of depression regularly. It was no mystery why he was violent. Men of many different walks of life abuse women for whatever reason; be it they were abused as a child, watched their mother get abused growing up, a drug or alcohol addiction, or whatever the case may be. The pimp subculture however promotes and excuses this behavior whereas other "square" occupations frown upon it. This lessens the reservations that a pimp may have when it comes to hitting a woman.

## The Businessman

The businessman can be a charmer and good with communication skills—as most good businessmen are. What sets the businessman aside from other styles of pimps is his method of initiation. He doesn't rely on charm or coercion to get his prostitutes. He uses logic and pitches a business plan as a means to convince a girl to work for him. He will clearly lay out the facts, and show the potential prostitute how they will make money together. Like myself, the girls that the businessman usually recruits are either money-motivated from the beginning or smart and believe in the plan.

Once the businessman has the prostitute(s), he operates his team like a functioning business. Violence is not his means of discipline or a tool used at all. The motto is, "If you have to beat her, you don't need her." He would rather get rid of a girl that does not comply with his program than put his hands on her. It is not so different from a businessman cutting out a bad investment.

## The Hefner

The "Hefner" style of pimp is close in behavior to the businessman. The difference between the two is in his relation to the women he deals with. The Hefner will be the one that usually owns the source that the sex is sold from. For example, he will be the owner of the escort service, website, magazine, or massage parlor. The Hefner will make his money off selling sex indirectly and from a perceived comfort zone. He is not a traditional pimp, although all of his income is derived from the exploitation of women and sex. The Hefner is usually protected by the law and operates as a legal entity. The Hefner is the real "American Pimp." Although a majority of the time this role is handled by a male, the Hefner can also be a woman. These women are commonly referred to as "Madams."

I often speculate as to why the Hefner is not referred to as a pimp and in many instances is praised and idolized—like the man Hugh Hefner himself. As a young teen me and my friends admired him and dreamed of being like him. He is still the biggest pimp that I know of that did it and got away with it. The Hefner pimp operates under the cover of legitimate business. He is the smartest of the pimp styles. He knows that he will get away with what he is doing and if he sets up his business correctly, he will get rich and never have to worry about jail.

## Female Pimps

In recent years the female pimp has become more and more common. I attribute this to a few things:

1. The new century mentality of women understanding that they do not have to be dependent on a man.

2. The growing number of lesbian women that have taken on the role of the pimp. The first time that I saw an example of

this was on the HBO documentary *Pimps Up, Ho's Down* with the female pimp Big Les. Over the years I've probably witnessed a couple dozen of cases involving female pimps, including in my own family.

3. The internet has also played a major role in the female pimping female game. With less need for a track, women do not feel the same need for the same amount of male protection. It's easier to go out of state with a group of girls to prostitute than it is to have a pimp with you.

Female pimping is not respected by traditional pimps. It is not respected because traditional pimping was always done by a man. To a male pimp, this should be a woman and man arrangement. Basically it's the same as in most male-dominated fields. Men feel threatened that they'll lose power. They don't want to be equal. This is built on inequality and the worst kind of power imbalance already. Due to its extreme growth in recent years in some circles it has become accepted. Many of the rules to this game have been changed or distorted. Many newer pimps and their network of friends have accepted this as a normal occurrence. Female pimps can also be Guerillas, Romeos, Business Women, and Hefner's in their methods of pimping. Some female pimps are actually prostitutes as well, who maintain a level of dominance over other girls. She will be the leader as they prostitute together.

A male pimp's bottom, or main prostitute, can also be a female pimp by job description. Based on her role in the stable/group, she may be responsible for the exact same things as the male pimp. She may collect the profits, transport other girls, post ads, and even discipline other girls that are in the group.

There is definitely a connection between how a child is raised and what type of pimp he becomes. I've noticed pimps that have had a better relationship with their mothers be nicer and more caring for their prostitutes. On the other hand pimps that were raised in foster homes or had bad relationships with their mothers can be way more aggressive and less caring for their girls. The person teaching or passing down the pimp game to the new pimp is also a determining factor as to what kind of pimp he becomes. As a child and young adult I was always into business and money. Although I personally never attached the pimp title to myself (I considered myself to be a Mac), if I had to say one of these described my style it would be a businessman. I never attempted to trick anybody that worked with me. I laid the scheme down plain and simple. Step by step. If she accepted then we moved forward. If not I moved on.

# Pimp Nicknames

Nicknames are common in American culture, but in the Black urban street culture nicknames are almost a requirement. In the late sixties and seventies when pimping was at its first peak in the urban communities, pimps were the only set of people that seemed to have nicknames, also known as handles, as a requirement.

As far as urban inner-city culture, the nickname explosion took place when the gang epidemic hit in the late seventies and eighties. During this time period, unlike the sixties where only pimps were fully taking on the nicknames, a new subculture of gangs joined in on taking on new handles. If you were a gang member you almost never went by your birth name. Instead, you were given a gang name to uphold; something that connects you to the hood that you represented. As you got older and younger gang members came up under you they would take on your name and add on the suffixes "young," "lil," "baby," or "tiny." Most of the time these nicknames were awarded to you based on physical or personality attributes. Sometimes the name came from a defining situation or event.

With the hip-hop culture and influence spreading as it did from the eighties and nineties, the use of nicknames became even more prevalent. Almost every hip-hop artist took a stage name. Some of the gangster rappers used their actual street names while others created names to brand themselves. I don't believe that the popularity of pimp nicknames had anything to do with its spread into the gang subculture. They were indeed totally separate. I believe that the nickname popularity explosion amongst young black males in the inner city was more about a group of people who had always been told, and believed, that they were nothing. It is no secret that this is the kind of treatment that black people have received in this country since the day they were first brought here. They have always been looked at and treated as second class citizens, unequal to their white counterparts. This treatment has psychologically damaged an entire race of people in this country leaving them scarred with a permanent identity crisis. The belief that they are less than human and worthless is a condition that I like to call PTSD or Post Traumatic Slavery Disorder. The people that we're talking about picking up these nicknames were people that had no true sense of self-worth or knowledge of their culture or ancestry, many of whom were fatherless. Taking on a nickname was a form of self-creation. Without knowing exactly what they were doing they were beginning to create their own identity. Largely because they did not have one already.  By the early nineties it was more than common for young black youth to have a nickname, whether they were gang affiliated, a rapper, or a normal teenager.

When the pimp subculture reached its second explosion in urban communities in the late nineties, most of the men involved already had nicknames. Their nicknames had either grown organically from their culture, or from having been previously connected to a gang or click. Because the gang culture and pimp culture were two totally separate lifestyles, many pimps had to change their old names and pick up new ones to fit the new lifestyle. For example, somebody that was once called "Big Knockout" from the gang could not carry that name into the pimp game. That name was once used to intimidate and scare other gang members. If used in the pimp game, this name would scare off girls and contribute little to the money-making goal.

The process of creating a pimp nickname is similar to choosing any other nickname. Physical and personality attributes, a situation, mode of conduct, or an abbreviated version of someone's real name. A lot of other pimp nicknames don't come from anything other than a person creating a brand or image for themselves in hopes of attracting attention and women. Somebody may use the name with the word "money" in it and have no money at all.

Nicknames are necessary when you're operating in any of the underworld cultures. Avoiding the law is a lot easier when you are going by an alias. Nowadays in the inner cities around America, unless you are super square you are known by a nickname, regardless if you're a pimp or gang member. People do not use their "government" name (legal birth name). I have close friends I've known for over ten years and have no clue what their real name is.

It is not common for people to drop their name when they leave the game. The name has surpassed the game and has been attached to the individual. Almost every friend I have still carries their nickname that they acquired from the gangster and pimp life— even if they haven't been involved in the game for a decade or more. This name has become their identity. It is not a front. Going by a different name didn't necessarily make being involved in the game easier internally, although it was a way to become another person. Once you were branded you had to live up to the reputation of that name. In a way it made things more challenging for you. Social media only furthered this culture of nicknames. Most people have created yet another or multiple names for their many social media sites. I personally have a different name on Facebook, Twitter, Instagram, and Snapchat.

# Richard

Richard was a very special young man. By fourteen years old he had already developed a charismatic personality that made women love him and guys envy him. The problem was that Richard knew it, and he used his attractive personality to his advantage. This meant he was very successful in using his persuasive smile and sweet talk to get girls and guys to give him money. Richard was forced into adulthood when he was only a child. By the age of six, Richard's mother fell victim to a toxic addiction and his father had passed away. Growing up impoverished meant that extra clothes, food, and toys were scarce for Richard. With a strong personality, Richard somehow found the courage to go out and hustle for money in any way that he could imagine. When he was eight years old, he and his childhood friend Demetrius would walk to the neighborhood gas station and solicit people to pay them to wash their windows. Selling candy for a non-existent field trip was another one of his more creative tactics.

By the age of thirteen, Richard's mother had cleaned her life up tremendously, and was heavily involved in her church. Unfortunately, their financial situation remained the same, so Richard began to use his charismatic personality in a new way: Richard used it to get money from girls. Richard began to request that the girls in his school give him money for lunch, and the girls would oblige. One dollar, five dollars, ten dollars—whatever they would give him, he would collect and add up to present to me and a small group of friends at school. Bragging, he would walk up and flash his wad of money. "Look how much I got! Look how much she gave me!" During Richard's sophomore year through his junior year of high school, having a girls that would buy him whatever he wanted had become even more important to him than sex. He and his friends called this "juicing." Richard would try to "juice" a girl for all that she could supply.

Towards the end of Richard's junior year in high school the concept of "pimping" had fully captivated his young mind. It wasn't exactly a new concept, but had been reborn as the next big hustle to get into. The current hip-hop world was both subtlety and outright talking about it. HBO was airing the pimp documentary *Pimps Up, Ho's Down* on a consistent basis. This documentary showcased the country's top pimps and showed them living glamorous lives with fancy cars and attractive girls catering to their every desire. It was a visual handbook of how to be a pimp. To a young, poor black male from the inner city this was an inspiration and a clear, achievable goal. The change from collecting food, money, and Nautica coats to the purchase of cars and large sums of money only seemed like an appropriate graduation.

At the age of sixteen, Richard was in a relationship with a younger, white female. She had been my friend from childhood and I knew that she would be perfect for him. I took it upon myself to hook them up. At first Richard was apprehensive about it because at the time he didn't feel comfortable dating outside of his race. I persuaded him to talk to her anyway, telling him about how I knew she would take care of him. This girl was from a well-off, two-parent household. She grew up her entire life in an upper-middle class community and had no idea what it meant to go without the things she wanted in life. She was infatuated with black men, and not just any black men—the more "street" they were the better. For nearly two years of her relationship with Richard she was his bread and butter. She would buy him his clothes, give him money, and allow him to use the car her father bought her as if it was his own. She did it all in exchange for Richard's time and occasional sex. She was in love with him and he was in love with what she did for him.

When the pimp business was introduced to Richard he felt it was the needed upgrade in his relationship with his girlfriend. Why live off a part-time job when you can make $1,000 in one night? Richard's mind was made up. He talked to his sixteen-year-old girlfriend about the "upgrade" and she readily accepted the idea. Within the week, Richard and his friends Kenny, Demetrius, and myself sat on the track and watched as she worked. Later Richard showed the growing young men substantially more than a few dollars for lunch money; this time he held a wad of $1,000 and hadn't even broken a sweat. The only thing our young teenage selves could think was, "Where do we sign up?"

Richard was by far one of the most charismatic and well known Pimps from San Diego. Richard took on the pimp nickname "Fantastic," and his name was ringing from coast to coast. Not only was he known for turning girls into prostitutes, but he also had a reputation of turning guys into pimps. His heart was big and he took care of many families throughout his career as a pimp. He had quickly earned a name for himself and was looked up to by many. His career ended quickly, when his life was taken by 4 minors that were on a shooting spree. His impact on the urban community of San Diego, and his presence in our lives, was so big that after 14 years his birthday is still celebrated every year by over 100 people at a gathering named after him, aptly named "Fantastic Day." This celebration has taken the form of a holiday for many people.

IN LOVING MEMORY OF
RICHARD LEON WILSON

# Chapter 3:
# Misdirection

# Motivations to Pimp

What motivates a person to be a pimp? Unfortunately, there isn't one, concise answer to this question. Through my own personal experience of growing up in this lifestyle, I have witnessed a variety of different personalities involved in pimping.

## *Money*

Having spent more than two decades in and around the pimp world I have known one thing to be the key factor that motivates individuals to pimp: money. Have you heard of that old saying, "Money is the root of all evil?" In the pimp world that is one hundred percent correct. In the impoverished communities around America where the urban pimp is created you will almost always find an individual who was searching for financial wealth, stability, and growth. It is extremely rare to find an individual who, as a child, had ambitions of growing up to be a pimp. Although, I have come across a few individuals that have been raised by a pimp or a prostitute who did believe that's what they wanted to do once they were old enough.

The youngest male that I've come across that wanted to be a pimp was around 12 years old. Even at his young age, he actually talked about himself as if he was a pimp already. I remember when he told me that he was a pimp, I laughed at him; I brushed him off, and told him that he didn't know anything about the game. I've never come across a girl under the age of 15 that expressed a desire to be a prostitute. I've only met these women after they were already adults—and they've told me about how they got involved at 12 and 13 years old. Most of them told me about how their parents were drug abusers and they were left on their own to take care of themselves. Prostitution was the primary means of them being able to put food in their stomachs. In these rare cases where a child *does* want to be "in the life," their inspiration seems to be their overwhelming exposure to that lifestyle. Outside of that, the majority of individuals are motivated to pimp for monetary gain. Pimping is seen as a means to living a life that would normally not be accessible to a person growing up in the ghetto.

How does a person come to believe that pimping is the way to make money? First, let's examine the person that is being influenced by money. Individuals growing up in the impoverished cities around America run a high risk of being affected by many negative factors: low-income, run-down housing, drug abuse, poor nutrition, inadequate schooling, and mental and physical abuse by family members only begin to scratch the surface. Yes, these same factors occur in all walks of life and not just in the inner cities, however, the difference is the sheer abundance found in the inner city. These factors are the norm, rather than the exception. To an individual who has grown up knowing nothing but poverty, money is seen as the only means of hope and survival. To an individual who has never known what it feels like to have the things they wanted in life, a desire builds inside to constantly reach for more.

Money is power to somebody that has been powerless. Money is respect in your community, your family, and a way to have some self-respect. Money is an impoverished person's way out of an undesirable existence that seems to have no end. To many, having money simply means the end of being hungry, homeless, and hopeless.

A person's initial contact with the pimp lifestyle is usually through some sort of monetary expression. As a poor individual, meeting or knowing a pimp that is making money off the sex trade allows that person to physically see someone succeeding or surviving off the earned money. A young man sees the cars, fancy clothes, jewelry, and other things that he can't afford. He is lured in because he wants these material possessions. He wants to have more than two pairs of pants that he shares with his brother and those worn down Nikes with the holes on the side of them that keep growing. If a young man doesn't meet a pimp in person, he doesn't have to look far to see monetary value in pimping. He can hear it in the music coming through the radio every day. From the early nineties to mid-2000's, "pimp rap" was so influential on the hip-hop scene that it became a type of rap style of its own. As a teen, I remember saying, and hearing others say, "I listen to pimp rap." Through this music I heard people bragging about the money that they made and the lifestyle that came with it. If a young man doesn't hear about pimping in the music, he could see it on television, movies, documentaries, and countless other forms of media. To a poor youth growing up in the inner city looking for an achievable means of getting money, pimping is definitely at the top of the list.

## Material Gain

Although accumulating as much money as possible may be number one on the list of motivation factors of being a pimp, coming in at a strong second is material gain. In my years of experience in and around the pimp world, I have noticed that many people stay in the lifestyle just to have access to the material possessions. I have seen men and women that once had money and were able to purchase the designer, name-brand items. Once the money isn't there and they are no longer able to buy what they want, they continue investing time into the pimp lifestyle in the hopes to have those items again. For many people, just having the luxury cars, jewelry, and designer clothes is satisfaction and motivation enough to pimp. I've known many people throughout the years who owned brand new, luxury automobiles, but didn't have money for the gas tank and couldn't put food on the table.

## Peer Pressure

My best friend "Fantastic" was extremely gifted when it came to speaking. He was very persuasive and convince somebody to do almost anything. Good or bad, male or female. I always knew when he was working on somebody, trying to convince them to become a pimp. For example, his cousin and my good friend who was the same age as me. Day in and day out I would hear Fantastic ridicule his cousin about being a square and having a girlfriend. I couldn't say much because I had a square girl at that time as well. Although I was occasionally ridiculed having a girlfriend, it was nowhere near as hard as Fantastic was on him. I believe this had to do with the fact that at this time I was making more money than everybody else that was a pimp. The man with the biggest bank could not be talked about. I honestly believe that because his cousin wasn't getting money and was doing poorly financially, Fantastic felt the need to constantly pressure him. Fantastic wanted to see all of his friends doing well.

The combination of being constantly ridiculed, pimping being socially accepted, every rapper you listened to talking about it as if it's the best thing in the world, and having financial problems equaled a form of peer pressure that was too much to contain. Even at a young age I could tell that Fantastic's cousin was not cut out to be a pimp. Similar to how it really wasn't the thing for me. But like me, the pressures were laid on him so thick that he finally did convert into a lifestyle of pimping. His girlfriend at the time was rumored to have been very promiscuous and we had teased him about that fact for the few months that they were dating. We all knew that he really liked her, but no amount of "like" was going to combat the opinions of your best friends. Within a matter of three months of dating, my friend turned his girlfriend out to the game. Four years later they were married with two kids.

One might ask, "Why would your peers pressure you into pimping?" Well, if your peers happen to be pimps already then it is not a far leap for you to join them on that path. If a young man is friends with a pimp or multiple pimps, they will likely continuously push their friend into the lifestyle. This may be because the friend that's pimping may honestly believe the way they are living is great and could be beneficial to his friends. This could also have something to do with the lack of emotional security within the pimp, which creates a desire in him to make his peers join him. By doing what he is doing, his way of life is now validated—at least inside of his head. Once a person is in the pimp lifestyle, his peers will continue to expect them to keep up a certain persona. If your peers are in the lifestyle you would be looked down upon if you're not in the game with them. Once a person digs into this lifestyle, he works hard at creating an image of himself. Deviating from that image leaves an individual vulnerable to being ostracized from his friends and others involved in the lifestyle. At times, many continue to pimp regardless of how much they really want to stop and get a "square" job, go to school, or just get out of the lifestyle because they don't want their peers to badmouth them.

## Social Status

Whether individuals are motivated to pimp for financial gain, material possessions, or peer pressure, they all want to increase their social status. If you are a pimp motivated by money coming from an impoverished background you are likely trying to break free from the shackles of poverty. In achieving your financial freedom, you will be advancing your social status. In the capitalist American society that we live in, money equals respect, power, and admiration.

For the individual motivated to pimp for material possessions, his status is upgraded from those around him with less. He could live in the same poor community that he grew up in, with the same people that he has known his entire life, but as soon as he has a nice car, nice clothes, and other accessories that are uncommon in his community, he is now looked at with honor. He's glorified. Acquiring material possessions can take a person from zero to hero in the blink of an eye.

Social status amongst peers can fluctuate in the pimp world. The friend in the circle with the most prostitutes is looked at with higher esteem than the one with none or less. In the pimp community, a pimp may never admit it out loud, but he cares how he is viewed by others in his field. Most pimps work on establishing a quality name for themselves and will literally fight to maintain their social status. The way that one is viewed in this world can affect a person's financial gain and safety. If a pimp is known for being untrustworthy, a liar, thief, or a scandalous individual, people in the pimp world will shun him. This means valuable information that could increase your profits or keep him and his prostitutes out of jail will be kept from him. A pimp wants to build and maintain a quality social status. After years of doing this, individuals can actually become caught up in this idea of their own personal social status and will remain in the lifestyle simply because of the fear of losing the false ideas of status that they have about their own value.

## Music and Media's Influence

They say music can calm the savage beast. I say that music can also create a savage beast. Looking back at my personal life growing up listening to predominantly rap music, I can see how it affected my views towards women, society, and life in general. Not just any rap music, but a specific sub-genre called "gangster rap." From the age of twelve, this was my primary choice in music. If you know anything about this genre, then you know that the belittling of women is a common trend. There's almost no way that you can go through any random five songs and not hear a reference to a woman being a bitch, hoe, or a variety of other demeaning terms. Some songs are more extreme than others. Songs are also usually sexually explicit when it comes to women. These songs tend to reduce women to merely sex objects in the minds of the listener. There were a few rappers in the late eighties and early nineties that based their whole music career on talking about women in a sexual or degrading manner.

As I write this, I can hear strongly in my head the chorus to producer/rapper Dr. Dre and Snoop Dogg's hit from 1993 "Bitches Ain't Shit." When this song came out I was twelve years old with a young impressionable mind that surely should not have been listening to music like this. Compound that song by 1,000 over the course of a decade being created by some of the most influential people in your life and you will discover that many of your opinions have been shaped by these music artists. For the most part my parents did control the music that I listened to as a young child. They would play reggae, R&B, soul, and jazz. They had total control, which was slightly different than most of my peers, who were allowed to hear anything they wanted. However, by the age of twelve, my dad was gone and my mom was more lenient; I started listening to all of the stuff my friends were listening to. My parents never talked to me about the lyrics being bad or degrading. For the most part they actually liked the music themselves. My aunts and uncles also would throw on some Too $hort, Sugar Free, Snoop Dogg, and others once I was older. The music was good music. The sound, the style, and delivery of the raps were all great. It's no wonder why many of my peers and others that grew up like me have a low opinion of women. This music added to an already existing male chauvinistic society where women were depicted as sex objects and less-than-men in all forms of media and entertainment. What has manifested is a mindset that sees women as objects rather than humans.

How important is music really to an adolescent black youth growing up in the inner city? How important is music to any human being anywhere? As a child, I would brush off the severity of its influence on my mind. "It's just music!" I would tell my mother as she half-heartedly attempted to control the sounds coming out of my stereo. Writing this book has forced me to face many truths about myself and my upbringing, and I can't help but acknowledge the impact that music had on me.

When we were kids my friends and I listened to the original form of hip-hop. As a child in the early 80s, we were exposed to Hip Hops beginning stages. Artists like Grandmaster Flash, Kool Moe Dee, KRS 1 and many other Hip Hop pioneers were still prevalent. When this was popular, it was common to dress how the rappers dressed, dancing how they danced, and mimicking the way they talked. All of our latest slang came from them also. This was in the early eighties. During this time "gangster rap" had not yet hit the scene as hard as it would later. Prior to N.W.A. launching its transformative album *Straight Outta Compton* in 1986, the world had yet to hear rap that talked about or glorified street gang life. N.W.A. hit the scene hard and opened up a new genre of hip-hop, which was termed "gangster rap." In reality, San Francisco Bay-area rapper Todd Shaw, better known as Too $hort, had started rapping about street gang life a few years earlier. Too $hort appeared publicly with his street sound in 1983 with his album *Don't*

*Stop Rappin*, but it didn't have the same impact as *Straight Outta Compton*. Too $hort is said to be the first rapper to use the word "bitch" in a recorded hip-hop record. Due to the fact that West Coast rap was really not looked at during the early stages of hip-hop's birth, artists like Too $hort were overlooked and passed over. That is probably why even Google search will not state him as the first MC to use the word "bitch" in a rap. Unlike N.W.A., Too $hort not only talked about the underground street thugs/gangs, he talked about the pimp, player, and prostitute elements of the street. Songs like "Pimp The Ho," "Mack Attack," and "Freaky Tales" in the mid-eighties introduced pimping into the minds of many urban youngsters that may have not had any exposure to it otherwise.

As gangster rap became more socially acceptable and was promoted heavily by the mainstream media in the early nineties, the more traditional hip-hop sound started to fade. The rap throne shifted from the East Coast to the West and the vast majority of the music coming from the West Coast was gang influenced. The lyrics were filled with vulgarities: murder, gang banging, drug dealing, and promiscuity were promoted as if it was an intentional campaign. In my opinion, this was very intentional by the major record labels. Major corporate record companies found this type of music extremely lucrative and put millions into it. It seemed like the more rappers promoted gangs, drugs, and sex the more successful they became.

Simultaneously, the communities where most of these rappers came from were being ravished by gangs, drugs, and murder. The music of this era was a direct reflection of what was going on in the inner cities around America and I lived this personally in my own community. I can remember rappers during this time period saying that they were expressing the life that was going on in the hood to inform the rest of the world of this tragedy. It was a cry for help to a world that seemed to turn a blind eye to the needs of the disenfranchised, underserved communities in the U.S.

Unfortunately, this cry for help went unheard. Instead, the reverse happened. By this style of music being pushed mainstream throughout this country and the world, people from all demographics, social backgrounds, and economic levels began to listen to gangster rap. Not only were they listening to it, but they were imitating the behavior that was being expressed in the lyrics. Instead of the music being seen a cry for help, it was seen as something cool, something to be admired, even glorified. Blood and Crip gangs were starting to pop up in little and big cities throughout America and overseas. They were appearing in places where they were unheard of previously. In the U.S. there were pockets of people that would protest this music being promoted and tried to ban its creation all together.

One of the most famous advocates against gangster rap music was civil rights activist C. Delores Tucker. Delores, who marched alongside Dr. Martin Luther King in Selma, Alabama, spent the last decade of her life taking on rappers, music stores, and music companies that produced gangster rap. Many rappers mentioned her name in their lyrics negatively. One of these people was Tupac Shakur. I remember listening to his song "How Do You Want It" and hearing him comment on her. Even though I didn't even know who she was previously to that, I grew a hatred towards her. I thought she was against my idol and hero, Tupac. At that time, anybody or anything opposed to him became my enemy too. This was a prime example of how deep music can and does influence the minds and emotions of people, and inner city youth in particular.

At the same time gangster and drug dealer rap was being promoted by the mainstream media, the prison system was becoming the largest growing industry in America. It is rumored that the top music executives and the executives of private prisons met privately and came to an agreement to promote gangster rap knowing that this would directly affect the growth and sustainability of private prisons. In early 2012 an anonymous letter entitled "The Secret Meeting that Changed Rap Music and Destroyed a Generation" was released online and immediately went viral. This letter describes in detail the accounts of this supposed private meeting. Either way, the facts from my own experience validate that the promotion of gangster rap did and does affect the minds of people. Music does in general. Unfortunately gangster rap came from the pain of a hurt community, and rather than it being used as a means to help uplift the community, the lifestyle was glorified. Instead of communities receiving help, major corporate dollars backed the music, incentivizing people growing up in these gang areas of America to dig deeper into the street life. The soundtrack to many real life murders was gangster rap.

Rappers failed to realize how powerful their lyrics were and how much it encouraged us to do harmful and illegal things—things that led us to jail. So many times I've heard rappers say that they're just artists talking about real life situations that occur in the inner city. They claim that people don't do the things they do (or say they do) in their lyrics. In actuality this is a complete scapegoat from personal responsibility. Rap, for the record, is extremely influential and has helped guide tons of people in the wrong direction.

Right around the time of the assassination of Tupac Shakur, West Coast gangster rap lost its prestige. Gangster rap was shoved off the hip hop throne and replaced by music from the Southern region of the United States, from places like New Orleans, Atlanta, Texas, and Mississippi. The influence of gangster rap was there but there was a lyrical shift from bragging about murder and drugs to bragging about money, cars, and clothes. Rap music went from glamorizing West Coast gangster life to down south hustler life. Rap labels like No Limit and Cash Money emerged. You would still hear the rap about guns, violence and even gang affiliation in their rhymes similar to their West coast gangster rap predecessors, but that was not the dominant sound. One thing that remained the same throughout this transition was the dehumanizing of women. That part never changed—if anything, it got worse. With the down south dominance you now had an element that may have been peeking around the corner before but now it was on full display. That element was music geared toward strippers and strip clubs. In the urban communities throughout the South, strip clubs play a major roll. They are where many people, both male and female, hang out, drink, and enjoy their leisure time. In hip hop history the first example of this strip club rap that emerged was from Uncle

Luke and The 2 Live Crew from Miami. He is crowned as the pioneer of "booty shake strip club rap."

Around the time of the genre shift, the urban streets of America also experienced a shift. Youngsters in the inner city no longer sought out lowriders, but expensive cars with big, shiny rims. I remember growing up and experiencing the switch. Our clothing style also switched from Dickie's suits to wearing labels like Polo, Nautica, Abercrombie & Fitch, and even Urban brands like ENYCE, FUBU, and Karl Kani that had an appearance of upper class and wealth. On a mainstream level, southern rap was taking over and getting the corporate industry dollars that once was going to gangster rappers. Although this was happening, California never let go of its love for gangster rap. It still held a major influence on the minds of youngsters, just on a more underground level. As a youth loving gangster rap in California, you would no longer get to see your favorite rapper on TV or receiving awards. Being from the West Coast we not only noticed this but we're angered by it. I was really into West Coast rap so I took it to heart. I would refuse to listen to almost all music that wasn't from California. Only a few artists from outside of California would get my attention and money, but they still had to sound like they were from California. This was serious to me and I was vocal about it.

During the late nineties there was a branch of gangster rap that emerged focusing almost exclusively on pimping and prostitution. This break off genre was called "pimp rap" by the urban community. With this genre, many new rappers emerged. Their lyrics focused primarily on the pimp subculture. Rapping about this lifestyle was not totally new to the rap scene; Too Short began rapping about pimping in the mid-eighties. He practically branded his entire image off of being a pimp. One key difference is that during the late nineties period there were a lot more than just a few rappers talking about pimping and prostitution. This was becoming an epidemic.

Packs of rappers making music about pimping began to emerge during this era. Established rappers who may have mentioned the word "pimp" here and there before, now made pimping the main focus of their music. Even Snoop Dogg, one of the world's most famous rappers, transitioned from strictly gangster rap to the new "pimp rap." Not only did his lyrics change, but so did his image. He began to dress like a pimp, talk like a pimp, and make appearances with women who appeared to be prostitutes. On one occasion I remember him appearing on an award show with women on leashes next to the famous pimp Don Magic Juan. Don Magic Juan had become Snoop's pimp mentor. Along with Snoop Dogg, other mainstream rappers began to create songs that either referenced or were solely dedicated to pimping. Nelly's song "Pimp Juice" and Jay-Z's "Big Pimpin" were a couple of incredibly successful tracks. While the world may have been dancing in their cars on the way to work with these songs playing, the people who were actually living the lifestyle that this type of music glamorized, saw this as validation to continue doing what they were doing. The music being created helped plant the idea that women were to be viewed as hoes and bitches—that women were property.

The fact that urban culture had been moving back to the seventies pimp era is indisputable. I lived it, watched it, and felt it from coast to coast. I was one of those young kids that was pumped up and directed by the rap artists that I loved. When I wanted to attack my own people or involve myself in gang activity, I would put on the most violent murder music that I could. When I was hustling I would put on the artist that was talking about money and hustling. When I wanted to be cold hearted to a girl or feel what we called "Pimpish," I would play the artists that were rapping about pimping. I remember how my friend Lawrence, who was a young active gang member, would listen to Brotha Lynch Hung and CBO to put him in the mood to go out shooting. I myself would also listen to similar music when it was time to fight or to feel encouraged and tough. Too short, Mac Dre and Sugar Free are still rappers that I currently listen to when I'm trying not to be emotional over a woman. When I was in the game they would keep me in a zone of not having feelings about pimping, and always inspired me to pimp. Through my life and many lives like mine, rappers were our guidance. They were our teachers, preachers, and mentors. We learned more and were influenced more by them than our own parents. It's not surprising that I can recite word-for-word every Snoop Dogg line from his 1993 album, but can't tell you one thing that I learned in a high school classroom.

Here in San Diego towards the peak of the pimp and prostitution epidemic another growing trend started to arise. Somewhere around 2001 I began to notice that more and more of my peers from inner cities throughout San Diego started to become rappers. Many of which actually had talent. More and more, the local rap culture and the pimp culture began to merge into each other. Pimps, gangsters, and other young black men had started to rap. Creating music videos, albums, and even performing shows. The really good ones would actually make a name for themselves, which in return made more girls attracted to them. This led to bigger stables for those that were already pimping, and a popularity for those that weren't pimping that would ring throughout the city that caused many to get into the game. The merger between the genre of pimp rap and the actual pimp and prostitute subculture started to majorly spread in my city. Almost every pimp friend that I had in the early 2000's had begun to rap. This rap epidemic had not just affected the guys who were pimping but it had become the new cool thing for young black males in San Diego. It seemed like at one point everybody was striving to be a rapper. I often joked that rap had no longer been a form of music but a new form of communication because everybody was doing it. In my opinion this was happening because a lot of young black males from my community that had attempted to pimp or never got into it still were looking for a way out of poverty—still living in underserved communities with no visible options or opportunities to get out. Rap was beginning to seem like the only possible breath of fresh air. This mentality is still going on today, but it's substantially lower than it was in the early 2000's.

With this merger of pimp and rap culture came some unforeseen consequences. Everybody talking about pimping in their raps (whether or not they were actually doing it) created a very thin string when it came to legal issues. Several of my close friends here in San Diego have run into some small legal issues, parental custody fights, and huge indictments, where the music they created about pimping or gangs was used against them as evidence to convict them. Law enforcement agencies quickly caught on to both social media and the local hip hop music scene here in San Diego to build their most compelling cases. In 2014, my childhood friend Brandon 'Tiny Doo' Duncan was indicted under California Penal code 182.5 facing a life sentence with the only evidence being the lyrics in his album. Just recently, I was in Federal court advocating for two of my mentees who were violated for the content of their music—most of which was pimp related. The saddest thing about this situation is that both of the young men that I was advocating for were not pimps. Both were new fathers, had girlfriends, worked jobs, and one of them had just made the Dean's list at City College. Unfortunately I'm in court often, advocating for or supporting people all of the time and what I've noticed is that even if the music they created wasn't directly used as evidence against them, it is still brought up to make them look bad. Frequently, they were not even involved in the activities that they were rapping about. On the flip side of that coin, when you have people that are actually living the pimp lifestyle, that they then rap about, they have just handed the prosecution all of the evidence they needed for their own conviction.

The question stands unanswered: Does rap music influence the streets and create its trends, or do the streets set the trends and influence rap music? Now as an awoken thirty-seven-year-old man, I look back at being fifteen and being angry with C. Delores Tucker for her fight to ban gangster, misogynistic, hip hop and wish that she would have succeeded. To this day gangster/pimp rap is the most listened to music in my car. It's been embedded in me. Only now I know how to listen to it with understanding. I also can recognize how it's still helping to mold the minds of youth from the inner city. Knowing now that this music affects them in the same way that it did me, it's imperative that I stay up to date with musical trends.

# Music and Me

As a young teen growing up in the hood I did understand that music affected my mood. I just didn't realize how much. I can actually think of a few situations where we purposefully put on certain music to alter our mood. The instance that sticks out the most was one filled with murder.

I remember the night like it was yesterday. At the age of fifteen, I was in the neighborhood park that was home to the gang that Lawrence was from. I didn't normally hang out there, but that night I was with him and somehow that's where we ended up. I was at the park with him and several other gang members. I was smoking weed and drinking a beer. I rolled my own joint, being extremely cautious not to smoke anybody else's weed—I knew that they were smoking weed laced with sherm (PCP). I sat back for about an hour and 30 minutes and watched what looked like a gang meeting taking place. That is exactly what it was. When the meeting concluded everybody simultaneously got into 3 cars and started caravanning. I was in the backseat of Lawrence's car riding when I heard him say to the passenger, "Change this shit! Put that Brotha Lynch on. I need that murder music." It was at that point I realized what was going on and that I was about to be on a gang mission with Lawrence and his friends. More than likely this was going to be a drive-by shooting. I was scared out of my mind, but couldn't speak up. I was afraid to let Lawrence know that I was even a little bit scared. The more the Brotha Lynch album played in the car the more I felt my fear going out of the window; I started hyping myself up for whatever was coming next. However, what came next was Lawrence pulling up to the house we stayed at and telling his passenger to let me out. Lawrence looked at me and said, "Armand you don't need to be a part of any of what's about to go down. I'll see you later." I got out of that car relieved, but worried at the same time. Worried about Lawrence. That next morning, on our way to work, we walked up to his car. I remember seeing bullet shell casings in the back seat. Lawrence chuckled and said, "I gotta clean this shit out."

# Media and Television

Right alongside music's influence over the streets was the visual imagery that coincided, further growing the seeds planted by the music. Imagine listening to lyrics constantly telling you how to pimp, how prosperous pimping is, how cool pimping is, and then having the visual images to back this up. For a poor, young man growing up with little to no positive guidance, these images become your most influential mentor.

As the shift was occurring in the inner city from gang banging to pimping, a special documentary premiered on HBO called *Pimps Up, Ho's Down*. This was a landmark documentary produced at a time when most of us had just started hearing about prostitution and pimping but never had a true visual on what this lifestyle was like in reality.

In my neighborhood there were not any known pimps that I looked up to or even knew existed. My only exposure to pimping at an early age was through music and *Pimps Up, Ho's Down*. I remember being a sophomore in high school when my friends and I would gather in front of the TV, right after school, and engulf ourselves in this documentary. We'd watch pimps from the seventies and the nineties talk about the game, and explain what their lives were really like. For once, we had something tangible to show us what we had heard about in the rap lyrics. It was almost like a starter guide to the game—Pimpin 101. All of my friends found one main character that we related to the most; for most of us it was "Pimpin Snooky." We mimicked his charisma and characteristics daily. It was on this documentary we heard firsthand how lucrative pimping and prostitution was. We learned from prostitutes how much they enjoyed being involved. Pimps were shown as prosperous, happy, and intelligent.

I've recently re-watched the documentary. It's been over a decade since I've seen it. What I found is that even now that I've matured and seen the depth of the destruction that the pimp subculture brings, I was still attracted to it. Watching the pimps featured in the movie after so long was like watching a childhood superhero. I heard them speaking about the game, but this time around I could actually relate to everything they were saying because unlike before, I had lived a similar lifestyle. On top of watching the film repeatedly, quotes from the documentary frequently popped up in rap lyrics, further validating the lifestyle: "Gold is for the honey and green is for the money," "By choice, not force," "Barbecue or mildew," and "You need some new guides in ya motha fuckin life" are just a few of the sayings that stick out in my memory now.

The pimps became not just my idols, but my role models. To my group of friends, this life was something we now felt we had to have. The conversations that we had while watching this documentary were as if we were classmates in the same group project at school—and we were very interested in the subject matter. Gang banging was played out to us. As we were approaching adulthood and looking for a way to pay the bills, this new life that had been presented to us seemed to be a logical next move. Here was a group of black men with money, fancy cars, expensive clothes, jewelry, and women that catered to their every desire. These men didn't go to college to do this. They didn't have to be on someone else's clock, listening to rules from some asshole boss. At the age of sixteen, this was the most appealing life I had ever seen, and it wasn't a life I had to wait for. I could start now. I was practically living on my own, raising myself anyway. How hard could this be?

Within a year of *Pimps Up, Ho's Down* being released, many young men from my community had begun to experiment with this lifestyle, myself included. I was still in high school when I first sat on El Cajon Boulevard—San Diego's famous "hoe stroll" or "blade." I sat amongst a group of my friends at a bus stop as we watched my friend's girlfriend make her first dollar from a trick. I don't actually remember much from that night, except feeling an adrenaline rush. I was scared, excited, and curious. Actually applying what we had learned from *Pimps Up, Ho's Down* and rap music gave us a sense of accomplishment—a feeling that I had never felt in my life up until that point. We thirsted for more knowledge.

The next visual guide my friends and I used was the seventies blaxploitation film *The Mack* starring Max Julien and Richard Pryor. Even though this fictional film was created over thirty years prior to us entering the pimp life, it served as our guide on how to behave as pimps. It furthered our knowledge on the rules and regulations of the game. Although the star of *The Mack*, Max Julien, was only an actor, this role created an idolized image for him that lasts to this day for black men entering the pimp lifestyle. He was our superhero. *The Mack* showed us a young, black man who came from poverty, went to prison, came out, and learned the pimp game. Even though he was a pimp, he was still depicted as a good guy who loved his family and wanted to provide for his mother.

As I re-watched *Pimps Up, Ho's Down* recently the biggest thing that stuck out to me was how easily we were misled by the pimps in this movie. How they all ended up going to jail at some point, but we never knew that. The biggest thing that stuck out to me about this movie that I didn't know then, but I know now, is how the main character that we admired the most, Pimpin Snooky, has recently come forward and admitted to being an FBI informant during the time the movie was being filmed. He claims that the FBI was well aware of his human sex trafficking and did not care. He felt that by working with the FBI, he had a free pass to Pimp.

A little more than a year after the release of *Pimps Up, Ho's Down* another major documentary on the pimp lifestyle was created, called *American Pimp* by the Hughes brothers. With the respect and clout that the Hughes brothers had already, releasing a pimp documentary had our immediate attention and money. This documentary, while very similar to *Pimps Up, Ho's Down*, strayed away from just glorifying the black male street pimp by adding an interview of Nevada's Bunny Ranch owner, Dennis Hof. It also showed a little bit more of the legal ramifications of pimping.

Just as *Pimps Up, Ho's Down* was our introduction course into the pimp subculture, *American Pimp* was like the continuation course. By the time of its release we had already had a lot of hands on experience and could relate to the things that were talked about in this documentary. What this film did differently, was that it inspired us to not just stay still in our city, but to begin thinking about pimping in other states. I actually liked this documentary more than *Pimps Up, Ho's Down*. I used to keep it on special display on my bookshelf in my dorm when I was in the military. It was a prized possession.

Both documentaries were two of the leading inspirations for young black men growing up in the late nineties to start pimping. These two documentaries also opened up the floodgates for a slew of low budget producers to follow in their footsteps and attempt to create similar documentaries, specials, and interviews with pimps. With all of this material being released on the internet and television glamorizing pimping and prostitution, it appeared as if it were legal and acceptable. I knew that it wasn't legal, but it seemed like the safest way to hustle and the best possible option to do as a young black man growing up in the hood. At this time law enforcement only seemed to be concerned with gang activity and drug dealers. As long as you followed the rules of the pimp subculture, I didn't think getting in trouble was an option.

Mainstream music entertainers like Jay-Z, Nelly, and Snoop began releasing hit music videos exhibiting pimping. *MTV*'s release of *Pimp My Ride* in 2004 only furthered what seemed to be the stamp of approval of the pimp culture. Imagery can be incredibly influential, the question is only whether that influence is going to be positive or negative. In the late nineties and early 2000s, all forms of media not only promoted pimping to black youth, but helped create an atmosphere that would seduce the desires of a better life for both males and females. Instead of true positive black imagery that would help lift us out of the condition we were in, we were force-fed the pimp lifestyle with a shovel.

## The Nutty's

Welcome to sunny San Diego! A tourist destination for people around the world, known to have the best weather of all American cities. Nicknamed "America's Finest City," on the surface, San Diego is an ideal place to raise children and have a family—

and for the most part, this is true. In many San Diego communities, children grow up in the middle and upper classes.

Now, welcome to the Nutty's! The official map of San Diego will have this place listed as "North Park." North Park is technically a "low-income, urban area," but unlike other urban areas, this part of town is unique. For those of you familiar with the present-day community, let me point out that over the past ten years North Park has gone through some major gentrification and it is a very different place today than it was for many years. For the sake of this book, I will be referring to the version that I grew up knowing.

This urban area is home to one of the United States' most popular streets used for prostitution—El Cajon Boulevard. This boulevard runs through both the residential and commercial areas. This boulevard is the key factor that made growing up in this area completely different than other San Diego urban communities. In many other San Diego urban communities the children are surrounded with and influenced by poverty, gangs, drugs, and crime. In the Nutty's you have these same obstacles, but with the added bonus of pimping and prostitution. That is not to say that pimping and prostitution don't also influence other poor urban communities, but unlike the North Park area, it is not directly in the children's faces.

Growing up on or around one of the nation's biggest prostitution tracks, you find yourself walking down the boulevard regularly. You'll find yourself conversing with and observing prostitutes and pimps at the corner store, gas station, or street light. The likelihood of one or several members of your family being involved in this lifestyle is almost guaranteed. Walking to and from school, observing a trick picking up a prostitute, or watching the interactions between pimps and prostitutes are commonplace. Recently I came in contact with a young 21 year old pimp that grew up in the North Park area. He's never known his biological parents and has grown up in several group homes. The group home that he stayed in the longest was in the North Park area. In that home, he was raised and mentored by the pimps his foster mom said were her brothers. He grew up calling them "Uncle." He had a deep respect for these men. They were the most prominent and consistent male role models that he had in his life. They would always have money and occasionally gave him some. That feeling and image stuck out to him as he aged. He never knew what these men did for a living until he ran into his favorite "Uncle" at the corner liquor store. When he ran into his "Uncle" at the store he was with two beautiful women dressed as if they were high end fashion models. The kid asked him if one of the women was his girlfriend and the "Uncle" happily replied with "Hell no! Pimpin doesn't have girlfriends." Those words sparked his interest and later on that week when he saw his "Uncle" again he asked him a serious question: "What is a pimp?" That day his Uncle explained to him what a pimp was without reservation of details.

I didn't know what pimping was until I was in my teens. This was less likely if you were a kid growing up on or around the track. When I found out what a pimp was it was as if all of the people I knew found out around the same time. My mother and I never had a full conversation about it, but she and all of my friends' mothers knew what we were into. They never addressed it as if it was a bad thing and most of the time seemed to encourage it.

Children are like sponges, ready and unknowingly soaking up information, actions, and experiences of others. The environment that children grow up in can be so influential in the person they become. Growing up in an environment where pimping and prostitution is glorified and commonplace would make any child believe that it's alright, that it's normal. A child's future may rest on proper parental guidance to tell them that what they're observing is wrong. Unfortunately, positive parental guidance is lacking in most poor, urban communities for a number of reasons. Combining poverty, environment, peer pressure, and bad role models encouraging a person into a pimp or prostitution lifestyle, the likelihood of a child attempting to pimp or sell themselves is extremely high.

The 2014 indictment and prosecution of young men and women in the Skanless Black MOB (Case No. 13cr4510-JAH) demonstrated how young men and women easily wind up living the lives they've observed in their community. In this federal case, twenty four individuals were charged with a RICO conspiracy largely involving sex trafficking. Although a majority of the people in this case had not actually been involved in sex trafficking, they were still grouped together for associating with others who were involved. Some individuals were charged for being involved in a related incident that occurred ten years previously. The RICO law was passed in 1970. RICO, which stands for Racketeer Influenced and Corrupt Organizations, refers to the prosecution and defense of individuals who engage in organized crime. This law was passed by congress in an effort to combat mafia groups. It is a United States Federal law that provides for extended criminal penalties and a civil cause of action for acts performed as part of an ongoing criminal organization. This law was intended for people such as Al Capone and the Italian mafia. How the young, disenfranchised individuals of Black Mob and Skanless received this is beyond my understanding. Nothing about them was organized or ongoing. These young men were guilty by association and affiliation to the same clique. Most of these men had grown up friends since they were children. When you closely examine this case and look beyond the surface you can clearly see a group of young men and women that had potential to be great in whatever they may have chosen to do in life, but instead became a product of the environment they grew up knowing.

Like many of the recent recipients I know of this RICO law it seems as if it is a thinly-veiled attempt to incarcerate a large amount of people at once. Once you're involved in one of these indictments, you are not sentenced off of the individual crimes you may have committed, you are now liable for the crimes of the group whether you were involved or even had knowledge of the crimes. In my humble opinion, this is not helping the lives of the individuals involved, or the plight to end human sex trafficking. The communities that they came from are still impoverished and without lack of resources or options to improve public health. All that it seems to do is continue to fuel the massive prison industrial complex and its gluttonous appetite for poor bodies. As I will repeat throughout the book, if we really want to put an end to sex trafficking, we must attack it at its roots.

# Tony

Tony was born in Chicago but moved to San Diego at a young age. He was a very smart and athletic kid who could have done anything with his life, had the proper resources and guidance been available to him. When Tony was old enough to attend middle school he was able to attend a school in a nice middle class neighborhood. That neighborhood was not the same neighborhood that he resided in. Tony lived in a community in San Diego called North Park, also known as the Nutty's. He lived in extreme proximity to the main track. In order for Tony to get to school every day he would have to take the bus. On his daily route to the bus, he would witness and observe prostitutes and pimps in their own daily routine. Tony told me that he wasn't sure at first what they were all about but quickly learned. While waiting on the bus one day, Tony was approached by a much older female who he would later discovered was a prostitute. When she approached him she began to tell him about how cute he was. She continued to talk to him about how he would be a good pimp one day, and taught him how to treat ladies. Conversations like this, constantly coming across individuals in the game would continue occurring in Tony's young life. The lifestyle of pimping and prostitution became normalized in his young mind. It was inevitable that he would become involved in the game himself as a young teen. Tony entered the subculture of pimping and prostitution and excelled at it.

A little over ten years after Tony entered the game he was wrapped up in a major RICO indictment for organized crime dealing with human sex trafficking. At the time of his arrest, Tony had been out of the game for many years but the Federal Government found a way to use evidence from his teen years against him to link him to the racketeering indictment based out of North Park. After spending five years in federal prison, Tony has now returned home and has recently interviewed with me for my documentary on the epidemic of pimping and prostitution that took place in San Diego. One of the things that hit me the hardest when talking with him is the fact that he knows if he could have grown up in a different environment, he would have never entered the game.

# The New Boulevard

With the internet's ever-expanding capability to sell sex, the actual El Cajon Boulevard track slowed down and has almost completely died. Ten to fifteen years ago you could have driven down several blocks, at any given time, and count more prostitutes than you had fingers. Now, driving down those same blocks it's more likely that you won't even see one. That was until the signing of a new law called FOSTA or Fight Online Sex Trafficking Act. From this new law on April 10, 2018 the Department of Justice seized backpage.com, the website that was once the most accessible online marketplace for sex workers. All that remains is a large banner announcing the shutdown under a row of law-enforcement logos. The site was a target for groups opposed to sex work. Close to a dozen other sites were also shut down that also offered sex ads. This immediately caused many women who were using the internet to make money in a safer environment back out onto the street corners. El Cajon Boulevard and other tracks around San Diego are now being repopulated.

When the new FOSTA-SESTA law was put in place I first thought that this would was a good thing. That is until I received my first of many phone calls from female friends of mine, crying hysterically, all saying that they had no idea how they would be able to feed their babies or pay their bills. Those phone calls got me thinking about the unforeseen repercussions from the Backpage shut down. After much thought about the situation, and many conversations with some colleagues of mine, I formed the opinion that I have now. Backpage at its time of shut down was already an old outdated form of online trafficking for the pimps and prostitutes that I know. The only people left online that I knew of were people that couldn't really manage on the newer sights or out call services.

Regardless of the people that were hurt by this shutdown, it needed to happen. Backpage needed to be shut down for the simple fact that there were children across this world that were being sold through this platform. My only wish is that before it happened that there had been some sort of outreach to the people that were stuck using that source telling them of other resources or opportunities that the Federal Government had set up. In my career of helping people out of a life of street crime, I've come to the conclusion that you cannot tell somebody to stop engaging in illegal activities that they use for survival, unless you plan on replacing it with another option. Something should have been done to help the ones that were still stuck in the game.

# Chapter 4: The Playing Field

# Recruitment

Since I've been actively involved in anti-human sex trafficking work, I have heard many colleagues speak about how girls are recruited into the prostitution lifestyle. Most of the stories/scenarios are based in reality, but oftentimes take far turns into drama-filled, alternative facts. A common story I've heard from multiple sources is the story of a pimp that was patrolling a mall for new recruits. The pimp sees a girl and compliments her eyes. She responds with a "thank you" and smiles. The pimp moves on and doesn't pursue her because she's too confident. He repeats this compliment to other girls until he runs into one that, once complimented, stares off to the side and looks down. The pimp then pursues this girl because she shows signs of being weak. I have heard a few different versions of this story, all of which were told as if the individual telling the story had learned the information firsthand. Now this may be a big coincidence and all of these people may have met the same girl or pimp. Pimps could be big mall recruiters, following the same playbook, or these people telling the story are lying to sound educated on the subject matter. Hopefully people are using this narrative to show the skill in recognizing human behavior and the subtlety of coercion without revealing a particular person's story.

When choosing who to recruit into prostitution, there is no girl that is above initiation into the life. It doesn't matter what you look like. It's often said, "Oh my niece is so pretty I worry about her being recruited." Plenty of unattractive girls are in the life too. Every body type, skin type, no discrimination. A saying that pimps have is "I'll put a pig in a wig." This means that the girl could be overweight and not attractive and still be fixed up for work. When I would recruit there were obvious people who I believed to be more susceptible to turning out into the game. The only way to find this out was through conversation. You would be able to see if there were any weaknesses that could make them susceptible. When a pimp is trying to figure out who to recruit, he is thinking about if this girl would be an easy turn out, or if more work would have to be applied. Depending on how bad the pimp wanted the girl would determine how much he would pursue. When recruiting the girl he's listening to everything she says, looking for any opening at which to strike. Depending on where the girl is discovered or her appearance everything the pimp may want to know may already be on display. How poorly she's dressed, working in a strip club, living in a homeless shelter, or walking away from a greyhound bus station with bags and nowhere to go.

A pimp is going to recruit anybody willing to follow their instructions and make them money. In the recruitment process there is no specific place to find a potential prostitute. Yes, it could be a mall, nightclub, grocery store, frozen food aisle, or law firm. The key to recruitment is finding a girl that gives you an indication that they like you. A simple "hello" from a pimp that gets a "hello" back can open the door to a conversation. If a pimp catches a girl staring at him with interest, that is an indication to move in. A pimp will only recruit a girl over the age of eighteen if he is following the rules of engagement correctly. Only a desperate pimp with no values for the lifestyle will recruit a minor for prostitution. Unfortunately, this does happen, but it is far from being the norm in the pimping world. Prostituting a minor is shunned by other pimps. If found doing this, the pimp recruiting a minor will be ostracized and slandered by other pimps. Pimps that conduct activities with minors will oftentimes do it in secret because of the fear of being rejected by his peers.

## Where?

Most of the places are learned how almost everything in the pimp subculture is learned: through the passing down of knowledge by more experienced pimps. Although a pimp can recruit anywhere, there are some key places that are often targeted.
Pimps often recruit women at bus stations, particularly the Greyhound station. At this location pimps find women in transition from home to home, or with no home at all. A lot of women are running away from bad situations, abusive ex-spouses, broken

families, or may have just gotten out of jail. After you've seen people freshly released from jail, you develop an eye for these things. It's not hard to tell if you know what you're looking for. There's a look that both males and females have when they are fresh out. Sometimes it's certain articles of clothing like grey sweats or khaki pants. They could be carrying a manila envelope with the belongings they were released with. Their clothes could appear as if they don't fit them. These women are easily susceptible to a pimp's charm, help, and plan for a better life. To a pimp, the story he is feeding the new potential turnout is completely true. He believes wholeheartedly about the dream of a better life free from financial worry and stress. The more a person believes in a dream or vision, the easier it is to sell it to another and convince them to follow. Similarly, homeless shelters and other women's shelters can be easy targets. Here, pimps find women that have also been through a lot and are looking for a better life. To a pimp, he is doing this great thing, getting these women out of a life of poverty. He is not thinking about the psychological damage that a life of prostitution can bring. The only challenge of recruiting women in homeless shelters is weeding through the ones that are addicted to drugs or clinically insane. Most of these women are emotionally broken and in need of something to build them up. The women that are not emotionally broken, just financially broken, and are ready to take a chance to get rich. In my experience, I've never personally seen a pimp just hang out outside of a shelter and try and talk to girls, although I have heard of people doing this. Most of the time, recruitment is usually done by driving by the shelter or other areas that homeless women frequent in the hopes of spotting a prime target. I remember being 18 years old while out looking for girls with a pimp friend. We actually parked near a shelter, got out of the car and walked into the lobby. He knew a girl that worked at the reception desk. She used to be a prostitute herself. She had given up the lifestyle, but still believed in the subculture. My friend told me that she had called him in the past when she came across girls that had potential of being turned out. I remember being really uncomfortable, but my friend wasn't—this was one of his preferred recruitment sites.

"The Track" or "The Blade" is where most prostitution recruits are found. Where better to find and recruit a new prostitute than the place where current prostitutes work? A pimp can find his next prostitute just by patrolling the areas where sex is sold. At some point he is guaranteed to find a girl that is mad at her current pimp and ready to jump ship. He may even find a girl that is working on her own and in need of a pimp.

Pimps will also often stake out hotels known for prostitution to find a new recruit. Oftentimes between 10am-12pm; oftentimes, this is the time that girls might be checking out of hotels by themselves, making it a perfect opportunity to recruit them.

Most of the pimps that I have come across have used the strip club as a watering hole to recruit new women. Throughout the U.S. there are plenty of gentlemen's clubs. These places are perfect arenas for a pimp to relax and get a good conversation in with a girl that is already in the adult/sex industry, but who has not fully crossed over into selling sex. After finding the perfect recruit, a pimp can move out of the club and into further money-making ventures. Throughout my years of growing up around pimps and strip clubs I have noticed more and more that pimps began to stop recruiting out of strip clubs as much and began to just hang out there. Not by choice, but because many of the girls stopped talking to them. Many girls became tired of pimps coming in and either belittling the work that they were doing and saying it wasn't enough, or just trying to get them to come work for them. In gentlemen's clubs that are in cities heavily influenced by pimps, the girls will not even talk to you, and assume that if you're a young black male dressed nicely, that you are a pimp.

## Creating an Image

As a pimp, the biggest recruiting tool is the image he creates of himself. If he is telling a girl about how much money she could make with him and he's looking like his entire wardrobe came from

Goodwill, he's not going to get the girl. If he doesn't have a car or money to pay for lunch it is hard to believe that he could improve her situation. The best recruitment a pimp can have outside of the gift of gab are his "tools." Tools are the nice cars, fancy clothes, jewelry, and money. Even without words, these tools will recruit prostitutes.

Fame, toughness, and intelligence are also good things to have for a pimp's image. These characteristics will recruit new girls for him. Pimps styles may differ slightly depending on not only their upbringing, but who they were before they even got involved in the lifestyle. For the most part I would say that most pimps seem to take on a lot of the same characteristics. Many girls that I had just met would ask me if I was a pimp, just based off of how I talked. To this day I still find myself speaking in the flow and manner of a pimp. After so many years of learning how to become a pimp, studying pimping, hanging around other pimps, and listening to pimp music, it has become a characteristic trait that is not easily shakable.

## Using Prostitutes to Recruit

Depending on the particular female a pimp is dealing with, she may or may not be into recruiting other girls. If the girl is with the pimp because she has deep feelings for him, or is a jealous person, she will not recruit at all. She may even run other girls off that the pimp may acquire. Once a pimp has trained a prostitute that is down for him and the mission they are on, she will begin to recruit other prostitutes. All of the places that the pimp would recruit, the female prostitute will now do so as well. Females can recruit even better than the male pimp can. They can get into places that he cannot, and they are more believable to other girls. Girls can also recruit inside of jail in the event that they get arrested—pimps cannot. Girls are oftentimes in the same areas where sex is being sold with other girls that they can befriend and eventually sway to their pimp. If a girl is telling you how good she has it, it is going to seem ten times more believable than coming from the pimp.

## Elementary, Junior High, and High Schools

Even after my full exit out of the game I remained closely associated and around people who were trapped in the life. In my time in and around the game I have traveled through over 20 states, including Hawaii and Puerto Rico, dealing with and learning about the game in different areas. I have met and talked to over a hundred pimps and even more prostitutes. I currently work almost daily with people who are currently still pimping and prostituting, or used to be involved in the game. With the work I do and the communities that I serve, it is imperative that I stay current on the trends of both the gang and pimp/prostitute subcultures. Now with that all being said, I must truthfully say that I personally have never witnessed, or even heard of a pimp recruiting directly at any school—but it does happen. According to a friend who works as a Deputy District Attorney in the Juvenile Court here in San Diego, there are many cases of kids being recruited at school. However, I cannot speak on this from my experiences or knowledge as I do on the other areas in this book. As Dr. Jamie Gates from Point Loma Nazarene University said, "We have evidence that such recruitment has happened in middle schools. I'd agree, that to say that this happens in elementary schools is an exaggeration. The danger in saying this too emphatically is the reality that kids as young as 12 and 13 are being recruited while in Junior High, and to say it's not happening there is to divert attention where at least a modest amount of attention needs paid. If there is prevention work to be done to get out ahead of this, we have to be at least in the middle schools." In order to help stop women from being recruited from any school, it is going to take educating all of the school staff.

1. Everyone on the staff need to be aware on how to look for the signs of recruitment. If the signs can be spotted early on, then more intervening can take place in the student's life.

Hopefully the proper information can be given to the child to make them second guess the decision they are potentially making about going into prostitution or trafficking.

2. The school staff, as hard as it may be, must know the student's home situation. Schools in impoverished communities like the one I grew up in should almost act more like typical non-profit organizations. Instead of school counselors, they need to have case workers who can work with the students. The status of the home that these students come from has a direct effect on the behavior that they exhibit and the susceptibility of them being misled. Unfortunately, school is one of the most important places for grafting America's future, and it is one of the least funded so actually implementing a system like this is more difficult.

3. Students should not only be taught academic material, but also must be taught about self worth. They must be shown early on that they have options of other pathways in life. Again, this is more the case for children that have come from impoverished communities. This may seem like the roll of the parent, and it rightfully should be, but unfortunately in the case of many "at-risk" kids, parental role models may be lacking or nonexistent.

4. The students, particularly those "at risk" should be trained about what to look for as far as signs of prostitution and recruitment. The better informed that they are about the subculture of pimping and prostitution, the better chance that they have to recognize it when it's being presented to them. The students should be informed of the negative side of the game from men and women that have actually lived it, to combat any positive misinformation they may be receiving. Schools need to inform and prepare students so that they will be able to make the right decision and avoid becoming a pimp or a prostitute.

Junior high and high school levels are the most valuable places to train and inform students and staff about the dangers of human sex trafficking. This is where we, as advocates against human sex trafficking, can have the biggest effect on lives. However, ultimately the biggest motivator for people to move into the world of pimping and prostitution is poverty. If we can find the solution to that problem, then we will put a huge dent in the trafficking industry here domestically.

# Grooming

## *Grooming a Prostitute*

The intent of the following is to put you in the mind of a pimp. These inner thoughts and tactics are being shared with you so that you can understand intent, motives, and thought patterns of the pimp when grooming a new turn out. I believe that if you know the thoughts behind the actions, you can better serve the population of people in the game. For those of us who want to prevent people from entering into pimping and prostitution in the first place, I feel it is important for you to know exactly what this grooming process looks like, and to know what is on the mind of the person doing the grooming.

In order to groom a prostitute, a pimp must be knowledgeable himself. How can you teach somebody that which you do not know yourself? At the start of any venture you may have an idea of how things are supposed to work, but you truly do not have a full understanding until you've actually been involved and have a first-hand experience.

Prior to a pimp sitting a new prostitute (new turn out) down on the track, strip club, entering her into an escort service, or other trade, he will give her all of the information that he has about the job she's about to encounter. He will let her know his do's and don'ts. These can differ from pimp to pimp but are primarily the same. The "Do's and Don'ts" can be a variety of different minor details or ways that the particular pimp runs his operation. For example, how he likes his money delivered to him or even the direction that he wants his women to walk when on the street. The pimp will give her the instructions on how to conduct business as he sees fit. The pimp will also teach his new prostitutes safety techniques. All of this preparation will prevent a poor performance.

Outside of verbal training and mental grooming there may be a need for physical grooming that takes place for a new prostitute. These things may include, but are not limited to, buying clothes for work, hair styling, nails being done, and the purchase of makeup. Another physical tool that may be used for safety are pocket knives and pepper spray. A pimp will supply his girl with these tools to help her feel more secure while engaging in prostitution. When a pimp is in the process of grooming a girl into prostitution he is fully aware of what he is doing. To create the ideal prostitute he must groom her correctly, or the results will be a girl with a very limited time span in the game. While the majority of pimps know that the actions of pimping and prostitution are wrong, they have become so deeply involved that they have ultimately lost the understanding of right and wrong. The longer that a pimp has been in the game, the more and more he convinces himself that his actions are justified and that there may even be a special God that will bless him if his "pimping is correct."

## Grooming a Pimp

A pimp must also learn how to conduct himself within this profession. A person must learn how to be successful at it. Some may feel they can do it because they saw a documentary or movie on pimping, while others heard about the game from their favorite rapper. The smartest pimps find themselves a pimp mentor. This mentor will be somebody who has been in the game for a while. A seasoned vet they are called, or an OP, an "Original Pimp." This mentor can and will be willing to share an abundance of knowledge with the new pimp. This information is invaluable and can set a pimp on a path with less pitfalls.

Although a new pimp can be groomed by an older, more experienced pimp, the true grooming and learning takes place on the field—experience that no movie or documentary can teach. After a short period of time, a person who was intrigued by the lifestyle will find out if it is really for him. The streets hold no punches. I've known people that have been arrested for pimping/trafficking in their first week in the game.

It takes a lot of manipulation and communication skills to convince another human being to do something outside of what they are naturally inclined to do. Selling your body to strangers for monetary gain is not a natural instinct for anybody. However, under certain circumstances people can and will do anything. With a convincing groomer who knows how to use a person's weaknesses against them, the process of turning a woman out is easier. To do this properly there must be a manipulator. A pimp grooming a prostitute knows that he's manipulating the girl, and prides himself on how good of a manipulator he is. When you're in the mindset of preparing a girl for prostitution, you don't feel bad. You actually feel as if you are doing the right thing in most situations. You convince yourself you are saving her and yourself from a life of poverty. This lifestyle is the answer that will bring your American dream into reality. Yes, you are manipulating the girl into selling her body, but you don't feel as though you're lying to her. You just want to get her ready to get in the game, so that she can see for herself that the vision that you have and the words that you are telling her are true.

A pimp will tell the girl he is grooming everything that he can about prostitution. It would be no good for him to hide the bad side of the game from her only to have her discover it on her own through experience. If and when this happens, the girl looks at the pimp as if he's a new to the game, or she is so shocked by a bad experience that she leaves him. Knowing how to deal with situations such as rape, harassment from other pimps and prostitutes, police encounters, and more must be discussed up front. These situations are almost inevitable. If they are not discussed during the grooming process, the consequences can be detrimental to the continuation of their relationship.

# The Web of Distraction

During the rise of the internet, a new major factor entered virtually every facet of our culture, including the pimp subculture—social media! Facebook, Twitter, Instagram, Tumblr, Snapchat, and YouTube. Not to mention the countless dating apps. Who would've thought they would be such a vital part of transitioning into the game? Social media has been utilized in recent years by people all over the world as a tool to express yourself, confess, and invite the public into your life. You can say and show whatever you want without any filters, literally. For some reason, people who had been in the game were not wise enough to hold on to the unspoken code of conduct they had before the social media trend of posting anything and everything. In previous generations, the pimp subculture was not something to broadcast to the world. A lot of the participants in the culture even called it "the secret society." This new generation has taken on a total opposite stance. Many fell right into the trend and began posting incriminating words, videos, and transactions for the entire world to see, including law enforcement.

For several years many individuals in the game began to use social media as an outlet to display themselves as a pimp or prostitute. The thought that these posts could be used against them at a later time never crossed their minds. Real pimps, as well as people who were fascinated by the lifestyle, began to make social media posts to make themselves seem like super pimps. Many people say that they did this to lure more girls to them to prostitute out. This may be partially true. I know a few pimps that would post false propaganda online—posting pictures of cars they were renting as if they owned them. It's common to see pimps posting photos of big bundles of cash that were either fake or modified to look like it contained all $100 bills. The larger population of the people who were putting themselves out there in the public eye as pimps were actually putting on the facade of somebody they were not. This was done out of vanity, bravado, and simply a desire to look cool. In the young, black community, being a pimp was thought of as cool. The idea is dying fast, but the flame is still there.

Prostitutes also used—and still use—social media to express their involvement in the game. Girls you would never think were prostitutes if you met in real life, would actually be women of leisure on the net. The world may not recognize the codes that they are using but those of us that know the game can decipher what it is that's going on. When I see this behavior my first reaction is usually that of a big brother who has been there, done that and is seeing a younger sibling going down the same wrong path that I did. I think, "Dummy, what are you doing? You can and will go to jail." The feeling that follows is sadness that this madness is still occurring. Many times, the people that I'm witnessing are people that I had influenced in my past to live like this.

Although social media has been used to glamorize and promote the pimp subculture, it has slowed down significantly lately. This is due to the many indictments that have come down throughout the country based largely off of social media. Sites like Facebook and Instagram have been the major component in many people standing trial for human trafficking. Large groups, mostly men and some women, have been charged by both the federal government and state system based off of evidence found on social media. The crazy part is most of these cases are based on evidence that the suspect put out there themselves, making it almost impossible to beat. I mean, how can you tell the jury that you're not a pimp when you have Facebook posts that state, in your own words, that you are a pimp? What is the jury supposed to think? Even worse is how many people are using social media videos to rap or just talk about how they're a pimp. Videos where you are going into details about the subculture of pimping that you're involved in. In those situations there's not much more the prosecution needs to convict you.

When it comes down to it I will say this makes understanding the issue so much harder for a prosecutor or someone not involved in the life. They're not embedded in that community. To them it doesn't make sense that someone would post about being a pimp if they weren't. How are they supposed to learn what is really going on? Some of them do want to understand.

Most people don't want to ruin lives. How do they get a better understanding if this is all they're seeing? Reading this book is the start. Prosecutors are not all terrible people trying to lock everyone up. This is the world that has been presented to them. How can they be expected to turn a blind eye to that? It's hard for them to be able to separate the real pimps from those faking it. It's even hard for the people in the subculture of pimping to tell the difference sometimes. How would they know? The fact is there are still people out there, trafficking girls.

113

# Inside, Outside, Carpet

There are many different styles of prostitution in the world. When it comes to my personal expertise and experience in the American domestic pimp subculture, there are three arenas. The "Inside," which includes escort services, the internet and other incall services; the "Outside," which is the traditional track or blade; then there is the "Carpet," which are typically casinos but can be bars, nightclubs, and strip clubs. The method that a prostitute or pimp uses can depend on their preference, where the money is best for them, the level of their education, the look and race of the girl, or what city that they are in at the time.

## *The Internet*

In the early-nineties my friends and I thought of the internet as some mystical device only talked about in school. By the mid-nineties it was becoming better known, but still seemed to be something out of a science-fiction novel. When the nineties were coming to a close and the 2000's were rolling in, we began to realize exactly how the internet could be used.

When it came to criminal activity, a few friends of mine began to realize you could easily use somebody's credit card number to order those overpriced Jordan basketball shoes that you wanted. When the internet first hit the crime scene it was much easier to take advantage of it. There were not as many security checks online as there are today. As we were becoming more involved in the pimp subculture in the late nineties, we knew about websites where girls could sell sex. Sites like *Eros* and *City Vibe* were talked about, but not really utilized. In our opinion, those were just for "escorts." Pimps didn't have "escorts" they had "hoes" and hoes don't sell sex on the computer. This seemed like exposing yourself. At this time in the game most pimps still looked at the game as a private culture—a culture that wasn't meant to be exposed to the public as it is now. In this current era, it is common to find a pimp, or somebody who takes on the image of a pimp, talking about themselves pimping on social media or other sources that many people can see.

As in all business areas, there are always those individuals who think outside the box. What may seem like bad business to many, may seem like a great opportunity to a few. When it came to the early stages of the internet there were a few pimps and prostitutes that saw the benefit of promoting their business on escort websites and removing themselves from the blade. Some saw the benefit of using both. While a girl was on the blade or track they could have an ad posted on one of the many sites. If they received a call, they would get picked up from somewhere near the track and when finished, get dropped right back on the track to continue working. The individuals that I know that got involved with the internet early in the game were the ones that were the most successful at that time. Their concentration on the internet boosted their game to the extreme. A few of these individuals realized how lucrative it was and started their own websites. It was starting to seem like the best thing for the game, a much-needed transition. Why live on the dangerous, wild side of the outdoors when you could have a girl sit in a hotel room, post ads, have the trick come to her, pay her, and leave? This seemed like the way to go for the subculture.

Just like every genre in the business world, the internet was quickly taking over everything. From 2001 to 2003 I was in federal prison, serving time on a conspiracy charge. From the time I left San Diego, until the time that I returned, I noticed the amount of action on our main track drop by about two-thirds. This wasn't because of people going to jail or the decrease in the demand for prostitution. This was only due to the industry shift to the internet. By 2013, the same blade that I got my start on had completely changed. In 2000, at any given hour you could drive down El Cajon Boulevard and count no less than fifteen prostitutes. If you make that same drive currently for a week, you may only see one.

## Girls on Their Own: The Breaking of the Pimp

Up until the major internet explosion all prostitutes no matter if they were black or white, attractive or unattractive, were prostituted on the track. As the internet became a prostitution option, I did start to notice that pimps would become a little more selective on where they would operate and who they would send. Depending on the look of the girl and the marketability of her, a pimp would determine the best route to make money. In reality, the ultimate decision was on the pimp. Some pimps would prefer the blade regardless. This could've been because this was the only avenue that he knew or he just wanted to stick to what he thought was true pimping. However, times were changing and the internet was new. As the internet became a competing force—and also an attractive force for girls that wanted to get off of the blade—many girls began to request working strictly online. The thought of just working on their own soon followed.

With the World Wide Web came a new widespread mentality of prostitutes: *This is so easy, I can do this myself*. This mentality caused many girls to leave their pimps (if they had one) and it also caused girls that were brand new to the game to never have a pimp in the first place. This phenomenon of not needing a pimp caused many pimps to change their operational tactics. Many are known to take percentages of the profit these days rather than the whole pie as before. Girls are more likely to leave a pimp who is too tough, so many pimps play nice to keep their money flowing.

The average pimp today is not built the same as they were twenty years ago. Unlike the pimps of the pre-internet era, today's pimps are more lenient and accepting of behaviors from prostitutes that would have been deemed unacceptable before. With strict laws that are now enforced on pimping and pandering, or what's now more often referred to as Human Sex Trafficking, pimps have become more aware and scared of the potential consequences of their actions. The average pimp today is not successful. He is almost non-existent.

*"I have yet to discover one social media site including online dating platforms that has not been used for the selling of sex. Yes, Christian Mingle also." — Lived Experience Expert Yasmine*

# Strip Clubs

The Gentleman's Club. The place where a man (or woman) can view another woman's naked body legally for a small fee. These clubs are spread out throughout the U.S. Thousands of these clubs operate in our country with varying rules, regulations, standards, and appearances. In my 20 years of experience in strip clubs, I've found that most of the girls who work as strippers/exotic dancers in these clubs are licensed, independent women without any pimp at all. I personally know or have met close to 300 club dancers throughout Mexico, the United States, and Puerto Rico. The majority of the women I've known in the club despise and reject pimps. The girls that are in the club are there to make money. They know that a pimp is only there to get their money. The dancers that seem to be fond of pimps are usually only because of developed relationships that grew over time.

Clubs operate differently depending on region and management. I've known places where a little extra money could get you a hand job, oral sex, or intercourse. Most, however, fully operate by the rules and won't allow you to touch the girls. One common factor among these clubs is that the entity makes money, sometimes huge amounts of money, off of the sexual exploitation of women. This is a form of legal pimping. There's a big difference between stripping in a club and prostituting. The girls' lives aren't at risk. They're not risking major health problems, and they're less likely to be raped or abused. All of these places pay taxes and licensing fees to the city and state, which also makes the government a beneficiary of sexual exploitation.

Some pimps choose to have their girls work in strip clubs exclusively or in addition to the other forms of prostitution. The strip club is a good source of recruiting both new prostitutes and tricks.

In the club a girl can acquire a regular customer who eventually may want a little more than a lap dance. That is when an outside deal occurs. Also, while hanging out in a club, a pimp may spark a conversation with a trick and tell him about a girl that he may have that's willing to do a little more for the same amount of money than the trick is spending in the club. He may also meet a dancer who may like him and can set up an outside conversation where he can recruit her into the lifestyle.

# Escort Services

Most people are familiar with what an escort service can provide. For those that don't, an escort is a person who goes on dates with another person for money or property. What occurs on those dates can differ vastly. It can be an actual date out to dinner, or it can be a sexual experience. These services are run by many types of people from many different backgrounds and classes. The owners and operators are basically legal pimps. This country largely recognizes this as a legal business. Yes, some street pimps have their prostitutes with these services, but in my experience, most of the girls involved in the escort services tend to be independent workers selling their body of their own free will. In most states, girls need to register and be licensed to be an escort—a legal escort, that is. Many of the escorts and prostitutes that use escort services have registered in many states so that they can operate legally. This is the city's way of making money off of prostitution. Similar licenses are given to girls that work in strip clubs.

There are high-end escort services that cater to politicians, celebrities, and other wealthy clientele. There are others whose customer base is the regular middle-class man that would want to hire an escort for whatever reason. At each level of escort services there is usually one main person or owner that makes money off all of the girls for providing them with a platform to solicit themselves. A majority of the owners I've seen have been mostly white women. This is the safest form of pimping that I know, with relatively low likelihood of legal ramifications—with the exception of the owners and shareholders of Craigslist and Backpage. Getting caught or charged with pimping and pandering is not likely at all.

In my experience I have known most escorts to sell sex to the client, but many do not. Some girls truly live up to what an escort is supposed to do and only supply companionship. Massages are also very common with many escorts that don't have sex for money. I know of a few pimps that have moved from the streets to legit escort massage services, and I also know a few that weren't so legit. Usually this is just a starting point until they get comfortable enough to go all the way or are offered an amount of money large enough to make them reconsider. The basic massage escort business is like a gateway drug. Once you're hooked and comfortable, sooner or later you will try something else.

## The Prehistoric Blade

I can't speak for all tracks and blades around the country, but as far as San Diego goes, the blades have essentially turned into ghost towns. Over fifty pimps have been indicted in recent years, combined with the internet boom, and the mental growth of individuals that were in the game, have all played a role in the quietness of the tracks. During my era in the pimp world, many of my peers were young and in need of an option to eat and survive. As most grew older, wiser, and more exposed to other options of revenue, they grew out of wanting to be a pimp. There was a huge pimp and prostitute epidemic that lasted a solid decade, from about 1996 to 2006. During that time many misguided boys and girls entered the game. The blade was the initial point of entry. Most of the individuals realized that life on the blade and the game itself wasn't for them. They chose to make their exit. Unfortunately, a lot of pimps that grew out of the life fell into indictments years later, from cases that reached back into their past to link them to human trafficking.

To the ones that made it out of the game alive, the blade is old news. There is no need or desire to go back. When I drive down the blade now, it's like traveling through a land of broken dreams and death. A land of young men and women without resources and guidance trying to make it out of their reality without knowing how. The dangers of the track are not really recognized until you are removed from it. All I can do now is think about the dumb chances my friends and I were taking and also the dangerous positions we put others in.

Last week I took a trip back to the blade with the purpose of filming an episode of a new internet series my team at Paving Great Futures is producing. The series is called "Take'em 2 Chuuch." This title comes from an old pimp saying meaning to teach. This series is being produced by PGF to reverse the negative teachings we were taught in the street life and in the pimp subculture and show the new generation how to use them for positivity and prosperity in life. This particular episode was entitled "Pimp Till You Die." My motivation behind this title and lesson came from the recent murder of one of my closest friends Kenneth McKnight or "MacOn" as he was known in the streets.

While I stood on El Cajon Blvd and expressed my feelings on camera I was mentally brought back in time to when I, MacOn, and a few other friends had our first experience in the pimp life. We were all young teens and on that same blade where I now stand 20 years later. Tears began to well up in my eyes as I thought about how young and misguided we were. How he allowed this damn blade to take his life. Although he wasn't murdered on the blade in San Diego, he was killed on a blade in Houston. It doesn't matter though. Here or there. This path can consume you. Kenneth wanted to get out. He wanted to leave this life. He knew that this was not the way. Unfortunately this blade life was the only way that he knew how to survive in this world.

There are blades, tracks, and stops all over this country, and every day there is a young man or young woman getting lured into its fast money and fast life. Before you know it you look up and your life is gone. Sometimes it's gone in the years wasted on the blade, or it's literally gone with your life breath taken, never to walk another track again.

When I was young I used to hate being on the blade, but I would never speak up. My friends and I used to be on it all of the time. No longer did we spend time at parties or hanging out with girls like we did when we were kids. Any hanging out we did was on the track. When I was a passenger in the car, I would just hope that they would drive past the El Cajon Blvd. exit—but of course, they never did. When I was young I used to hate the blade, and the same is true today. It will forever remind me of all of the loved ones I lost to the pimp life. "Pimp 'till you die," we used to say. At the time I didn't realize how true that statement would be.

## Viva Las Vegas

As a young man I remember taking that long drive into Las Vegas. The trip itself was an adventure, full of mystery and had my stomach turning. I would relate the feeling of going to Vegas the first few times to that of a little kid going to Disneyland. Excited, yet anxious, a whole lot of nerves, and some fear. Nervousness and fear were two feelings that I could not let my friends know that I was having. I was supposed to be a man, and even more than that I was supposed to be this young pimp that wasn't afraid of shit. At that time in our life it was go hard or go home. We were already too deep into the game and Vegas was the top spot for a pimp to embark on. Just to tell our peers that we pimped in Vegas was going to set us on a higher level. Las Vegas, in my opinion, is the largest hub of prostitution in this country. Every type of prostitute is easily accessible to anybody in the city. Everything from strip clubs, brothels, tracks, escorts, you name it, it's there. We were definitely not going to stay at home on our city tracks that all of the other emerging pimps were on. We were constantly in competition with our pimp peers, and even our peers that were not pimps. We may not have realized it at the time but indeed we were.

I remember the first time I came to Las Vegas as a young adult without my family. I was eighteen. At this point I had already been involved in the game for a little over a year. My eyes were now aware of what a prostitute looked like, how she moved, and how she talked. My friends and I entered our first casino on the trip, I remember my first thought being, "Wow, is every girl in here a hoe?" This may sound extreme, but the reality wasn't far off. For the first time my eyes were opened to the reality of what was going on around me. I knew that every woman in that casino wasn't a prostitute, but for every ten women I saw, at least six of them were prostitutes. That day will remain with me forever.

In my opinion the prostitutes that worked in Vegas casinos were the top of the line. They dressed better than most prostitutes, their hair and makeup was always done, and they were way more charismatic. The more I got to know the scene, my pimp friends and I realized that the casinos were where pimps only brought their best girls. Normal girls didn't do well in the casino and it was a waste of time to have them there. Another thing that I learned fast was that even if the prostitute was gorgeous, if she couldn't communicate well with people, she wouldn't make good money.

Since that day I've returned to Vegas several times, each time witnessing the same thing. People travel from all over the world to partake in the world of prostitution and gambling. Outside of the known sources of prostitution there are many elite clubs that exclusively cater to the sexual desires of wealthy customers. Human trafficking at its largest capacity in the country can be found in Nevada where prostitution is legal in some counties. What happens in Vegas, stays in Vegas, right?

In 2002 I was arrested for possession with the intent to sell marijuana. At the time I was caught, I had been making a large amount of money for a while—and had also acquired a large amount of monthly bills. On top of that I had a financial status that at my age was unheard of. At a minimum I was bringing in $10,000 a week, sometimes as much as $20,000. During this time period I had purchased a Lexus, BMW, new model Monte Carlo, and helped my friends purchase their expensive cars as well. I thought I was on top of the world. Now on bail and facing jail time I had to figure out a way to get money. There was no way that I could let myself fall off of the status I had gained. So without selling anything or getting a job, I resorted back to what I had known best: pimping. When the realization that I had to pimp to eat the same way came to my mind, the first place I knew to go was Vegas. I could've stayed in San Diego, but I knew without a doubt that Las Vegas was a sure shot because of how prevalent it was in the pimp subculture. In Las Vegas a pimp not even searching for a prostitute can end up with two in one day.

Once in Vegas, there was a girl pursuing me in one of the casinos within four hours of arriving. At the time it was as if it was meant to be. I didn't have to put out any effort, get a phone number and set up a date, didn't have to run my mouth and try to convince her that I was the best thing. She had chosen me and I was in desperate need of her. When something like this happens in Vegas, you must act fast or you stand the chance of losing her. She was ready to make a move away from whatever situation she was in, and my duty was to take her away to a new environment. So within one day of being in Las Vegas I was right back on the road to San Diego. Being from San Diego, "The Big City," it was perfect for a new recruit. They were always amazed by my city and I knew just how to use it.

That one story of how fast Vegas worked for me can be multiplied thousand times over with thousands of pimps and prostitutes. That city was faster than any city I have been in when it comes to pimping and prostitution. That's one of the reasons that it is so attractive to people in the game from all over the world. We would call Vegas "the guaranteed come up spot."

# Brothels

Brothels are not really an avenue of prostitution taken up by urban street pimps. These pimp roles are usually filled by a white male. While there are several brothels located outside of Las Vegas, there are none actually known within the city. It is actually illegal to prostitute in Las Vegas on paper, but those who know the unwritten laws conduct business as if it is. If you're in the area of Las Vegas you can drive sixty miles to the nearest brothel, Sheri's ranch.

The difference between prostitution in Vegas, compared to San Diego (and any other city in America), is that it has more of every type of prostitution and every type of pimp. Las Vegas is an attraction point for people in the sex industry throughout the world. There are only two basic arenas that an urban street pimp or prostitute can play in San Diego. The Track/Blade or the internet. With Vegas having such a large variety of different characters from different cities, you also have less regulation and following of the unwritten rules of the pimp subculture than you would have in a smaller circle of people in another city. Although nobody tends to follow these rules anyways these days.

# Chapter 5: The Untold Truth

# A Prostitute's Relationship with Her Pimp

A pimp/prostitute relationship it is not always very different from a "square" boyfriend/girlfriend relationship when it comes to what the girl is seeking from the man. The way that the "couple" carries themselves in public and the activities they partake in may be extremely different, but the same typical characteristics are shared between the two different types of lifestyles. These characteristics are mainly, but not limited to, attraction to personality or physical features, protection, father figure, or admiration. A woman's relationship with a pimp can be a culmination of some or all of these things.

## *The Protector*

A prostitute that is with a pimp for protection knows that the lifestyle that she's in is dangerous. The situations that a pimp is putting the girl in are potentially dangerous. A girl doesn't know what a trick is going to do to her when she's alone with him. However, it is comforting to believe that if something goes wrong with a trick or another pimp she will have somebody to come to her defense. Oftentimes, a man must exhibit his strength in front of her to continue his hold on his prostitute. With some pimps this includes beating her. This is also shown by defending her against other pimps that are viewed to be antagonizing her, or against anybody that may disrespect her. On a few occasions I have witnessed pimps confronting other pimps about badgering their girls. The majority of these incidents lead to the pimp aggressor backing off and allowing her to work in the future. The conversation can be as quick as a few sentences in public or a more extensive phone conversation. The harassment factor stops when others know that she has a pimp. Although her protection may not be immediate, a woman engaged in prostitution is comforted when she knows that she can call her pimp and he will show up at the scene. Women that I have been in contact with in my experience have often expressed the desire to be protected. Many have also told me that they have left pimps that wouldn't bother to show up to the scene after a traumatic experience. Girls in the game can also sometimes lie and over exaggerate about an experience just to see if the pimp will show up. Sometimes this is for attention, and other times it's to try to get out of working.

When a Pimp is courting a girl he will definitely explain how he will be there to protect her. It is a necessity that she must know how to operate correctly. When she's new to the game or "green," he will stay close to her in a nearby location for her protection and watch how she handles herself. He may do this for weeks, or until he is comfortable being farther away from her.

Protection does not necessarily have to be physical. Protection can include feelings; protection from outsiders' disrespect or ridicule of a prostitute's chosen lifestyle. A girl that chooses to be involved in the prostitution world can be looked down upon by former friends, family, and outsiders. I remember a girl coming to a friend of mine, crying about how her brother told her that she was no longer welcome around his kids because she was a prostitute. My friend had to comfort her for several hours and re-encourage her to believe in herself and the mission that they were on. Just like in a regular or "square" relationship, a girl is comforted just knowing that she has a force in her corner that will back her up with support and protection if needed.

## "Daddy"

The "protector" role can be fulfilled by the pimp acting like a boyfriend, meaning he's there to fulfill the woman's security, both physically and emotionally. Then there is another side of this protection that's more of a fatherly nature. Oftentimes this is referred to as a "Daddy" relationship. When a woman engaged in the prostitution lifestyle chooses the Daddy relationship it is usually because of the lack of a father figure in her life. She might be looking to replace the father she never had. On the other hand, sometimes a girl who ends up with a Daddy pimp may have actually had a good relationship with her father and is used to being "Daddy's Little Girl." Maybe the girl was extremely dependent on her biological father and does not know a life without that sort of figure. When a girl falls for this type of pimp, or rather, when a girl fills this daddy void with a pimp, she may view him as many things, but he has no doubt taken over the position as a dad in her life.

This type of relationship also makes the acceptance of discipline easier. Isn't a dad supposed to discipline you when you're wrong? The prostitute will accept these lessons more often than not when she views the pimp as her Daddy. The majority of the girls involved in the pimp subculture come from some sort of broken family background. If their father or male figure in the house was physically abusive of them or their mother, they grow up assuming that physical abuse is normal. Essentially, it's called being emotionally illiterate. She doesn't know how to respond to what she is now a part of. Her mentality is that it's acceptable to be hit when your man is mad, or punished physically when you've done something wrong. Being slapped is not typically viewed as violence.

## Admiration: The Cool Guy

In this society full of materialism, narcissism, and the overwhelming need for self-elevated status, you will find that in the pimp and prostitute world, many prostitutes will be with a pimp just because he's viewed as the "cool guy." This isn't very different at all from normal society. There are always those females that will do anything to be the girl with the cool guy, the popular one with the nice clothes and hot car. The cool guy is usually respected around town or in your circle. Everybody wants to be with a winner, right? Pimps strive hard to be that cool guy. They want to be the sharpest dressed, appear wealthy and successful, and be the one everybody is happy to be around. This is because they want to be viewed as the "cool guy" by prospective prostitutes and to make the women he is already working with stay with him. Girls that have no emotional attachment with a guy or a pimp that is lacking in the cool department will leave him quickly for another pimp viewed as cooler or in possession of more money. One day a well-known pimp walked into my house and saw my friends prostitute look at him. He looked at her and simply said "come on, let's go" while motioning towards the door. Without question or further conversation she was up and walking out with him. This guy was known around town for being a rich pimp. He had many fancy cars, jewelry, and nice clothes. Being the "coolest" out is always the goal. It attracts new prostitutes to the pimp, which equals more money.

# How Pimps View Girls

The way that a pimp views the women he decides to prostitute can vary. There are many different factors that contribute to the way the girl is not only viewed, but treated. Everything from race, weight, and mind frame become the deciding elements. The unfortunate and ugly truth is that the way that a pimp views a girl can sometimes be compared to a businessman with multiple products that must be treated differently based on value.

## *Race*

I know that that race and racial prejudice is a very sensitive subject, as are many of the subjects detailed in this book. I have been a victim of racial prejudice myself for as far back as I can remember. I will be describing the common view that pimps have of women based on race—I am not in agreement with these thoughts personally, or trying to reinforce cultural stereotypes. As mentioned before, one of the goals of this book is to bring you into the inner thinking of the pimp. In the pimp and prostitute lifestyle, race plus ethnicity equals value. Don't be too surprised—society created these unwritten rules far before the American pimp subculture was created. In so many societies across the world, not just America, the lighter skinned people are viewed as more valuable and desirable than those with darker skin. This plays a definite role in the pimp and prostitute world. To a pimp, the highest valued female prostitute to have is a Caucasian with blonde hair and blue eyes.

This should not come as shock; this Barbie doll image has been the standard of beauty in the minds of many Americans for decades. A pimp knows he is going to make a profit off of this type of girl. There is not a trick or John out there that would not bite at the chance to be with a Barbie doll. There are pimps that only exclusively seek and want white prostitutes. They are viewed as a prized possession. If a pimp has a team of white girls, he is celebrated amongst fellow pimps. If a girl does not have blonde hair, more than likely a pimp will have her dye it or wear a wig to increase her value. It's not uncommon to post ads online of light skinned black girls (or other nationalities) and claim that they are white. The pimps and prostitutes know that white male professional John's are primarily attracted to white girls—and they are the highest paying customers.

Oftentimes a black pimp will hear his black prostitute complain about being treated differently, or will at some point hear something negative, from the black woman, in reference to the white girl he has. I have known some black girls to actually like their pimp to have a white girl in the stable because she felt that she was actually benefiting off of her in some way. An unwritten rule is to keep the "prize" white girl away from the black girl. There is no blanket standard for how all pimps treat the different races in their team of girls. What I can say is that I personally have witnessed white women be treated better than any other race, with black women being treated the worst; not unlike American culture as a whole. When it comes to physical abuse, in my experience all races are treated about the same. No pimp wants to just beat on his woman, period. That's like damaging a product you intend to sell.

When a pimp's stable is mixed with different races, the girls do realize that there is a value and hierarchy. It is not a hidden issue and often talked about within the pimp subculture. Women in the game will usually treat each other as equals, but this could change depending on how the pimp manages his stable. He cannot show favoritism to anyone—except for his bottom of course. She's been with him the longest and has earned the right to be treated at somewhat of a higher level. I have witnessed many fights amongst women based off of racial jealousy, but then there are often fights amongst the girls for a lot of things that have nothing to do with race. I have heard many black girls complain about their pimp's white girls and also white girls complain about their pimp's black girls. Negative comments come from both sides. On the flip side of that, there are many black girls that applaud their pimp having white girls. They will even help recruit them. They know the value of adding a white girl to their stable and want them on the team. Race is just one of the issues.

White girls are the most valuable to have for many reasons other than simply the John's desire to be with the stereotypical image of beauty. Due to an underlying prejudice in our country, a white woman has a far easier time maneuvering through society than other races. She is viewed as innocent and law-abiding. People tend not to question her motives. This is extremely useful when operating in the underworld. A white woman can walk into nearly any setting in the business world and not be looked at as a threat. This helps when renting hotel rooms, conducting banking transactions, buying property, and more. Pimps typically refer to white girls in general with the name "snow bunny" or "snow" for short.

White girls are also viewed as easier to control and subjected to a pimp's orders. From my personal experience in the pimp subculture, I have noticed that a lot of white girls are more easy-going and gullible when it comes to the harsh realities of the underworld. I connect this directly to "white privilege" here in America. They carry less baggage than other races that have had to endure racism and poverty for generations as is the case with many other cultures. You will find that white girls that have grown up in middle and upper class communities have never been exposed to prostitutes or pimps. Whereas Blacks and Latinos that fill the ghettos around the country have had that exposure. This lack of knowledge combined with an easygoing attitude makes them easier to manipulate and control. Unlike other races, white girls from wealthier backgrounds seem to be accepting of prostitution. Whereas races other than white tend to be attracted to the lifestyle based out of financial necessity, many white girls from the middle class and higher backgrounds have come into prostitution out of pure rebellion and intrigue. Simply put, rich girls wanting to be bad. If and when they realize that entering the game was the wrong way to do this, they are often in too deep to get out.

The second highest valued prostitute for a pimp to have is an Asian woman, also known by the nicknames "chop," "China doll," and "Asian persuasion." The Asian prostitute is highly valued due to the fact that the Caucasian men seem to have an extreme fascination with Asian women. A vast majority of the Johns that I've known have been white males. Since white males are the number one consumer of prostitution, Asian women are a hot commodity. Similar to a white prostitute, having an Asian prostitute is celebrated and highly favored. Asian women and women in general are not necessarily recruited differently because of their race. To a pimp, Asian women are looked at as passive and submissive - attributes that are definitely favored in an industry based on male domination.

A Latina woman's value varies depending on a number of factors, most importantly the complexion of her skin. Latinas can look almost Caucasian, which of course raises her value in a pimp's eyes. A white-skinned, blonde Latina will easily pass as a white girl. Spanish-speaking Latinas can be extremely valuable in the United States due to the fact that many Johns, especially in the Southwestern region, are of Mexican descent. Latina prostitutes are sometimes avoided because they are known to be hard to control and feisty. For example, when it comes to a physical altercation with the pimp, Latinas are known to fight back and occasionally destroy property. Although they are profitable, they can also be a headache for a pimp.

At the bottom of the race totem pole (from a pimp's perspective) is the black woman. Although they seem to be more plentiful, they are the least desired choice for a pimp. Unlike the cute nicknames that are given to other races, black women are nicknamed with derogatory names. One of the most commonly heard is "mud duck" or "duck." Some pimps choose not to deal with black female prostitutes at all. It is rare to find a pimp that will not deal with any girl that will submit to him. However, when it comes to black females, this is not always the case. Why is this? I would say that it is for multiple reasons, some physical and some psychological. The physical being the pigment of her skin. In this society, racism is still very much in existence. Police tend to interrogate, stop, and harass black female street walkers more than other races. Through media's portrayal of the "crack whore" and black women being "ghetto," tricks tend to be more reluctant to pay a black woman as much as they would another woman of a different race, offering the same service. Black or African American women come in many different shades and variations of skin color. The lighter the skin color of a black woman, the quicker she will be accepted by a pimp. A light-skinned black woman can also be made to appear white, usually through a blonde wig or complete bleaching of her hair.

Some pimps choose not to deal with black women because the women come from the same impoverished communities that the black male pimps did. The women have many of the same negative psychological attributes that were developed from growing up in those communities: frustration, a short temper, and a poor work ethic. With frustration and short tempers on both ends, the result is oftentimes fighting rather than money making. In a pimp's eyes, fighting is a waste of time. On the other end of the spectrum, there are some pimps that tend to *only* deal with black girls because they find it easier to talk with and relate to people who grew up where they grew up. This pimp's mindset is similar to a person from the impoverished inner city who has never ventured into corporate America to deal with business professionals. They lack the confidence to try and relate to someone who appears to live a life so different from what they know. These pimps also view black women as more loyal and more economically motivated. Black prostitutes are more loyal because they usually are involved in the game for the same exact reason as the pimp—as a way out of generational poverty. They are a little more invested in the situation and might really have a genuine love for the pimp. In many cases, the black women who enter the life have an extremely low self-esteem, partly because they know that they're the lowest on the hierarchy of prostitutes. They may not feel like they can get out of the game and will stay in the relationship.

Psychologically, black pimps suffer from "Willie Lynch Syndrome," just like many black people in general who feel that white or lighter-skinned people are better than black. The "William Lynch Syndrome" is based off of an unconfirmed speech made in 1712 by a slave owner by the name William Lynch. The speech was to other slave owners about how to control their slaves. One of the methods being pitting the slaves against each other based on the shade of their skin. Whether the speech is true or not, there is an underlying self-hatred that has affected the minds of most pimps that they will never admit. All of these feelings can be traced back to the slavery of blacks in the U.S. In some cases, black pimps look down on black prostitutes because of a bad or non-existent relationship with their mother. The opposite of that is that some pimps will only deal with prostitutes of other nationalities because of the love they have for their mother, grandmother, or sister. It is hard for them to put a woman through the horrible lifestyle of prostitution when they look like their own family.

This hierarchy of race was learned throughout life as a black man in America. It is unspoken, but taught in every aspect of society via media, politics, and all other systems in this country. The idea that white is right and black is bad was verbally and physically forced upon black people in the past and now in current times it is still subconsciously instilled in us. The pimp subculture is just a lot more open with expressing these ideas and thoughts. This mindset must be first acknowledged to exist before a person can move past it. There's a point to be made: not only are black men socialized into these racialized half-truths and stereotypes, but so are buyers and the general public. I want to make that a strong point and call them out for what they are; they are half-truths at best nonetheless.

# The Pimp's Mother

Almost any man that has had the privilege to have been raised by his mother tends to honor her, respect her, and put her up on a pedestal. The manner in which a man looks at a potential mate can be directly connected to the way his mom was viewed and/or the relationship that he may have had with his mother. This is also true when it comes to a pimp and the way he views the women he's working with. Pimps that have had good relationships with their mother oftentimes take care of their girls, whereas pimps that have gone through abusive situations with their mother seem to be more strict and abusive of their girls. For example, my mother and I have had a great relationship for the most part. I didn't grow up watching men beat her. She has always taught me to respect women. To this day I have never put a hand on a woman in a violent manner. On the other hand, a close friend of mine grew up watching his mother get beat by the men in her life and he grew to be one of the most violent people that I've ever witnessed with his women. I've seen this pattern repeated throughout the pimp world.

An abusive or violent relationship between a growing young man and his mom can manifest in a variety of ways: physical abuse, mental abuse, neglect, or absence. The son may have even witnessed his mother being abused by another male. All of these forms of abuse can change and mold the perception of any man towards women, not just a future pimp. When you're a young man growing up watching your mother being beat, you hate it, you know it's wrong, and you may even tell yourself that you'll never do it when you grow up. Then when you grow up, it somehow creeps into your behavior patterns. It's similar to having an alcoholic parent. Pimping and prostitution is a lifestyle, but it does not mean that the individuals involved are any less impacted by normal human events. The idea that how a man treats a woman is directly connected to his relationship with his mother is without lifestyle boundaries. Like the old saying goes, "If you want to know how a man will treat you in marriage, just look at how he treats his mother."

# Dehumanization

Dehumanization is the psychological process of demonizing the enemy, making them seem less than human and thus not worthy of humane treatment. Throughout history we have seen this process lead to not only violence, but some of the most horrific abuse of human rights. I firmly believe humans are naturally born to be kind, love, and befriend one another. No human is born to look down on another based on race, sex, creed, or religion. These are learned behaviors that are thrust upon us, perhaps subconsciously, by the outside world. Unfortunately, in this world there are many individuals and groups that look down upon others that seem different from themselves, sometimes leading to dehumanization. This process of dehumanization is used to justify hate, to make a group feel superior, and sometimes even to kill.

To a pimp, a woman is not an equal. A majority of the time she is looked at as somebody lower than him. Pimps must constantly tell himself that what he's doing is correct, because he knows deep down that it isn't. Sayings like, "Pimpin ain't easy and hoeing ain't hard," are constantly recited amongst pimps and from pimps to their prostitutes. The music that a pimp listens to that confirms these thoughts, as does the many conversations he has with his fellow pimp friends. These conversations will be self-assuring and confirming that they are doing the right thing. A pimp must constantly say things to himself, his friends, and his prostitutes that dehumanize women, making them feel less than. He must feel like he's on top and they are on the bottom of the totem pole.

Amongst pimps you will hear them sometimes speak of a "Pimp God." This Pimp God is created as a replacement God to help them cope with a lifestyle and behavior that they know is wrong and against their nature. Pimps and prostitutes will both refer to the imaginary "Pimp God." It was usually when they achieved a new car, money, or another prostitute—anything that was viewed as an upgrade. When I was in the game this saying was one of the things that really irritated me inside and never felt good hearing out loud. If a woman is on your level as a human, you could not have her sell herself sexually to random men. If you view a woman as lower than you, as less than human, as an object, selling of her body for monetary gain is acceptable. You must dehumanize a person to be acceptable of this lifestyle. Although you may find some pimp/prostitute relationships that are nearly identical to boyfriend/girlfriend relationships, there is still some degree of dehumanization that is in effect. Like I mentioned before, this is not a natural human behavior. In my opinion, as a man growing up in America, I would say that the first initial thoughts of women being lower than men come from public media. As a kid I was subconsciously taught that women are sex objects and weaker than men. This behavior must be planted, grown, and nurtured to continue to live. As soon as these thoughts fade away or die completely, a person comes back into their right mind and realizes that their thought patterns were misguided. The dehumanizing of women for the purpose of prostitution is not a permanent mentality for those that make it out of the pimp subculture. When I look back at my mentality towards women and see it was incredibly misguided, it makes me sad and regretful. I do, however, understand that was the person I was, and that person is no longer living.

## Hailey's Tears

Sitting back in my desk chair my mind started to shut down. It was 3:00 a.m. and the thought of sleep began to overtake everything in my mind, including the two subjects that were always at the forefront of my mind—money and success. Ninety percent of my days were spent thinking about and working towards those two dangerous and powerful goals. I didn't see the danger then though, only the power. I couldn't wait to expand out of my walk-in closet of an office that my peers considered a great accomplishment. While having an "office" might be an accomplishment to many people in my community and circle, it was only small potatoes to me. I had always aimed for more. I never understood my friends who couldn't, or refused to, envision life outside of the streets of San Diego. I knew my planned business venture with my older friend was going to hit San Diego by storm and make us rich.

My eyelids started to close and my index finger pressed down on the "y" key, leaving the last sentence of my future project as, "yyyyyy." I quickly snapped back to consciousness. *I have to stay awake*, I thought to myself. My mind began to wander. Why am I drawn to this lifestyle again? Why am I not believing in myself enough to build this business without fucking with the game? My thoughts were interrupted by a long-awaited phone call.

"Hello?" I answered immediately.

"Hey Daddy. Where are you?" A voice choked out on the other end. She was crying and I could barely understand her.

"What's wrong? You okay? Where are you?" I jumped up out of my chair and grabbed my keys. Something was terribly wrong. What could have happened to her? Too many possibilities flashed through my mind. She could just be having another emotional breakdown. That's it! She's tripping again, thinking I'm with another bitch.

As she continued to cry I asked again, "Where are you?"

"I'm outside the office in the parking lot."

"What the fuck are you doing? Come up here!"

"No, I can't. Come down here."

Normally I would have refused, but her crying put me on edge. I rushed down four flights of stairs to my car. I pulled around to the back parking lot where I saw her standing. She climbed into my car with her head hung low and sobbing. Physically, she looked alright. What was wrong? She was still wearing the colorful satin skirt that we bought at the mall earlier, and the rest of her outfit looked perfectly intact. Her purse was there too. What had happened?

Then she said three words that I would spend the rest of my life trying to forget.

"I was raped."

I froze. This was not at all what I had been expecting. For the first time in my life, I was at a loss for words. *Come on, come on! You know what to say to this! You've learned from other pimps.*

My thoughts were scrambled. This had never happened before. One thing I did know was that I had to talk fast and say the right thing. You cannot seem like you don't know what you're doing in this game, especially in this situation.

She was a fresh turn out and had only been in the game for three weeks. Her words reminded me of the harsh reality of this world—a world in which I had introduced this young, gullible woman too.

Suddenly I remembered the words I'd heard other pimps use in the same situation and regurgitated them to her, "That wasn't rape. You were going to have sex with him anyway, right? He didn't rape you, he just robbed us. He got to have sex with you for free and didn't pay."

She stared back at me with a blank look on her face. Eventually she seemed to take in my words, reluctantly believing in my theory. Of course, I now know that this tactic didn't allow her to process her trauma, and certainly didn't translate to her feeling heard and protected. It was simply the reaction of a man that was scared and immature, completely lost in the mindset of the game. As I drove her home, I called a couple of pimps I knew who had girls working that same track and tipped them off about the sadistic trick that just raped my girl. I knew that if this trick raped once, he'd do it again and again.

She laid down for the night, only to go right back to the same track the next day. Only this time she was armed with pepper spray and I reiterated my instructions on how to better screen a trick as soon as she got into a car.

Our "run" continued for a couple more months until the day she got mad at me. She had finally realized that all I cared about was the money. She was right. In her anger she reminded me of that day she had been raped, and how I put her right back to work the next day. She yelled, and for once, I said nothing. The desire to talk her down or argue was gone. All I wanted to do was exit the game for good this time. When a person is truly tired of dealing with a particularly bad situation in their life, and they know better. The alternative is continuing to live in a constant state of being uncomfortable, something I no longer wanted to do. Finally, for me, this was the beginning of the end of the game.

# Rape

I can only imagine that rape is one of the greatest fears of any woman in this world, regardless of her profession. Unfortunately, it is not an uncommon occurrence. Regardless of age, nationality, or social class, women are taken advantage of sexually by men. Sick, sadistic males who know that they can trick and/or overpower a woman and will use any means necessary to fulfill their sexual desires.

A pimp knows that for a woman who sells sex for money, it is almost inevitable that she will be raped at some point. After 20 years of being directly involved in the game I have never really documented any statistics on how many prostitutes that I have knowledge of being raped. From my knowledge, I don't know a single girl who has been in the game longer than a year that hasn't been raped. It's a part of the life. The tragic thing is, I knew this before I would persuade a girl to sell her body and I didn't really care. I was blinded by my own greed. Yes, I would warn her of the chances but I would not press the issue like I would have if I truly cared about her well-being. No matter what level of precaution you take, at some point, some kind of unwanted sexual attack will take place. The only thing a woman can do is pray and hope to make it out of the experience alive. Women in the life have to be mentally prepared for not "if" but "when" the sexual assault will happen. As if there is such a thing as being mentally prepared for an experience like that.

In my experience in the life, I have known women who were raped at gunpoint, by knife, and/or just physical force. I have also known of women that were raped by their pimp. I have known women who have been raped by total strangers that were not soliciting sex. Most often, I have known women who were raped by the trick who picked them up or called out for them. The most tragic case that I personally know of is when a friend of mine went on a call and woke up three days later in another city. She had been drugged for the three day duration and sold to countless men for money and drugs. She was pumped with meth and other drugs to the point where she was frequently unconscious. She remembers waking a few times, always with a different man sexually assaulting her. She was incapable of fighting or resisting. After the experience ended, she found herself alone in an abandoned house coming to consciousness. When she was able to put the pieces together, she realized that the girl she thought was her friend had set her up for this to happen. This one "friend" had set her up with this call, telling the victim that this trick was one of her regulars.

The conversation with a girl about rape is a conversation that had to happen and I was trained to do that by other veteran pimps. It is definitely not the kind of "normal" conversation that you would have with a girl who isn't prostituting herself. However, once it's gotten to this stage, then nothing you're talking about is "normal". You are about to embark upon a lifestyle that is different than any other endeavor than you've probably ever been involved in. This lifestyle is crazy, but many people like choose to live it. I use the word 'choose' very lightly. My friend and Lived Experience expert, Jaime Johnson, says it's like having a choice between eating shit and trash but you have to choose one.

As I sit here writing this I continue to have flashes of that night when Hailey, a girl that I introduced to the game, came to me with the news. That night she came to me and told me that she had been raped I was saddened—but my desire for money overpowered my natural human instincts to comfort her. I attempted to coach her into feeling better. I asked her if she was good enough to go back to work or if she wanted to take the rest of the night off. She requested to go home and I proceeded to take her there. Although I felt sad I knew that as a pimp I could not show that. She sat in my passenger seat crying as I drove her home. I dropped her off and unlike most nights when I dropped her off, this time she didn't ask me to stay with her. I figured she just wanted to be alone. What she was really doing was testing me, to see if I really cared enough to stay with her. Unfortunately, I failed her in several ways that night.

Remorse, care, and sympathy for the women's feelings are things that a pimp hides so deep inside that they are almost non-existent. The only way to survive in this game as a pimp or prostitute is to become numb to feelings. When I eventually woke to the crazy behavior that I was involved in, I begged God to forgive me for all of the evil that I brought to the lives of many women. Not just from the days of me pimping, but throughout my continuous disregard for other lives since I was a young teen. I didn't care or understand at the time about the seriousness of rape, or what it would do to the their minds.

When rapes or assaults occur, a pimp's duty is to get the word out to other pimps. From the information he gains from the assaulted girl, he tells the other pimps that have girls working in the same area. Descriptions of the John, his car, and any other details are given to help prevent future attacks and to catch the assailant. Another precaution taken by the pimp is to re-instruct the prostitute on how to avoid assault and protect herself from future assaults.

# Minors

### Minors Pimped by Adults

To a real pimp or a traditional pimp that follows the unwritten rules of the game, prostituting minors is not acceptable or condoned. When and if a pimp is found participating in such behavior he is ostracized and slandered by other pimps. In my personal experience in the game, I have never witnessed anybody openly express that they are or had pimped on a minor. When I did hear about these types of cases it was through second hand information and when that individual was talked about it was never in a positive light. In a conversation with a good friend, and former pimp, a few months ago he brought up a mutual friend that was found out to have dealt with minors. I expressed how shocked I was because this individual had a clean name for himself and I was in disbelief that he crossed that line. My friend that was telling me the story began to tell me that that is why he and his crew parted ways with the person in question. I never had to personally see the pimp that had a minor to know that he was ostracized. My friends and colleagues would never condone such behavior when I was in the game. When a so-called traditional pimp is involved with a minor he is an exception and not the standard.

In the past year I have noticed a substantial increase in minor's being pimped. There are three cases I have had a personal connection to. The harsh unfortunate truth is that 2twoof the Pimps involved in these cases were people that were very close to me. One of the individuals is 26-year-old cousin of one of my best friends. He was charged with pimping a 15-year-old girl. His family, who I am very close with, told me that they told him to leave the young girl alone. They had even kicked both of them out of a family event where the minor in question tried to lie about her age. I have no compassion for him, nor does anybody else, and he is currently facing 15 years to life behind bars.

The second individual that was caught for having a minor was even more of a shock. He and I had been friends since high school. He's a little bit younger than me, but we entered the game around the same time in the late nineties. He was very popular as a pimp and was also a pimp rapper in San Diego who many admired. He was what I would have considered a "real pimp." Recently, he called me to come meet with him to discuss an emergency that he was having. The emergency turned out to be his discovery of a warrant for his arrest for the trafficking of a 14-year-old girl. He showed me the warrant on his phone and my stomach sank into my shoes as I read. He proceeded to tell me a story about how he was not aware of what he was doing and told me that the girl just asked him for a ride. I had known him too long, and known him to be way too smart for this lie he was telling me. After reading the charges and hearing his story I looked at him and asked, "Well what do you want me to do?" He asked me if I could help him and I immediately returned his request with a "no." He knew he had messed up and there was nothing that I would even be willing to do to help. He asked me not to tell anyone, meaning our mutual friends. He knew once the word spread that our entire community would ostracize him. Two weeks later he was picked up by the police and arrested on the warrant. The news has spread throughout our circles and he is looked down upon by everybody I've come across. The word on the streets are that his own friends in jail are waiting on him to punish him for pimping on a minor.

More and more recently I have been hearing about minors being pimped. For someone like me, who lived through the epidemic of pimping and prostitution in San Diego, this was rarely heard of amongst the circles I ran in. Recent reports has made me analyze the current issue of minors being prostituted in depth. Why is it so common now? For the past 6 months I've heard about a different case of a pimp being caught up with a minor at least once a month. In my opinion this growth in minors being pimped out is based on the current state of the pimp and prostitute subculture. In the current status of the game today it is rare for me to find a traditional "real pimp," like the ones I had grown up with. There are three reasons that I believe this transition has occurred:

1. Technology: With modern technology, specifically the internet and social media, the need for a pimp has become almost obsolete (I talk more about this in a later chapter).

2. Women's Empowerment: The social explosion of women's empowerment has brought many adult women into the mindset of not needing a man and being more independent. That same mentality has been adopted by women entering or already in the game when it comes to having a pimp. A lot of women that I know that are still in the game either refuse to have a pimp and work on their own, or will have a boyfriend that they give money to as they wish. With this current climate it is extremely hard for a "real pimp" to get an adult female to prostitute.

3. Learning from the previous generation: Unlike my generation, who had majority gang members, drug dealers, and drug users to look up to as examples, this current generation of 18- to 25-year-old women growing up in the inner city have lived under many close examples of people that were in the game. Their older cousins, sisters, brothers, and neighbors were in the game—and if not they were still influenced by it in some way. When we were coming up in the game it was almost like a brand new experience. There was nobody around to tell us about the game. The generation of today was born into the game and watched it at its height.

In my opinion, these three things have created a state of desperation in the game. A pimp is still trying to remain in control of people and money, but it has become harder for a pimp to control the situation. It has even become harder to convince a new potential girl to enter the game. In sick desperation some pimps find it easier to coerce and manipulate a naive minor girl.

## How Do Minors Get Involved?

What leads up to a minor becoming a prostitute? If that was known, maybe we could stop this tragedy before it even starts. I wish it were that simple. The situations and circumstances that create the pathway for a minor to get involved with prostitution are too varied and too big of a problem for a simple solution. It takes more than just awareness of human sex trafficking. Making children aware of sex trafficking—without working on the root of the problems that make them vulnerable to the idea of prostitution in the first place—is fruitless.

In a majority of the cases concerning young minors getting involved in prostitution, you will most likely find a child that came from an abusive home. That could mean sexual, physical, or mental abuse. The other common factors are that they grew up impoverished or have no home at all. Foster children are also at a high risk of becoming involved in the life. The "decision" to prostitute usually comes from a place of dysfunction, hurt, or a desire to survive. When a pimp comes along and persuades them to prostitute, their young, damaged mind is easily accepting. Sexual, physical, or mental abuse, as well as financial disparities are the roots of young girls gravitating towards prostitution.

One aspect that is often overlooked regarding minors becoming involved in prostitution is the fact that the guy that got them involved wasn't this big, bad adult man. Often he's a minor too. He was the kid who sat next to her in math class. The cute boy she had a crush on in gym. He was the slightly older guy she fell for on social media. In reality, he too came from an abusive home. He was also a victim of poverty, sexual abuse, or any of the other horrible upbringing scenarios that she was too. The only difference between the two minors is that he took on the traditional male role and she took on the traditional female role in this twisted lifestyle. They both need help. When I think back to the age me and my friends were when we entered into the pimp subculture known as "The Game" we were 15 and 16 years old. We were not turning out older women. We were getting involved in the game right alongside our female peers. This is still going on today, just on a lower scale. During my teenage years we lived in a domestic pimping and prostitution epidemic that has since slowed down considerably.

### The Vulture

The "vulture" is a male pimp that preys on underage girls in the hopes to make them prostitutes. I've heard stories and believe that people like this exist, but I cannot write about them. I cannot write about them because I've never been around anybody like this. In my decades of exposure to the pimp subculture and my personal relationships with numerous pimps and prostitutes throughout the country, I have never run across anybody that was targeting minors.

Multiple times while in human sex trafficking awareness meetings, seminars, media, and other related gatherings I hear stuff about pimps targeting schools for minor prostitutes and I want to scream. I wonder who they are getting this information from. Is this being said to scare people, or create a more dramatic speech? They must not be speaking about the urban black pimps. Yes, there may be isolated cases of this behavior happening, but it is spoken about as if it is the norm and a regular tactic being used by street pimps. In reality, it's only sick monsters who would do this, and these individuals would never be respected by society or by black urban pimps.

## The Deceiving Minor

Although a pimp is in the game and is supposed to be cautious of everybody he deals with for one reason or another, he may make the dumb mistake of not verifying the girl's age. There are occasions where I have known girls under age who approached pimps asking to join their team. The two girls that come to mind had been prostitutes for a few years already. Both pimps rejected them, or at least that's what they told me. In both instances the younger girl was hanging out with older girls and was introduced to the pimp—typically in a setting only adults would be in. Once I had a girl approach me with a younger girl trying to be with me. I immediately rejected her and sent both the minor and the older girl away from me and never dealt with either again. Ultimately the decision to accept a minor is on the adult. Period. I don't care how pushy the minor is, or how old they may appear, the adult should reject her.

Far too often I've witnessed a guy fall for a girl that looks like she's in her mid-twenties only to find out later she's a teenager and lied about it. Sometimes I believe that guys act as if they believed the girl was of age, when in reality they are just leaving themselves room to say they were lied to. The standing rule is to check all questionable IDs; yes, pimps will ask for a girl's ID in a heartbeat. It may be hard to believe that a guy would turn away a girl that he was recruiting, would turn her down because of a lack of identification, but it's the truth. Especially when dealing with a veteran pimp who is not willing to risk doing even more time dealing with a minor. This goes for the square world and the game. The dumb pimp believes the minor when she says she's eighteen or older. He doesn't ask her to see any identification or if he does, she says she has none. So hungry and greedy for money, he moves forward with her word. Yes, this is willful ignorance.

The following is an excerpt from the interview "A Girl Attracted to the Streets" I conducted with a survivor on my podcast *Raised in Pimp City*.

*Survivor: "When we had met him we told him we were 18 years old and you know we just went from there. He didn't ask for no ID or nothing like that."*

*Armand: "So you told him you were 18, but you weren't 18?"*

*Survivor: "No I was 17 years old, but I did tell him I was 18. And this is July 2003 and I wouldn't have been 18 until April 2004. Which is actually the same year I would've graduated high school. So we went out and the first day, I remember we went to an apartment in Spring Valley and in his stable he had two other girls, but he roommate with a P that had 3 girls. So it was all of us in one house, and uh, as soon as I went in he was like you guys gotta do her hair. So some girl immediately put a weave in my hair, like a ponytail. Those little fake ponytails and he was like tonight we are gonna go on the track. So the girls are explaining it to me, all my wifeys are explaining it to me. But the other girls,who were the other pimps, they were explaining it to me and they were like, "don't be scared." So I was like afraid, I was afraid. So the first night out there I hid. I was like this is too much. They took us to National City, somewhere on Main though. Not National City Blvd. but on Main, where it was that little short track that you couldn't walk on the other side because you would be on the base. So we're on the other side looking at the base. The Navy base right there. We didn't walk on the Navy base side because I guess you could get in more trouble or something. I don't know. I don't remember why we couldn't, but all of the women that were out there we were on one side of the street. There were so many. I remember sitting out there like 'oh my God, what am I into' while I'm hiding on a side street. Yea but because it was my first night I didn't get in trouble. I didn't meet my quota. Nowhere near it, but the girls that I was with she had turned a date and my wifeys, they had held it down. So he just chalked it up as I was scared. So the next night I was out there he had paired me up with my wifey. With the Bottom, like you know "She's gonna turn a date tonight because we have to break the ice and there's no way she's gonna be able to do this if she's hiding or afraid or whatever." So um, the first person pulled up and me and her hop in the car. She basically does all of the negotiation, but she was like 'You're gonna do this with him. So I'm in the car, turned my first date, scared as hell. I wasn't really sexually experienced like that, but I knew that I had to survive and at the same time I was like, "this is cool." I was like "I'm in a situation. I'm doing something right out of the books. I'm about to be a down ass chick. Like I'm about to be that chick." And... that lasted about a week… and the girl that I was with there was like some jealousy going on, because I started to make more money than her and she ended up telling my folks that I was 17. So he takes me out on a ride and he said "I need to know how old you are!" You know and I'm lying like "I'm 18" and crying. He's like "ok well we're gonna go to the DMV so we can get your ID." So I'm just crying, crying, crying. He's like "You need to tell me the truth." He takes me to some park. I can't remember what park it was. He was like "I'm gonna beat your ass and I'm gonna have the homies come out and hurt you! You gotta tell me the truth!" So I just broke and was like "Damn I'm 17."*

## The Use of the Word "Minor"

In recent years there has been a very noticeable intensification of the prosecution of pimps. Some of the recent cases here in my hometown of San Diego have been large group indictments. Federal RICO and state racketeering indictments have hit many urban areas with the common charge being sex trafficking. When these indictments first come down, and are made public, there is a world that I've heard on every occasion. That word is "minor."

Whether it be on the news as the indictment first comes out, or in the courtroom as the case goes through the system, the "minor" or "minor victim" is involved somewhere. Why is that? One would say maybe it is because there was actually a minor or minor victim involved. This is true to an extent. On the surface level there may be a minor that was trafficked or prostituted, but when you look further into many of these situations you find out a little more detail. On a few occasions where there was a minor involved you will find that the facilitator or pimp was also a minor. Does that make the offense acceptable or okay? No it doesn't. What it does do, is make the situation more understandable. My purpose for bringing this up is so that we can all start looking beyond the surface about these situations and stop being headline readers. Each situation is different and we need to know that because lives are being affected.

When the word "minor" is used or "minor victim" is used by media to the public or by a prosecutor to a judge and jury without explanation or details on the particular situation, it is damaging and can create a false narrative. It is also an intentional tool to make the listening party feel anger and dislike for the accused. Nobody in their right mind would want a minor prostituted. Most of the indictments that I'm familiar with where this was done had investigations that spanned over many years. One in particular used evidence from ten years back to connect one of the people involved. This means by the time this actually happened, an individual who is in his twenties when arrested could have been a minor pimp with a minor prostitute earlier in life. Only now, at the time of the indictment the perception is that he was an adult pimping a minor. In the courtroom this results in a merciless judge, a cold-hearted jury, and larger sentences.

I suggest that we all begin to look a little further into issues before casting judgment on anybody. Just because it was said on the news that does not constitute it being 100% truth. Even if you hear the words coming directly from the DA or Police Chief themselves. Often times certain words are used to paint a certain picture of an individual for motives other than actual truth and justice. We must stop being headline readers. Especially when it comes to another human beings life.

# Renegades

The term "renegade" is used to address a woman that is working for herself without a pimp. Someone that is an outsider to the urban domestic pimping and prostitution subculture would probably think that the word 'Renegade' is only a term used by the pimps or controllers, but in reality this term is used by the girls in the game as well. There really are no terms or verbiage that the urban pimp and prostitute don't share. They communicate in the same language in the game.

The thought of: "I don't need a pimp to do this" arises in almost every prostitute's mind at some point. Some choose to act on that idea. Most may think it, but for whatever reason choose to remain with a pimp. Some girls move on to doing it by themselves because of one or more bad situations with a pimp. It might have been something as traumatic as abuse, or simply a misuse of funds by the pimp. Sometimes a horrible physical experience with a John will send a renegade back to a pimp. Whatever the case may be, whatever caused a girl to go out on her own can either last for the rest of her career as a prostitute, or for only a brief period until another pimp wins her confidence.

Some prostitutes that choose to renegade do so just out of pure fact that they have been in the lifestyle for a really long time.

These girls have had multiple pimps in their career as a prostitute and have no desire for another. In some cases they're too old or may have a bad reputation; this makes pimps no longer want to deal with them. Some renegades may have already exited the lifestyle, but still choose to turn tricks with regulars that they have acquired when in need of extra money. They may even have jobs, be business owners, and even be married. After many years of prostitution being their only profession, many girls will continue to work out for survival. This life is all that they know.

A renegade will operate in the same arenas as the prostitutes that have pimps: strip clubs, brothels, tracks, and escort services. The way they typically see it is, if they are doing the work, why should they give all their hard earned money to a guy?

A typical renegade is usually condescending to other prostitutes that have pimps. Renegades frequently try to talk other girls into joining them in reneging. Pimps will refer to these renegades as "cancers" and demand that their girls stay away from them. They should not be interacting with them at all, and would be reprimanded and punished if they do. This is pretty standard, although there are occasional exceptions. For example, I have a friend who allowed a particular renegade around his girls because she was an old friend of his; a friend before the game. This renegade friend would help him to talk to his girls about how great of a pimp that he was.

### Benefits and Downfalls

Being a renegade has its benefits: you can make money as you please and do what you want with it. You don't have to worry about making a quota before work stops. You definitely don't have to worry about ever getting hit or cussed out by your pimp.

However, being a renegade has its downfalls as well. Unless you are great at saving money and self-discipline, you will not be successful. When I pose this argument some people ask me, "But how many pimps are actually great at saving money? It basically comes in and goes out on hotels, cars, food, and clothes right?" In my experience I have seen different kinds of pimps. Ones that did not know the first thing about managing money, those that were so afraid to lose a dollar that they saved every penny, and then there were those that grew their money. Yes, some of them spent most of their money on cars, houses, jewelry and clothes but when they did, it only made them more desirable and attracted more prostitutes to them. Of course when this happened, they made more money. I have never met or known a renegade that has shown a level of success. Not saying that there aren't some out there. Maybe the ones that were successful moved far away from the circles that I was in and I just didn't know of them. I do not know any prostitutes working without a pimp that are succeeding financially as a renegade in the US. However, I did discover many that were very prosperous in Puerto Rico. At this time, I know about 5 prostitutes that work on their own. They make a lot of money regularly and constantly brag about what they do, but showing any physical measure of financial success is non-existent. One thing that a pimp does is keep a regular work schedule, which maintains the accumulation of revenue. When given the option to work or not work, most prostitutes will not unless there is an immediate desire that needs to be met, like rent, a phone bill, or another current need.

Physical safety is one of the biggest downfalls if you are a renegade. Both pimps, tricks, and other prostitutes will know if you do not have a pimp. You have now become a target of verbal and physical attacks on a regular basis. A pimp that knows a girl is a renegade can and will physically take her money and feel no regret about it. This happened in front of me when I was younger many times. The culture of pimping and prostitution frowns upon women who renegade. It is looked upon the same way that society would look at a married woman for cheating on her husband. The game, as wrong and evil as it might be, has rules and a code of conduct. Being a renegade is a violation of those rules. It is not accepted on the streets. It will become a serious obstacle if you are constantly under attack by pimps and other prostitutes on the internet and on the track. This could hurt your revenue.

## The Growing Trend

Recently I was in deep thought on how much the game has changed since I was in my late teens/early twenties. I was reflecting on how many pimps and prostitutes were out in the open and in the game, compared to now—almost 15 years later. The number of renegades here in San Diego has increased substantially. Here in San Diego, where I have spent most of my life in and around the game, I can honestly say that most of the people that I know that are still in the game are women. None of which have pimps. This may be shocking to most of the people reading this. Honestly, it's shocking to me as I write it. I've really started coming to grips with the reality of how much the domestic pimping and pandering has changed here in my city and in this country. Sorry if this contradicts what you have been trained to believe or what the statistics are telling you. This is the reality from someone who has not only been a trafficker, but is still waist deep in the game as I work on bringing it to an end. Just last month I was with a friend that's still in the game in Florida and our conversation went like this:

Me: "Damn _____. When are you going to exit out of this life?"

Girl: "You too!! My boyfriend wants me to stop doing this. But I'm not gonna stop. This money's too good. He's just going to have to deal with it. Or..."

Me: "Or what?"

Girl: "Or leave."

Why things have changed so much, I will have to leave up to the researchers to gather the correct data. All I can do is tell the truth as I know it to be. A truth from actually being on the inside of the subculture. I believe that with the explosion of the internet and social media over the past ten years, there has been a large amount of women becoming renegades. With numerous websites like Craigslist and Backpage where women could post ads for themselves, the need for a pimp has diminished. I would also say that law enforcement's recent crackdowns deterred a lot of people from turning to the game as a means to make money. These crackdowns came at a time when most pimps were already exiting out of the game. Many people that have been arrested for pandering and human sex trafficking were already done with the lifestyle and had moved on, only to be caught up in an indictment anyway. This brings us to today where tracks around America have slowed down substantially in prostitution activity. Girls that would have at one time worked on a street corner are now on call sitting at home or in a hotel. Girls are often found working as renegades, sometimes alone or sometimes in groups. These renegades may have boyfriends, but pimps are non-existent. It has become a norm to be a renegade due to the internet. It is easy and extremely accessible to sell sex for money. Why have a pimp?

I want you to understand that the information I just gave you is very important, but I want to also make sure that you don't come away with the thought that there isn't anyone being trafficked, because that's false. There are still large amounts of people involved and caught up in the trap of pimping and prostitution.

*Survivor: "We were homeless, living in hotels. She ends up getting an apartment through her folks and then he ends up firing her for some ol' stupid shit. So now it's just me and her and we are getting it. All while I'm pregnant, which I'm not proud of, but I had to do what I had to do to feed my child."*

*Armand: "With no Pimp?"*

*Survivor: "No, No folks. We didn't have no folks, so now we're renegades. We end up moving into this house and when we move into this house, women ended up gravitating over there. We are living in a one bedroom apartment in La Mesa and it's like about seven girls there. Now we're like helping to turn these girls out because everybody wants a way out of their situation. So I started teaching them the game. This is what you do, this is how you do it…*

*Me and my sister and my other sister, well they're my best friends end up saying, "Now we have a clique and it's called Renegade Boss Clique." Now we're pulling in girls and now there's seven of us and we're all RBK. We were all like "We don't need no folks! We don't need nothing like that!" But you know how the game goes up and down and it had become a down time when we were really struggling. So and my best friend and I were like we need to find some more people to choose up with real quick just so we could be able to get a little status. So that we could be able to still be effective because right now we're tanking. This is when Craigslist came and I'm trying to remember if you had to pay at this point. I don't think so. We were on Myspace looking around…"*

*Armand: "So wait, why did you guys go? Why were you tanking? You said it was like seven girls. Renegade Boss Clique. You guys were the renegades. You guys were out working, turning dates, doing all of this on your own. Nobody has a pimp. Nobody has folks. So what made you guys tank?"*

*Survivor: "I believe well, one of the girls ends up getting folks, another girl ends up breaking off saying that this isn't for me. You know it just started to dwindle down like that."*

*Armand: "Were you all collecting money together? Were you doing it independently? How was that set up?"*

*Survivor: "We were living independently but we were all sharing one room. So everybody would put a piece in. You know what I mean. So I'm only paying like $15 for a hotel room at this time. At the nicer hotels. We were all able to put*

157

*in a piece. So as they all started to drift off and go here and there it was just me and my best friend. We're the only ones left and we were like 'Ok we're not making any money.' When you're a renegade the structure is different than when you have folks. So it kind of becomes a little bit like, 'Oh shit we're not forced, not every day do we have to work.' And not 'forced' either. That was the wrong word. But there's no quota. There's nothing like that. It's like we don't have to get up and go. We could sit there for like three days and not make no money. But what we didn't know because we were still young and stupid, if you sit there for three days and you don't eat your money dwindles. You have to spend your money. So by the third day you're hungry and broke all over again."*

# Chapter 6: The Trap

You see Devon, I'm telling you all of this so you can have an understanding. An understanding that I wish we had growing up. I know Richard dying was not a direct effect of the game. He didn't die while pimping and he didn't even get into any sort of confrontation with the little kids that killed him. However, we all must learn from his experience. In both life and death there are lessons to be learned. The kids that murdered him were all your age. They are all now serving 100 years plus for what they did. Every decision you make can affect your life for the rest of your life. Even in retaliation for something done to you.

Nephew, I know that this life is hard and that there are some people that hate their own life and will choose to take their own frustrations out on you, but I must warn you to fight against the temptation to do something stupid that could have your life taken away by a bullet or a prison cell.

Just to be clear with you, I know it's hard to be growing up in a community and a society that makes being wrong look cool and easy. I still fight temptation to do wrong everyday. I am not "Mr. Perfect" by any means. You would think that after Richard's death I would've learned my lesson and been scared away from any wrongdoing. Nephew, I was in prison at the time he was killed. I really should've gotten out and tried hard to do right. That was not the case. When I got home all of my friends were sad and in mourning, but they were all still in the game. Even people that weren't in the game when I went in were now acting as if they were super *pimps or the baddest hoes out there. The life had consumed them. As it does. It wasn't long before I fell right back in with them. It wasn't out of necessity; it was unfortunately because it was cool and I still had the hunger for fast money. I felt that I had to catch up to my friends.  Even though I had a job, a car, and a home, the game was still calling me...*

# Relationships

There's a thin line between being in a boyfriend/girlfriend relationship and being in a pimp/prostitute relationship in recent times. The majority of guys that I have come across at this new stage of the game have only one girl and maybe a possible second. That second girl is really temporary and seems to be there primarily for the benefit of the main girl and the pimp. When I was growing up, this was less likely the case. Most pimps that I knew of were in a race to have as many girls as possible. Things have changed dramatically. Even seasoned pimps from my era are operating like boyfriends these days. Pimps that once demanded to be the leader of the team are now making deals with the girls, in some cases even letting her dominate the relationship. The difference that remains from my era and this new era of pimping is the fact that the motivation to be together is still money—whereas the main focus of a boyfriend and girlfriend is love and emotion. Occasionally you may very well find a pimp/prostitute relationship based on both the pursuit of money and a strong love connection between the two. Many pimps/prostitutes started out as a typical boyfriend/girlfriend relationship before entering the game. This goes for both males and females.

To many in society outside of the pimp subculture it is extremely hard to believe that a man can love a woman that he is allowing to prostitute. It is also hard for them to believe that the love a woman feels for her pimp is real. Is their love true or is it fake? Who can truly be the judge of that? You would have to be that individual to know how you feel. One may wonder if the odd pair has each other's best interest at heart. In my opinion, the prostitute in this relationship would surely have the pimp's best interest in mind—even more than her own. The pimp in this situation is less concerned about her well-being and more about the financial come up. In a weird way, this may be his way of having her best interests at heart. He may truly believe that by taking part in these acts, it may give them a financial security that they have never had and would never have if they were not doing this.

## My Boyfriend Turned Me Out

Oftentimes males and females in relationships turnout to the game at the same time. Most of those times the male somehow gets introduced to the pimp lifestyle and brings it to his girlfriend as a way for them to make money. Not just any money, but large amounts of money. This begins with boyfriends and girlfriends because they are already involved with each other. The bond has already been created and the trust is in place. It is easier for a man to approach a girl that you are in a relationship with already than it is to find a new girl. As a man you may really like and have feelings for the girl that you are with, but the desire to acquire money and improve your life can take over all feelings. If the man is still fairly young, like I was when I started, you truly haven't even grown to understand what true love and feelings are. As a young black male growing up in the inner city, my friends and I were brainwashed to not respect women and to look at them as objects as opposed to fellow humans. From the music that we listened to, to the way the older men in our community treated women, we were trained to not truly value women. These ideas were instilled at a young age. Thinking back to the few girls that I was involved with and girlfriends that I had prior to entering the game, I may have had feelings for them—but I didn't truly care enough about any of them to not use and cheat on them. Another major component of this is peer pressure. If an older brother, friend, or somebody that you looked up to encouraged you to pimp out your girlfriend, rather than love her, you would be more inclined to listen.

When the day comes that the boyfriend tries to talk the girlfriend into getting involved, emotions are high. The girl may already be deeply in love with the guy, and out of fear of losing him she accepts the trial of prostitution. Around 18, I witnessed both my male best friend Roy and my female best friend (who was also his girlfriend) turn out to the game simultaneously. They were both young and on their own. Not sure where their next meal was coming from. He fought the peer pressure that we applied on him to turn her out for a long time, then eventually the pressure of life got to both of them and a strip club license came soon after. The girl may say that she's not willing to do it, but she doesn't mind if he gets another girl to do it. Some girls that are willing but don't want to go all the way may just want to strip. If it's already come down to the boyfriend having this conversation with his girlfriend, he is ready and will accept just about anything the girlfriend is willing to do as long as it's a movement forward into the game. Some girls are disgusted by the fact that he even brought this up and their relationship ends.

If the boyfriend is in love with his girlfriend and cannot stand the thought of her having sexual intercourse with any other man, he will usually talk her into the strip club or go as far as becoming an escort. Not all escorts have sex with their clients. Topless massages, lingerie modeling, hand jobs, and simple conversations are often the only requirements. The boyfriend may be willing to cross those lines with a girl he has strong feelings for or even loves.

Pimp and hoe relationships that started as boyfriend/girlfriend relationships do not typically last. There are too many emotions involved from the beginning. If the new pimp ends up with multiple girls besides the initial girlfriend, problems usually follow quickly. Once a girl gets deeply involved in the prostitution world, at some point she may begin to hate herself and blame the person that got her involved in the first place. She may not even recognize that is why she's mad, but the resentment will eventually emerge. I remember arguing with a girl that I had turned out about little issues and she would always find a way to bring up the fact that I was the one that got her into this lifestyle. That fact would come up in most of our arguments. That was usually when I was a prick and started fights out of aggravation. Looking back on it, money was probably slow because she wasn't trying to make any. She was probably frustrated about the entire situation and chose not to work knowing that this would irritate me. This would lead to a fight and then her feeling like she finally had an opportunity to come down on me for getting her into the game. In a situation like this, the resentment never really leaves—it's just masked until eventually it is revealed in some sort. By the time their relationship has dissolved, both parties will have been exposed to the game and be ready to continue. Only this time, when they proceed, the words "boyfriend," "girlfriend," and "square" will be out of the equation.

## When the Girlfriend Turns Out Her Boyfriend

"No way!" is the common response when people not in the life learn a girlfriend turned out her boyfriend. How could a girl possibly do that? Why would she want her boyfriend to be her pimp? Although this may seem absurd, it is actually more common than not these days. After over a decade of this major pimp/prostitute epidemic that took over my city, a lot has changed in the mentality of the girls. Nowadays, it is not only the guys wanting the fast money and things that come with it, the girls do too. There has always been an occasional girl that's asked her boyfriend to be her pimp, it's just more frequent now. Girls that are in the life already and have years of experience under their belt feel that if they turn out their own pimp they will be in control of the situation. This is typically true. Many girls believe that they need a pimp to conduct their business; although this is becoming less and less the case. Women in the game that have operated as renegades (women without pimps) for long periods of time, and have no desire to have a pimp, may still have the natural desire for a companion. Because of this desire, they will acquire a boyfriend. This boyfriend can remain a square boyfriend without knowledge of his girl's profession, or she can be up front and let him know. The reaction of the boyfriend can vary greatly:

1. The boyfriend is in love with the woman and tries to talk her out of her life as a prostitute

2. He is interested in the money and gives her some stipulations if she is to continue, for example not being allowed to kiss the male on the lips

3. The boyfriend leaves her.

165

Unlike the boyfriend turning out the girlfriend scenario I discussed, where both are usually new to the lifestyle, the typical situation of a girlfriend turning out a boyfriend typically occurs when the girl is a veteran prostitute. Even if she hasn't had many years as a prostitute, she has had some involvement. This girl may really want a regular boyfriend, or she may be planning on making him her pimp from the very beginning. Either way, she will bring it up to him. Most guys in the urban communities from which I'm speaking of are more than likely, living in poverty, to jump at the chance to make a fast buck.

So you may wonder how this works. First, the girl will proposition him to be her pimp or daddy. This conversation typically starts with the girl telling the guy what she does, if he doesn't already know. She will then tell him how much money she is making, and how she couldn't make nearly as much working a square job. She will then convince the boyfriend that she doesn't have feelings for any of the tricks, and that she loves him, to secure his self-esteem. This conversation usually ends with: "Please do this with me. You will never have to worry about money again. I know this sounds almost identical to what a pimp would say to a new turnout prostitute and it is. This is just the beginning." Now she will make the money and he can protect her. The guy may have never believed that he could be a pimp, or had no desire to be, but once it's brought to his attention he jumps at the idea. It's almost like a gift that fell out of the sky, right into his lap.

Just like a seasoned pimp will train a new prostitute the prostitute would do the same for him. She will teach him how the blade works, how to post ads on the internet, and anything else to do with his role in the game. Although I was never the boyfriend turnout, I have had a couple girls teach me things about the game and ways that we could make more money. The new turnout boyfriend will usually not hesitate to accept this opportunity, even if the girl is offering it to him with a deal. The deal might be that she gives him 50% of what she makes and she retains the rest. A real pimp would never accept such a deal. This new pimp turn-out does

166

not realize that if he's caught by the law he will be doing all of the time and the girl will labeled a "victim." Although I have personally seen this done on many occasions, especially in the federal system, this is not necessarily always the case. He would likely do more time, but if the girl is an adult she would still be prosecuted. The women are actually prosecuted more frequently than the men. It's easier to prove cases against the woman too. If there isn't any force, fraud, or coercion involved then he's just facing pimping/pandering charges.

## Bonnie and Clyde

If you know what it's like to grow up in the inner cities of America then you may know what it's like to grow up in poverty, homeless, hungry, and all of the other issues that come along with it. The "land of opportunity" can sometimes seem like a fairytale or something out of a fiction novel. As a human there are three natural desires that are essential to your life: food, clothing, and shelter. If at any point those essentials are denied or viewed as unattainable, then there are no limits to what somebody is capable of doing to obtain them.

Growing up in the ghettos of America as a young, black man my options seemed slim. I only thought I would be capable of one of three things: a drug dealer, gangster, or a pimp. As a female growing up in the same conditions as me, I would imagine those options would be a single mother on welfare, finding a man to take care of her, or working a low-paying job. If the girl was a little more edgy her three options would be almost the same as mine were: drug dealer, stripper, prostitute, or escort.

When two people come together who are from the same impoverished conditions, a mutual understanding and bond is there. The desire for success and wealth are in them both. They have a common goal and mission to achieve these things. College and business ownership seem like a far-fetched idea. They've been broke for too long, and life is demanding they do something. They could sell drugs. They then realize there is too much risk in selling hard drugs and you would have to move way too much product to be profitable. *What can we do?* the couple thinks. *How can we get the things we want without hurting anybody?*

Bonnie and Clyde figure out that they can hit the pimp and prostitute game together. They have found the solution to all of their worries. There are many different angles they can use to achieve this. The girlfriend herself can prostitute. Or she can work at a strip club and dance. They can start an escort service together where they can both recruit girls to work for them. They can remain a couple and attempt to pimp girls together. She may even act as if she's the bottom bitch that's working too, just to persuade the other girls to work and pay. They may both post fake ads on the internet to rob tricks that they reel in. They may both sell their bodies for money. Personally, I have known of one couple that did this together. Both the boyfriend and the girlfriend escorted to make money. Their relationship lasted for many years, although I believe it was extremely difficult on them. They would argue all of the time. She was actually the violent one in the relationship, and he was frequently abused. At any point in time he could have overpowered her, but chose not to. One time I had a conversation with him and asked why he was selling himself instead of just letting her. He looked me dead in my eyes and said "Because I really love her and if she's willing to do this for us to live better, then I can too." Both male and female can go on calls, strip, and bring the money home to each other. Either way, Bonnie and Clyde are one and there is no manipulation of mind, except that which they do to themselves. To dwell in this world and have your mind involved in this sick culture you must manipulate yourself into believing that what you're doing is alright. In my experience I have seen a few of these relationships, but this is a far from common in the pimp subculture. They are on a mission to get rich together.

## Pimps Having Girlfriends on the Side

In some cases I've known pimps to have square relationships on the side with girls that they have feelings for or were attracted to. These relationships were kept secret from their prostitutes. These relationships start off as square but usually ended up with the girl being turned out to the game in some way. Sometimes it was the pimp's plan from the beginning to lure her in and make her like him before introducing her to the lifestyle. Other times it just ended up happening for different reasons. Real pimps, when sticking to the rules, would never lie to a girl about not being a pimp to trick them into a relationship. Growing up in my era there were a lot of square girls that wanted to be the girlfriend of a pimp. They would reap the benefits with no work. At one point in my life I had a square girlfriend that was attending a University while I was in the game. She enjoyed the stories I would tell her about me and my pimp friends. One day I had lost all of my girls and was losing money. I asked her if she wanted me to get a job and to be a square with her. She told me no, to go get another hoe. Her exact words to me were, "I don't care if you pimp, just don't f*** them." We broke up about a year later and she began dating another pimp shortly after. She was attracted to the pimp subculture, like many of her friends were around that time. Most of them ended up prostituting or stripping, but she remained a square.

## Emotional Pain

Relationships are already an emotional experience in the square world. Whether those emotions are good, bad, or a combination of both. When you add the stress, heartache, drama, and degrading sexual acts of the game to the equation, you will have an eruption of emotions. Most people, no matter how hardened they may seem, can be hurting on the inside. Both pimp and prostitute will mask their true feelings and press on in the lifestyle. Yes, both can love each other. Just because it is not the way others may view love, that doesn't mean that it's not love. On the flip side, what may feel like love at the time may be false due to the fact that neither partner has never truly know what love is. Once this is realized, a person may never recover. Most girls that I know that have made it out of the lifestyle choose to never talk about it, or relive their past in any way. The emotions are too much to deal with.

## (FLASH BACK)
### *9:10pm*

*I check my watch for the third time, heart rate increasing and stomach starting to turn. Damn, only one minute has gone by, I think to myself as I crouch deeper into the driver's seat of my car. I adjust all of my mirrors, making sure that I can see the surrounding area, but never taking my eye off of the hotel window of the room my girl just walked into. Why the fuck isn't she calling me to let me know that everything is okay? We went over this a thousand times! Frustrated, I sit and wait as each second feels like ten minutes. Thoughts of what could be happening in that room with the woman I love and some man I've never seen. Did he attack her as soon as the door closed? Is she having sex with him? She was only supposed to give him a massage! She better not be! Is he a cop? Is he raping her?! My other thoughts vanish and the only thing I can think about is making sure she's okay.*

*With that final thought I call her phone. After one ring, I'm sent to voicemail. Frustration quickly turns to anger, which then becomes fear. I don't want anything to happen to my girl. I envisioned her beautiful face and small body being attacked. Making sure she's okay is the only thing I can think about. Even worse are my jealous thoughts of her with another man, period. Why do I let this continue? This shit doesn't feel good but damn we need the money.*

*Slowly I begin to get out of the car, leaving the keys in the ignition just in case we need to leave in a hurry. I put my phone on vibrate and softly closed the door behind me. The hotel is quiet. Too quiet. I can hear a couple having a normal square discussion as I walk by, attempting to be unseen and yet look as normal as possible. En route to the room my girl is in, I must climb a staircase. Why does this shit gotta be on the second floor? As I think this to myself, I spot a camera aiming dead at me. Damn. I try to avoid it, keeping my face focused on my destination, only to spot another one right by the room, staring directly at me. My adrenaline is racing*

170

and I'm too close to turn back. She may need me. I have to continue.

As I get closer to the room I strain my ear to hear everything coming from the room's direction. Finally by the window, I try to increase my hearing capabilities as if I'm in a sci-fi movie, to hear any indication of a problem. All seems to be quiet. Not knowing if this is a good or bad thing, I decide to go back to the car and wait it out.

When I reach my car I immediately try to call her again, only to be sent to voicemail. Just as I place my phone down I notice the hotel door beginning to open. My girl was coming out of the room— safe, smiling. I watch her smile as she says "bye" to the guy now in plain sight standing behind her—tall, mid-forties, business-type, clean-cut, white male.

### 9:39 pm

I watch as she makes her way back to the car and my stomach's finally settling down. It seems as if both of us are uncomfortable as she gets in.

"Hey, you good?" I ask as I pull out of the parking lot.

She hesitates to answer before finally saying, "Yeah, I'm straight."

Now knowing she's okay I being to grill her with a tone of a jealous boyfriend. "I tried to call you! How come you didn't tell me when you got inside like I told you…?"

She quickly cuts me off and replies, "Look, there wasn't a need for that. It would've looked weird and that dude was already nervous."

She looked as if she had just went through a horrible ordeal and didn't want to talk about it. Her face was blank and emotionless. My curiosity raged. I wanted to know what took place, but not enough to put her through the pain of retelling it.

She continued, "He was a banker from out of state here on business. All he talked about was his wife back home and their adult son. He paid me $800.00 for twenty minutes."

Twenty minutes of what? I thought.

The car ride was silent for a while until she picked up her phone urgently.

"Shit I forgot to check in." She proceeded to call the service that had arranged the call. "Hey girl. Sorry it took so long… Yes, he was easy… No he wasn't as weird as the last guy… Yes, I'm still

171

*available… Thank you and I'll make my drop in the morning… Bye. Yes, please call me."*

*She hangs up the phone and quickly turns to me. Her facial expression is hard to decipher. Was she happy, sad, upset? Probably a combination of all three.*

*"Hey that was so easy. All he wanted was to be in my panties as I gave him a massage."*

*Even hearing that made my heart hurt. But I couldn't show that emotion, not even a little bit.*

*"Oh yeah?" I asked. "Damn for $800?"*

*"Yup. He thought I was the most beautiful escort he ever called."*

*"Shit, you were."*

*For the remainder of their ride home the only noise in the car was the music coming from the stereo. All I could think about was how deep I had gotten her into this life and how I wished we could stop and lead normal lives together. How did I get to this point in life? Why am I now dragging the woman of my dreams into this madness? I'm not even in control of the situation. How can I stop? Is it too late?*

# What Keeps Pimps and Prostitutes Trapped in the Game?

## *Stuck in the Cycle*

People always ask me, "Why do people remain in this lifestyle? Why don't they get out like you did?" The truth of the matter is that there is no one reason that a person remains in or leaves the lifestyle. There is no easy fix. The same reason I stopped may be totally different than the next person. You would think that a person that has never even been successful at it would give it up and get a job. You would think that a person who lost their family, years of their life, and gained a criminal record would throw in the towel and run away. Still, countless people remain stuck in the cycle. I have life-long friends who were involved in pimping who became homeless and beg me for a few dollars just to eat, only to return to the lifestyle that got them into their mess in the first place.

Once a person has been engulfed in the underworld of sex trafficking it begins to be all that they believe they can do. I see this more so with men rather than women. Women suffer so many more challenges than the men in the lifestyle: rape, disease, violence, the constant fear of being arrested or killed. These situations can scare them straight and/or make them constantly regret their situation. Men do not have to deal with the mental anguish, sexual abuse, and other malicious things that come from being a prostitute. One saying that is constantly repeated in the pimp world is, "All I do is dress, rest, and finesse and let these bitches do the rest." Yes, there are hardships and headaches that come with being a pimp, but these "hardships" are absolutely no comparison to what the women suffer.

Because the pimp doesn't face the same trauma that a prostitute might face, he has a greater chance of staying in the lifestyle. The longer he is in, the more the lifestyle takes over his character. All of the repeated, self-convincing mantras that he's repeated for years keep him going. In my efforts to reform people and get them out of this lifestyle, I've seen many people want to leave, want to do something different, but after going without money, food, shelter, and clothing they run right back to their old ways and go after money the only way that they know how.

Prostitutes, as well as pimps, find themselves stuck in the cycle of this life like a recovering drug addict. In all cases, a person in the lifestyle must want to get out badly enough to make that move. Unfortunately, some women have been brainwashed to believe that they are worthless and can never be or do anything else with their lives. They are told by the pimp, and sometimes by their own family, that they can never be normal again. If they do leave, they carry with them the shame and stigma attached to being a prostitute. Until something eventually frees a woman's mind of this feeling of worthlessness, she will remain trapped. Even without a pimp, many women will continue the path of prostitution or other forms of selling their body. They may have broken free of the pimp, but the mentality is still confining their ability to see themselves as anything other than a hoe.

## Having a Good Run

All it takes to re-motivate a person to remain in the pimp and prostitute lifestyle is a "good run." A good run is any amount of time where the lifestyle proves to be lucrative or successful. This good run could be three days, three weeks, or three months. The time span doesn't really matter as much as what the person is able to accumulate during that time frame. These runs may come at a time when a person has been thinking about getting out of the lifestyle after a bad stretch. A pimp or prostitute may have been questioning their decisions and future, but when money starts pouring in their doubts are washed away. This can happen in one night. When this happens, the person is re-motivated to continue pimping or continue prostituting. The better the run, the longer the person is likely to continue in the lifestyle. Even when that run ends and troubled times come, that one good run will keep a person chasing the carrot, in the hopes of reliving it. This person may think that *this* run will be the one to never end and that the dream of getting rich will finally become a reality.

## Acquired Reputation

Throughout their time spent in the sex trafficking world, a male or female may gain a reputation amongst their peers. A reputation for getting a lot of money, driving the nice new cars, dressing in the best clothes, or even just keeping girls on his team. With this reputation, the person starts to be admired, not only by others involved in the lifestyle, but others in the community, neighbors, business owners, and even the families of the prostitutes and pimps. Once these reputations have been established, it is hard to walk away from the lifestyle and characteristics that got you the reputation. As a pimp, you've likely acquired a network of support, from the toughest thug in town to the luxury car dealership owner. The tough thug will give you street credit and protection and the car dealer will give you a new car with no money down, job, or credit. These are the perks of a good reputation as a pimp. These reputations and perks will keep a pimp motivated to continue in the game.

Acquisition of a negative reputation can also keep someone involved in the game, not necessarily inspired in a positive way. For example, once a male or female is viewed by people outside of the subculture as a "bad" or "dirty" person, the one who is inside can oftentimes remain inside the game to keep from facing that other world. Their reputation has become so bad that they begin to feel like they will not be accepted into the regular square society. Their self-worth has been lowered within themselves, to the point to where they believe that the game is all that they can do with their life.

## Addicted to Fast Money

They say fast and easy money leaves you faster than money that you had to work hard to gain. This is often the case with pimping and prostitution. Like many other illegal means of getting money, the people involved in pimping and prostitution become addicted to the fast buck. Once you have been on the receiving end of fast money it is hard to go back to any other lifestyle. It almost seems illogical. Of course the things you're doing may be immoral, unethical, dangerous, and illegal, but at the time the reward of easy money overrules any moral qualms, and you continue your pursuit of the fast cash. The fast cash is not only appealing to the person earning it, but also to the people around the guy or girl making it. I have witnessed many people who hated the idea of pimping or selling their bodies for money, but changed their minds after one of their peers began to acquire lots of fast cash.

In this capitalistic society, the dollar rules. The person that finds a way to make the most money is the one on top. After you have experience being that person, it is hard to stop, especially if you're in your prime and nothing seems like it's going wrong. Why would a person give up easy money that takes little to no effort to gain to work a minimum wage job? A job where the person has to listen to a boss and follow the rules. The person is lucky if he or she makes one thousand dollars at the end of two weeks, when they could have made two thousand dollars selling sex. A person doesn't have to pay federal or state taxes on the money that comes in from pimping either. This person isn't thinking about the drawbacks of not having a savings, or a retirement plan; they're blinded by the money that is right in front of them. To an individual involved in making money like this, the chances of stopping are slim, although they can happen.

Some people do see their way out of the life even in their so called "prime" of making fast money. For example, I have had a few friends that left the game at the prime of their careers and chose to invest the money that they had into legitimate business ventures. Two of them actually married their bottoms, and started a family. It's been several years now and neither one of them has looked back. There are many factors that can change somebody's mind and make them leave the "game."

## "Daddy I Don't Want to Do this Anymore"

What happens when a girl wants to stop prostituting? Is there a retirement plan? Does she put in a two-week notice like other "square" occupations? Is it as easy as just quitting as soon as she decides she wants to quit? Is there a process?

From my experience I have witnessed many different girls quit their pimp and the game. Many of these situations are the same and rarely am I shocked at how they take place. Usually there are a lot of emotions involved with both the pimp and the prostitute. The longer the two have been together, the harder the split is—very similar to a regular relationship. Sometimes just because the girl stops, it doesn't necessarily mean that the relationship stops between the two of them. One of my best friends was told at one point by his prostitute that she wanted to leave the game and would leave him too. She knew and believed that he loved her, although he never told her this. So when she told him she was leaving, she had hoped that he would leave the game too. He did exactly that. Two years later they were married and had their first son. Another friend of mine, who was a prostitute for over 10 years, has been out of the game for almost 8 years now. She is currently a successful business owner, a strong woman, and a community advocate. While talking with her recently, she expressed to me how she and her former folks (Pimp) were still super close and that she still hung out with him occasionally and still had strong feelings for him.

When the girl approaches her pimp saying that she wants to quit prostituting the pimp's first reaction is going to be trying to convince her to keep going. His mind is going to be concentrating on the money that he's making with her. Depending on the relationship between the two of them, the pimp may feel emotional about losing the girl. Her telling him she wants out may be just what it takes to get him out as well. Although, most pimps have built up enough false pimp pride to counter any possible feelings that he may have about leaving the game too. Depending on the situation it can be both personal and emotional for him too; it's not necessarily only about the money. These issues can play a role when she approaches him and wants to leave. He may or may not be successful in convincing her to continue working. If he is successful, he must begin to watch her even closer. If she really wants out bad she may begin to do things like hold out on money and start stashing it away so she can stop on her own. She may even purposefully not try to make money out of spite, or because she's just no longer motivated. She may even just out right leave the pimp, or "blow up" as it's called in the pimp subculture.

I can remember only one girl that was with me that actually had a conversation with me about stopping. I was her first introduction to the pimp subculture. She really had strong feelings for me and in another world we would have just been dating. When she told me she wanted to stop she said it in a soft, comforting tone in the hopes of keeping me from getting mad, and to appeal to my sympathetic side. It was almost like a girl trying to break up with a boyfriend nicely. I, of course, responded with every reason as to why she should continue for "just a lil while longer." I was able to convince her into continuing, and we lasted for about a month—until she disappeared one day, running off with another pimp. In a later conversation with me she told me that she had to leave me because she was starting to have too many feelings for me, and she knew that I would never be with her in a regular relationship. She told me she was hoping that she could get me to leave with her by saying she wanted out but after seeing how relentless I was for her to continue, she knew it would never happen.

In some situations, if the girl really wants to quit and has been with the pimp for a significant amount of time, he may allow her to. I've seen many situations where the pimp had true, genuine feelings for the girl and would quit the game with her and begin a square relationship based on her desire to stop. Deep down inside he probably wanted to stop too, but was caught up in the lifestyle too deep to admit to or face that fact.

A girl becoming impregnated by her pimp is another common circumstance. A few people close to me had this happen. In a couple of these situations, the girl said that if they both didn't quit the game she was having the kid and leaving. The pimps all quit. On the flipside of that, there are many pimps that would continue to work the girl pregnant for the first few months or even more—likely only allowing her to only give oral sex and hand jobs until the baby was born. Once the baby was born and she healed, they would go back to business.

The guerilla pimp responds with force after a girl/prostitute approaches him with the idea of quitting. He may or may not start with verbal manipulation. He may try and talk her into continuing but if those efforts seem fruitless, he will beat her. There is no particular level or extent to this beating. It may be a slap or it may be more severe. Outside of physical abuse it may also be verbal and mental abuse that's used as a tactic to keep her working. For example, he may remind her of how she's a hoe now and tell her there's no going back to regular life. He may tell her things like, "Nobody will accept you!" or "Your family won't want you back!" and other verbal put downs to keep her in a weak enough position to continue working. Some of these tactics may be passed down by other pimps, but I believe most of what he is saying to her differs from situation to situation. Unfortunately, most of the things that he uses to hurt her have some basis in truth. That is why he says it, and that is why it works.

Like I mentioned earlier, how a pimp handles this situation could be the reason he keeps his girl or loses her. Sometimes the woman may just say that she wants to quit to test the pimp to see what he will do. If the wrong response comes from the pimp, this can be a guaranteed way to lose his prostitute to another pimp. If she wanted to quit the game for real and is sent back down on the track or put back to work, she may be open to finding another pimp who is more willing to listen to her.

# Kenny

Kenny was Roy's younger cousin and unlike the others in this circle of friends, the girls and guys he hung out with didn't find him physically attractive. He had always been shorter and not as "cute" as the other kids in school. Although some might have seen his growing up in an upper-middle class neighborhood as an advantage, it shook his confidence. The neighborhood was filled with White and Asian people, making Kenny stick out like a sore thumb.

Throughout life Kenny was often made fun of in school and picked on by the bigger kids. However, Kenny was not one to sit back and accept the physical attacks; Kenney would fight back violently. He would use physical aggression when met with confrontations. Usually beating up the kids that verbally hurt him. One time he actually brought a knife to school to address a bully that was bigger than him. In the instance Kenny was caught by school officials and was expelled from his school. The consequences were very negative for him when it came to school. He started to find that it was not a place of comfort and security for him. It is important to have a supportive school environment for a child growing up with pre-existing insecurities. Otherwise, it can be detrimental to their future. The violent behavior he exhibited was positive for him when it came to building street credit.

Raised primarily by a single mother who had to work long hours to support their household, Kenny learned early on to be the man of the house and to take care of his other siblings. He would clean up after them, cook for them when needed, and most importantly protect them against any bullies. As a kid, Kenny felt as if he was already a man. Although this was far from reality, his current situation dictated otherwise. That is until his mother moved in a new boyfriend. Suddenly, Kenny was no longer the "man" of the house. This situation made him extremely uncomfortable and drove Kenny away from the home. He would stay out in the streets with friends until the latest time possible. As a young kid, he had witnessed his mother in several different relationships with men. Some were decent, others were verbally and physically abusive to both Kenny and his mom.

As Kenny's home life, worsened so did school. The more he was made fun of in school, the more insecure he grew. He began to be shy and reserved in school. The teachers didn't understand what was going on with him, nor did they try to find out. Instead, he was diagnosed with a learning disability. This only made him more reserved and insecure as a person. As a child when you're told by people in authoritative positions that you have a learning disability you not only believe it, but you begin to use that as a crutch to lean on, rather than trying to excel in school. His home life played a role in his school behavior as well. Running around in the streets with your friends until it's time to go to sleep doesn't really leave much time for homework, study, or further development. Not to mention all of the inside distractive noise that was going on in his head about home life. Caring about doing well in school was the last thing on his mind.

In his early teen years his family uprooted and moved to a far poorer, more urban neighborhood. This neighborhood was not completely foreign to him. His father's family lived in this area, so he had visited often. At this point in his life, he was making more changes than you could count on two hands. One week he was a tagger, the next week a skater, the next a gangster. Kenny was searching for some sort of identity. At fourteen years old, he began to hang out with his cousin Roy and his circle of friends—which I was a part of. Although he was still constantly made fun of, it was a circle he felt good in. School was already far from his mind. By his freshman year in high school he had already decided to drop out.

Shortly after Kenny decided to stop going to school, an incident occurred that would drive him further away from family and into the streets. One day while breaking up a fight between his mother and her alcoholic boyfriend, Kenny was attacked by the boyfriend, resulting in the loss of two teeth. Abuse was starting to become a regular occurrence in this young man's life. At school being verbally abused by the staff and kids, in the neighborhood, and by the men his mom brought around the house.

For Kenny, becoming an adult faster than normal was a must. His skin had to be thick to withstand the mental, physical, and emotional abuse that was coming from the world and his inner circle. As he grew older, he became more in need of an avenue to channel his inner rage and desire to be fully accepted. He met these desires by joining one of the biggest gangs in his city. Although he was now a gangbanger, he would still hang out with our clique. Kenny had obvious personality changes depending on his emotional and financial state at a particular time. When he had money and was feeling good about himself he would hang out with us. When he was broke and down, he would spend more time with the gang.

When Kenny was eighteen he watched disheartened as his friends began to graduate from high school. Here he was, eighteen years old, a ninth-grade dropout with no job who had been made to believe he was dyslexic. His self-esteem was crushed even more as his friends earned their diplomas. The answer to what he thought was a hopeless life came when he learned that his friend Richard had begun to make huge profits off of selling sex from a girl he had known for years. Kenny had been around his friend Richard and his girl for a couple of years now. He and Richard were close friends that told each other everything. He and I were there when Richard first put his girlfriend on the track. What he never expected was that there would be as much money as there was in this new business.

"Wow, I can really do what I heard my favorite rappers talk about?" Kenny thought. "And it works?"

From that day of realization Kenny sought out to learn everything that he could about the trade called "pimping." His current girlfriend at the time, who was in a similar state of despair, was easily convinced to become Kenny's first prostitute. Who knew that this was the beginning of a life-long career? When Kenny started pimping, like most young black males, they don't have any true plans for the future and where they are going to do with it. All you know is that you've discovered a way to make money that can help you survive—and even overcome—poverty. The more that a young man like Kenny gets involved, the more evolved the plans and ideas are. Many pimps young and old say that they are in this field "for life." They mentally convince themselves that this is the only way for them. None of the young men that get involved in the pimp subculture have thoughts about what comes next or a retirement. Their vision is clouded with money and they live in the moment. The consequences that come along with this lifestyle are not yet visible.

Fast forward 19 years. Kenny has been in and out of jail several times. The longest time spent was two years in the State penitentiary. He has been out on the streets, trying to find a legitimate way to earn money—but without a high school diploma, inability to read, criminal record, no work history, and extremely low self-esteem, Kenny is on the verge of giving up on life. The game is all he knows, but he's tired of the bumps and bruises. He wants out, but it seems hopeless. He's trying hard not to go back into the life, but times are getting harder. He lowers his pride after not eating for two days and comes to me to ask for some money. He knows that I love him and he can get a few dollars from me. After getting some money he says fuck it and takes off to Las Vegas with intentions on getting back in the game. He is stressed and really wants a way out for himself, but sees no possible solution… "One more run"

# Chapter 7: Solutions

Devon the last time I spoke to Kenny I had just returned home from Puerto Rico. Kenny told me about how he was stuck in this hotel in Houston due to Hurricane Harvey. Although he was a bad situation, he remained joyful. I felt bad for my friend, as I often did. I knew that no matter how much I believed in his capability to do good things outside of pimping, he had to believe in it for himself. Before we got off that last phone call with each other, he said to me "Armand this is my last run. After this I'm coming to Paving Great Futures." I heard the sincerity in his voice, but I can't lie, I didn't really believe him at first. The more he continued to talk, I heard the exhaustion in his voice. I could feel the misery and pain from nearly 20 years in a game that can only produce a temporary joy. For decades, Kenny chased a carrot that he only nibbled every so often.

Two weeks later, when I got the call that he had been murdered on the track in Houston, it felt like an entire piece of me had been destroyed. I felt like I had let that happen to him—like I didn't do enough to get him out of the game. He would have listened to me if I pressed him more, but now another one of my brothers had fallen victim to the game. My other brother, Will, had died less than two months before. At that point in my life, I was mad at myself, because I felt a responsibility to help him more, to get him out of the game. Although I was heartbroken, I understood where to place my anger and sadness. All of these painful feelings and tears had to be redistributed into something positive. Now I have to go even harder, to save lives *from falling into this destructive path of pimping and prostitution.*

*Devon, I will never get another opportunity to talk to Kenny, Will, Richard, or Lawrence again. I can't ever look them in their eyes and tell my loved ones that the path of gang banging and pimping would lead to their deaths. I can still tell you. I can show you how to be a man. The way you should treat others. The way to treat a woman how she should be treated. I can be the living example for you—or a true friend, father, brother and husband. All of the examples that were missing from our lives.*

*Devon please call me back. At least text me so that I know you're okay. I would die if I let something happen to you. You do not belong in these streets. I'm not going to get on you for anything. Believe me, I understand everything that you are going through right now—even if you don't. Just come hang out with your Uncle and let's talk. You know that I am working day and night on a solution to this madness. I want you to build a brighter future, right alongside me, beaming like the light God intended you to be...*

Life and Legacy of

KENNETH DWAYNE
"LIL KENNY" "MAC ON"
MCKNIGHT
NOVEMBER 1, 1982- SEPTEMBER 19, 2017

# From Pimping and Pandering to Human Sex Trafficking

Growing up in and around the pimping and prostitution subculture in America around the mid-nineties and early 2000's, I never heard the words "human trafficking" or "sex trafficking." These words were not used by those of us in the game or heard from those with authority. When a person was ever caught by law enforcement, accused, tried in a court of law, or convicted, the crime was known as pimping and pandering. If somebody would have asked me in the year 2000 what I thought "human sex trafficking" was, I would have said it was something people from foreign countries did—some group of men that kidnapped girls and made them sell sex in basements. I would've pictured a bunch of Eastern European or Asian girls in storage containers being shipped to another country to be sold on the black market. These are the types of images that would immediately come into my mind. I never would have thought that what my peers and I were involved in was considered human sex trafficking. We were pimps, not traffickers. The girls were hoes or prostitutes, not victims. They were willing participants in the lifestyle that we were all a part of. Those were my thoughts until a new harsh reality hit in 2011.

Somewhere around 2011 the term "human sex trafficking" was brought to my attention. There was an indictment of a Northern San Diego County gang; the news reported that this Crip gang was involved in drug sales and human sex trafficking to make money. I remember watching this story on TV and being amazed that a local street gang was importing and exporting girls to other countries. As I looked into their case a little more I began to realize that the human sex trafficking that they were referring to was the same as the "pimping" term that I was accustomed to hearing.

From this moment forward, I recognized the game was drastically changing for the urban youth that were involved in the pimp and prostitute subculture. After hearing this new term, I began to notice that I would rarely ever hear the term "pimping and pandering." The only time I would even hear the word pimping was from the urban community and hip-hop artists. When it came to media, law enforcement, and politicians, they would only use the words "human sex trafficking."

People tend to underestimate the power of words. We don't realize how much of a psychological impression specific words have on people. The context and delivery method of words can plant impressions in the mind that can trigger many types of emotions. When I hear the word pimp, I know that it's negative, but the feeling inside myself is not negative. Maybe this is due to American culture making the word almost like a term of endearment, or maybe it's because for so long my particular culture has made this word positive. I have the opposite reaction when I hear the words "human sex trafficking." When I hear those words I feel anger inside. I feel negativity and evil. I'm sure that I'm not the only one that feels this way. Stop reading for a second and say the words "pimping" and "human sex trafficking" out loud with a brief pause in between. Did you feel differently inside? Now let's take this one step further by saying out loud, "Gangs and Human Sex Trafficking." How did that phrase make you feel? When I personally hear the words Human sex trafficking I feel saddened and emotional. This new term has a horrible internal effect. My friends who were also involved in the subculture of pimping have expressed to me very similar feelings.

## *What is the Difference Between "Pimping and Pandering" and "Human Sex Trafficking"?*

Is there even a difference between sex trafficking and pimping? In my past, the things that I was involved in and around were only known as pimping. To be honest, I am still confused as to what the difference is—if there is even one in the first place. For those that are interested, the following is what California state law defines the two concepts as:

## Pimping and Pandering

*Penal Code 266h (a) Except as provided in subdivision (b), any person who, knowing another person is a prostitute, lives or derives support or maintenance in whole or in part from the earnings or proceeds of the person's prostitution, or from money loaned or advanced to or charged against that person by any keeper or manager or inmate of a house or other place where prostitution is practiced or allowed, or who solicits or receives compensation for soliciting for the person, is guilty of pimping, a felony, and shall be punishable by imprisonment in the state prison for three, four, or six years.*

*(b) Any person who, knowing another person is a prostitute, lives or derives support or maintenance in whole or in part from the earnings or proceeds of the person's prostitution, or from money loaned or advanced to or charged against that person by any keeper or manager or inmate of a house or other place where prostitution is practiced or allowed, or who solicits or receives compensation for soliciting for the person, when the prostitute is a minor, is guilty of pimping a minor, a felony, and shall be punishable as follows:*

*(1) If the person engaged in prostitution is a minor 16 years of age or older, the offense is punishable by imprisonment in the state prison for three, four, or six years.*

*(2) If the person engaged in prostitution is under 16 years of age, the offense is punishable by imprisonment in the state prison for three, six, or eight years.*

*(Amended by Stats. 2010, Ch. 709, Sec. 8. (SB 1062) Effective January 1, 2011.)*

*Penal Code 266i (a) Except as provided in subdivision (b), any person who does any of the following is guilty of pandering, a felony, and shall be punishable by imprisonment in the state prison for three, four, or six years:*
*(1) Procures another person for the purpose of prostitution.*

*(2) By promises, threats, violence, or by any device or scheme, causes, induces, persuades, or encourages another person to become a prostitute.*

*(3) Procures for another person a place as an inmate in a house of prostitution or as an inmate of any place in which prostitution is encouraged or allowed within this state.*

*(4) By promises, threats, violence, or by any device or scheme, causes, induces, persuades, or encourages an inmate of a house of prostitution, or any other place in which prostitution is encouraged or allowed, to remain therein as an inmate.*

*(5) By fraud or artifice, or by duress of person or goods, or by abuse of any position of confidence or authority, procures another person for the purpose of prostitution, or to enter any place in which prostitution is encouraged or allowed within this state, or to come into this state or leave this state for the purpose of prostitution.*

*(6) Receives or gives, or agrees to receive or give, any money or thing of value for procuring, or attempting to procure, another person for the purpose of prostitution, or to come into this state or leave this state for the purpose of prostitution.*

*(b) Any person who does any of the acts described in subdivision (a) with another person who is a minor is guilty of pandering, a felony, and shall be punishable as follows:*

*(1) If the other person is a minor 16 years of age or older, the offense is punishable by imprisonment in the state prison for three, four, or six years.*

*(2) If the other person is under 16 years of age, the offense is punishable by imprisonment in the state prison for three, six, or eight years.*

*(Amended by Stats. 2010, Ch. 709, Sec. 9. (SB 1062) Effective January 1, 2011.)*

### Human Trafficking

*Penal Code 236.1        (a) A person who deprives or violates the personal liberty of another with the intent to obtain forced labor or services, is guilty of human trafficking and shall be punished by imprisonment in the state prison for 5, 8, or 12 years and a fine of not more than five hundred thousand dollars ($500,000).*
*(b) A person who deprives or violates the personal liberty of another with the intent to effect or maintain a violation of Section 266, 266h, 266i, 266j, 267, 311.1, 311.2, 311.3, 311.4, 311.5, 311.6, or 518 is guilty of human trafficking and shall be punished by imprisonment in the state prison for 8, 14, or 20 years and a fine of not more than five hundred thousand dollars ($500,000).*

*(c) A person who causes, induces, or persuades, or attempts to cause, induce, or persuade, a person who is a minor at the time of commission of the offense to engage in a commercial sex act, with the intent to effect or maintain a violation of Section 266, 266h, 266i, 266j, 267, 311.1, 311.2, 311.3, 311.4, 311.5, 311.6, or 518 is guilty of human trafficking. A violation of this subdivision is punishable by imprisonment in the state prison as follows:*

*(1) Five, 8, or 12 years and a fine of not more than five hundred thousand dollars ($500,000).*

*(2) Fifteen years to life and a fine of not more than five hundred thousand dollars ($500,000) when the offense involves force, fear, fraud, deceit, coercion, violence, duress, menace, or threat of unlawful injury to the victim or to another person.*

*(d) In determining whether a minor was caused, induced, or persuaded to engage in a commercial sex act, the totality of the circumstances, including the age of the victim, his or her relationship to the trafficker or agents of the trafficker, and any handicap or disability of the victim, shall be considered.*

*(e) Consent by a victim of human trafficking who is a minor at the time of the commission of the offense is not a defense to a criminal prosecution under this section.*

*(f) Mistake of fact as to the age of a victim of human trafficking who is a minor at the time of the commission of the offense is not a defense to a criminal prosecution under this section.*

*(g) The Legislature finds that the definition of human trafficking in this section is equivalent to the federal definition of a severe form of trafficking found in Section 7102(9) of Title 22 of the United States Code.*

*(h) For purposes of this chapter, the following definitions apply:*

*(1) "Coercion" includes a scheme, plan, or pattern intended to cause a person to believe that failure to perform an act would result in serious harm to or physical restraint against any person; the abuse or threatened abuse of the legal process; debt bondage; or providing and facilitating the possession of a controlled substance to a person with the intent to impair the person's judgment.*

*(2) "Commercial sex act" means sexual conduct on account of which anything of value is given or received by a person.*

*(3) "Deprivation or violation of the personal liberty of another" includes substantial and sustained restriction of another's liberty accomplished through force, fear, fraud, deceit, coercion, violence, duress, menace, or threat of unlawful injury to the victim or to another person, under circumstances where the person receiving or apprehending the threat reasonably believes that it is likely that the person making the threat would carry it out.*

*(4) "Duress" includes a direct or implied threat of force, violence, danger, hardship, or retribution sufficient to cause a reasonable person to acquiesce in or perform an act which he or she would otherwise not have submitted to or performed; a direct or implied threat to destroy, conceal, remove, confiscate, or possess an actual or purported passport or immigration document of the victim; or knowingly destroying, concealing, removing, confiscating, or possessing an actual or purported passport or immigration document of the victim.*

*(5) "Forced labor or services" means labor or services that are performed or provided by a person and are obtained or maintained through force, fraud, duress, or coercion, or equivalent conduct that would reasonably overbear the will of the person.*

*(6) "Great bodily injury" means a significant or substantial physical injury.*

*(7) "Minor" means a person less than 18 years of age.*

*(8) "Serious harm" includes any harm, whether physical or nonphysical, including psychological, financial, or reputational harm, that is sufficiently serious, under all the surrounding circumstances, to compel a reasonable person of the same background and in the same circumstances to perform or to continue performing labor, services, or commercial sexual acts in order to avoid incurring that harm.*

*(i) The total circumstances, including the age of the victim, the relationship between the victim and the trafficker or agents of the trafficker, and any handicap or disability of the victim, shall be factors to consider in determining the presence of "deprivation or violation of the personal liberty of another," "duress," and "coercion" as described in this section.*

*(Amended by Stats. 2016, Ch. 86, Sec. 223.5. (SB 1171) Effective January 1, 2017. Note: Prop. 35 is titled the Californians Against Sexual Exploitation (CASE) Act.)*

On paper, there is a thin difference between actually being a trafficker and a pimp. That line is so thin that it is almost non-existent. In courtrooms, media, and law enforcement conversations around the country, you will hardly ever hear the words pimping and pandering or "pimp" alone without the tag of human sex trafficking or trafficker. Here is a short list of some of the differences between the subculture of pimping and prostitution that I'm familiar with and human sex trafficking:

1. No one is kidnapped or forced into prostitution. There was an unwritten law that's quoted by pimps that says "By choice, not force." Meaning if the girl did not choose to be with you, you could not make her.

2. Prostitutes in the game leave pimps that they're with often and "choose up" with another pimp that they want to be with.

3. Before a girl can be claimed by a pimp she must pay a choosing fee. Which acts as a buy in to be with the pimp of her choice.
4. Minors are not to be prostituted.

5. Pimps do not share prostitutes physically or financially.

6. There is no organization that collectively benefits from the selling of a prostitute.

Human sex trafficking and urban domestic pimping and prostitution should be considered two different issues, rather than thrown under the same umbrella. Over the past three years I've attended many different anti-trafficking conferences, been a part of many different anti-trafficking groups and boards, and I've trained several human sex trafficking awareness groups throughout this country. The more I hear and learn from others about the complexity and variety of types of human sex trafficking issues and situations, the more I have to acknowledge that the subculture of pimping and prostitution that I come from is in a category of its own. Most often I do not even hear it talked about in its true reality. What I do hear is a hybrid form of it. I hear it filtered in with other types of sex trafficking which does not help the pimps/traffickers or the prostitute/victims.

The research that is out there about trafficking that I have witnessed has not yet specifically looked at the subculture of pimping and prostitution either. This is a part of the problem, and leaves a lot of the survivors that I know off the radar and keeps them from feeling a part of this anti trafficking movement. Just recently I was a part of a training conducted at the University of San Diego where we conducted a mock call to the national trafficking survivor helpline. In that phone call, a survivor sister of mine called as if she was a prostitute who wanted to get out of the game and was seeking help. From the very beginning, the automated recorded message made my survivor sister want to hang up the phone. The message states that they "are able to help adults or minors who have been forced to work against their will or have sex for money or something of value." My survivor sister said to the group we were training that "this message alone would not be relatable to her and she would've hung up." Most people in the game do not feel as if they are forced to work by their pimps, not to mention the women that are without a pimp and working on their own. This is just one small example of the different mentality of people that have not been a part of this culture.

Throughout this book I speak of different unwritten rules, codes of conduct, and even a whole language used by the people in this culture that are totally unrelated to other forms of trafficking. I honestly even hate using the words trafficking, traffickers, and survivor, but I use them for the sake of others, outside of our world, to be able to understand what we are talking about. Although the man-made definitions may fit the lifestyles that we lived in the game, I don't believe that makes them right. I am not a "Trafficker," a "Controller," or a "Facilitator" in my mind. I am a former pimp. I am a lived experience expert. It's sad to me that any outside group of people, researchers, or law enforcement can come in and brand us with what they feel is appropriate—then rebrand at any time, to whatever they want to change the terminology to. I do understand for communication and legal purposes that we need to have some labels to identify the issues, but maybe the people closest to the pain could create their own labels.

I cannot and will not ever try to take away from anybody's experiences in trafficking as a whole. Each person's way that they entered, the pain that they may have experienced while they were in, or the way they got out of the game are all viable. I empathize with anybody forced into sexual exploitation. I am striving to get anti-human sex trafficking advocates to break away from thinking everything is cookie cutter and falls under one big trafficking umbrella. I believe that once we look at every subset of trafficking for its individual truth we can better analyze it and come up with true solutions to help all that are involved.

## Attack on Urban Males?

The fight against sex traffickers may seem to be a glorious cause. In fact, sex trafficking and the exploitation of any human being is wrong. I can't help but notice that the majority of traffickers I see targeted in this country are urban, inner-city males—more specifically, black males. Why is this? Are black males doing a majority of the trafficking, or is the focus primarily on them when it comes to the sex trade? According to a 2016 study done by Dr. Ami Carpenter and Dr. Jamie Gates called, "Measuring the Nature and Extent of Gang Involvement in Sex Trafficking in San Diego," their findings ran counter to the local perception that "pimping" is primarily associated with African American Street Gangs. The study states, "We found that gang involved facilitators were tied between white, black, and hispanic." Further, this same study goes on to say, "African Americans are overrepresented in the California prison system where the majority of our interviews took place. African Americans make up 6% of California's population but 26% of the incarcerated population" which implies that African American males would actually be less likely to become involved in sex trafficking than other races.

Many people believe that the fact that black men are targeted for criminal behavior more than others is not by coincidence but by design. Mass incarceration of blacks and latinos is at an all-time high, with numbers that continue to climb. The shift from simply using the term "pimp" to "trafficker" appears to be a deliberate play on the mentality of the public. Yes, it still sounds negative to turn on the news and hear that someone was arrested for "pimping," but to hear that the same person was arrested for "human sex trafficking" invokes an even worse perception of the individual. To hear that the trafficking was gang-related might cause the average person to want to lock up that individual forever. Any mention that there was a minor involved, and you would want the facilitator/pimp tortured and then locked up. All of this without even looking further into the individual's situation or even verifying if the accusations are true.

Human sex trafficking is being used across the country at this time to incarcerate large groups of black males. This is the same way that simply using the terms "gang member," "gangster," and "drug dealer" were used in the eighties and nineties. Yes, I do know and understand that many individuals who have been involved in these indictments are guilty of these disgusting crimes, but I also see how the transformation of terminology is being used to give harsher punishments and incarcerate larger numbers of urban youth.

My organization and I deal first hand with the population of people targeted by the war on drugs of the 80's, the war on Gangs in the 90's, and now with those targeted by this new fight against human sex trafficking. I see and feel the detrimental repercussions that come from these deliberate attacks on my community. The fathers that have been incarcerated and taken away from the home for lengthy periods of time, leaving a single mother to raise their kids on her own. Raising kids alone in San Diego is significantly difficult due to the high cost of living. A single parent must work twice as hard to keep a roof over their children's heads and food on the table. That extra work takes away from time that the child needs to be parented. Now the kid basically has both parents gone and is left to learn life from the streets. Compound that with knowing that your father was incarcerated for pimping, and that usually leads the child towards curiosity into the game. As much as the anti-trafficking movement thinks it's helping to end trafficking, it is actually helping it to continue.

We will not arrest our way out of this problem. The same way it did not work with the war on drugs and gangs. The common hashtag I see used by the anti-trafficking movement is #EndSexTrafficking. In reality, we should be working towards ending poverty. I am speaking solely for the inner cities of color here in the United States. This may also apply to other places around the world, but I cannot speak with authority on that issue. I do know for a fact that the black community here in San Diego reached out towards pimping and prostitution as a means of finally getting a piece of that American pie that we've watched others eat, while we had to settle for the American crumb.

To be clear, I do not condone the lifestyle of pimping and prostitution for my community or anyone. What I do—and we as a collective—have to face is the reality of why pimping and prostitution would even exist for a community like the one that I am from. The people that I grew up with are not monstrous people. They are not evil men. Although they have been attacked and treated as such. The media has painted a very specific (white) face of the young victims of trafficking. What about the black women that are attached to trafficking? After all, they make up the majority of those arrested for prostitution. Is this because the masses that are in financial and political power in America do not care as much for black lives as they do Caucasian lives? Is the mentality of 'stop the big, black man from taking our daughters' still present in modern society as it has been for hundreds of years? The vehicle of incarceration may have changed but the methods are still very familiar. What I believe we have been living in over the past three years of this overwhelming amount of "awareness" is the ripening of the people's minds for a lot of major arrests and indictments of black and brown men. It is already happening across the country and has definitely been happening in my city.

For the record law enforcement has always been aware of pimping and prostitution or what is now called human sex trafficking. It just not been a major concern to them. In fact, some were known for dating the girls on the blade. I remember times when the police would see me and my pimp friends on the track and address us by our pimp names just to make sure we knew that they knew who we were. It was extremely rare for someone to be arrested for pimping and pandering. If you did not have drugs or guns, they didn't want you—and this was at a time when domestic pimping and pandering was at its height. Why is this now such a big issue? From a person growing up in impoverished communities in San Diego and traveling throughout this country, I know that this is far from a great explosion of pimping and prostitution in my community. The big epidemic came and went. The numbers and statistics are only showing extreme heights because people are now becoming aware of what has been kept in the shadows for so long in American culture; now law enforcement is being pressured to do something about it.

Rather than arrest, bring resources.
Rather than indictments, bring opportunities.
Rather than awareness, bring quality action.
Rather than focusing on problems, let's focus on solutions.
Rather than feeding prisons, invest into building better education systems.
Do this and in time you will see an end to human sex trafficking in the inner city!

# Life After the Game

*How to Help a Person Get Out*

Once you're involved in the game it is often hard to get out. After years upon years of doing nothing but living in the subculture of the sex trade, you have isolated yourself from the regular world. You've continuously brainwashed yourself into believing that squares were bad and "pimping and hoeing were the best things going." Oftentimes people have been involved in the game throughout most of their young-adult life. The years when people on the square side were going to college or working, building resumes and careers, you were in the streets hustling and building a criminal record. Once you're in this deep you feel as if it's all that you can do. How else are you going to eat? Society doesn't hire felons, or people with no job experience, skills, or education. People want to get out, but it seems almost impossible. A common phrase we would say in the game was, "Pimp till I die." Damn, is that really what I want to do? At twenty-four-years old that sounds cool. At forty-four it seems like you're forced to. What does a person who has been in the game for a majority of their life put on a resume? What happens in a job interview when you're asked what you've been doing for the past five years? Unless you're shown how to manipulate answers to your benefit, you feel lost. Fortunately I have been studying how to transfer the skills that we were utilizing in the streets into the business world, but the average person in the game would see their time and life as a waste.

The best way to help a person get out of the game is to catch them at a low point. When someone has just been locked up, is going through the court system, is getting released, just lost a loved one to death, or is violently attacked. At these times the person is the most vulnerable and open to a change in the lifestyle. If approached correctly, and with the proper support-system in place, you have better chances to get a girl out of prostitution or a guy out of pimping. Other than low points in a person's life, if you catch them at a high point—like the birth of their child—you may still have a good shot.

When I started to entertain living a square life and no longer hustling, it was due to me being put into federal prison for three years. During that time I was transferred throughout 8 different institutions across the country, where I witnessed some of the most disturbing things in my life. I heard stories from people as young as 19 serving 25 years and more on this evil conspiracy charge. This experience had me reflecting and thinking about my life up to date and where I would be taking it in the future. Two months before I was released, my best friend from childhood and fellow pimp was murdered. Richard Leon Wilson. He was only 21 years old. This man was the closest person that I had in my life. I have lost many friends and associates to murder throughout my life, but this pain was like no other. If I wasn't sure about living a life of legality before that dreadful day, I definitely was after. When I was released I jumped straight into the legit business world, but within the year I was already back in the game attempting to pimp. I was soon reminded of how hard life was out on the streets. Working jobs that barely pay you enough to get by. Scraping for pennies, meanwhile watching your friends who are still pimping appearing as if they are happy and financially secure. Off and on for the next few years I would bounce around between the legit life and the pimp life. I would work square jobs, and have a girlfriend. Then as soon as finances got tough, I would be right back in the streets running with my old pimp friends. Soon after I would have strippers, escorts and prostitutes. During this time I was mentally off balance and was conscious of that fact at the time. I knew this wasn't the life for me but yet in still I did it. I guess at times I felt like I was behind the ball on where I wanted to be in life and this was the only avenue that I knew of that I could use to catch up. Before I went to prison I had become accustomed to living a wealthy lifestyle. I did not go to jail for pimping and my money wasn't coming from prostitutes. I was actually making the bulk of my illegal money off of the sales of marijuana. That experience in itself will need its own book. When I finally made a complete and final exit out of the game I had three prostitutes working with me. All of them seemed like a handful of problems. Problems that I no longer had the mental energy to deal with. I was tired. Tired of the stress. Tired of the hotel life. Tired of dealing with these different personalities that didn't mesh. I no longer even wanted to apply my time and energy into this industry. After prison I had come to a point of change and learned so much about myself as a man and about life in general, and I could not allow myself to continue down this spiral. Walking away was the only way. Why did I even get back into this lifestyle in the first place? The truth is that that lifestyle is all I had known as a means to get money for all of my adult life. Like any drug addiction without proper rehab I found myself sucked right back in.

If only the proper mentorship was brought to me in prison and immediately after. Things could have been much better, with a much smoother transition. Although I did have a better start than most when I came home, I can see where a trained mentor would have definitely helped me. Once you've got a person's attention you must help them to realize that the path they are on is leading them to self-destruct. Prisons, continuous loss, and early death are no strangers to the game. Chances are if you catch a person at one of those low points, they are going through at least one of those situations at the time. This will enable them to not only relate to what you are saying, but to have a strong desire to save themselves from further pain. It is much harder to reach a person in the game when they are having a good run or experiencing any level of prosperity. They may listen to you, but they will not let go of the dream that they are grasping at. Pain and loss are the foreground of serious change.

## Support Systems

Support systems must be in place to aid them in leaving the game. Immediate housing, food, clothing, and another means to make money are necessities in this lifestyle transfer. The better these services are administered, the better your chances are of helping somebody leave the sex work lifestyle. By better, I mean that the housing could be sharing a room with four other individuals or a single-person apartment. Of course somebody would want the single-person apartment. Either would be good, but one would definitely be better. The same theory applies with the food, clothing, and money. The better the support system, the better the transition.

Once a person is receiving these services, which are more than likely temporary for a fixed amount of time, the individual must receive training. Training on how to be reintegrated into society. This training must come from people that were in similar situations and have learned how to maneuver into society and the workforce. This training can also be administered by others as long as they really care about the people that they are helping. A future venture that I would like to work on is a separate male and female focus/support group of people who have been involved in the game to come together and help each other during their transition into living better lives. These groups will operate similarly to AA meetings, led by individuals who have been vetted and have been removed from the lifestyle for a sufficient amount of time. Most importantly, they must be trained on how to apply the skills and knowledge they acquired in the subculture to their new life. They must not only be trained in these applications, they must be shown and made to believe that these game-acquired skills make them competitive, if not superior, to their college-educated counterparts.

## Transferable Skills

In the game there is no retirement plan, no IRA, no stock investments, or life insurance. When you're five-plus years into the lifestyle of pimping and prostitution, you miss out on building an employment history. Once I was removed from the game and got more into the business world, I could honestly reflect back on the mentality, experiences, and traits that I used in the game and realized not only was I skilled, but I had been in an intense training course on business. There is not one university standing that could equate.

A few of the main skills and traits a person in this subculture can acquire are the art of negotiation, relentless drive, marketing, communication, supply and demand, networking, and more. Once a person is made aware of the fact that they have not only acquired these skills but have, in many situations, mastered them, they are now open to the belief that they can still have a prosperous life. Going to school doesn't seem so far-fetched once an individual realizes they already have an abundance of knowledge in these areas. An individual can be motivated to pursue a business venture that's legal and morally correct if they can believe they have the abilities to excel.

Entrepreneurship is one of the best ways for an individual to transition out of the game. With the skills they acquired while in the subculture, as well as psychological traits they have developed, they can reach any level of success that they want. Similar to the game, they can get out what they put in. Only in the legal business world life-threatening risks alleviated. Having a criminal record is typically not a factor as to whether an individual can become a successful entrepreneur. Institutional education can help but it's not a determinative factor on your success. Yes, many years of your youth may be gone, but once you believe that they are not wasted, you can emerge from the ashes into greatness.

*"If you can set up a Green Dot, Netspend, or Bitcoin account, you can set up a bank account. If you can edit photos for an escort ad, you can edit and create graphics for social media networking. If you can create an ad on Backpage, you can create an advertisement for a business. If you can manage multiple tricks or prostitutes throughout the day, schedule dates, and negotiate prices, you can run a full business. It's all about recognizing, understanding and learning how to transfer what you already know, into what you want to do. You have so much power already through your experience in the game. Let's start using it for the things that make your soul light up"* — Lived Experience Expert Jaime Johnson

## Memory Blocking

Many female friends of mine that have left the game and transferred these skills into the business world; I have noticed that rather than acknowledging their past, many choose to block it out of their memory. They will not talk about it or reminisce like men with similar backgrounds do. The game is far more painful for women, and I can understand why the thoughts of things they've gone through would be hard to relive. Those conversations are best left for a therapist. Unfortunately, many survivors don't receive that help and are left to memory blocking.

I also have many male friends that have made it out and choose to not acknowledge their past life in the game. Continuously, I try to get them to come forward with me so that we can help save more young men from entering into the lifestyle, but time and time again I am turned down. Recently when I asked a good friend of mine to be in my documentary on the game, he aggressively said to me, "Why do you keep bringing this shit up? It over. The game is done." Another close friend of mine who was one of the biggest pimp rappers in San Diego refuses to be a part of any of the human sex trafficking events, trainings, or anything that has to do with HST. He has been out of the life for 6 years now and has done everything possible to remove his old image from his new square image. Both of these friends could be extremely valuable to the anti-trafficking movement—with more lived experience than me and stronger voices in my opinion. However, I completely understand their stance. As a former pimp if you live long enough and have not managed to get a lengthy prison sentence you are lucky. These men do not want to flirt with the idea of something from their past coming back to haunt them legally. Especially with families, careers, and future plans. Although I wish I could say that they were off of the legal hook now that they are out of the game I cannot. All three of us have mutual friends who have had pimping evidence used against them in their 30's, from when they were 18.

# Some Make It Out and Some Don't

The longer that you've been in the game the harder it is to leave. Especially if you entered at an early age. The following are a few personal stories of close friends of mine that have left the game. I have changed their names to protect their identities, but they are in fact real-life former pimps and prostitutes who have been lucky enough to get out of the game with their life and sanity.

Donald has been a friend of mine for over ten years. He slightly older than me, but was not involved in the game until about four years after me. In his career as a pimp he was actually very prosperous and was very smart with the way he managed his time and money. For some reason he was an attraction for the police. No matter where he seemed to go, the county jail would follow. Of the twenty times he was put in jail, none of those stints were for anything related to the game. Every time that he would get out of jail was like hitting the reset button on a video game. This was starting to break him down until he eventually gave up on living the fast life. Now in his early thirties, he found himself on probation and working at a supply store as an overnight stocker. This kept a little money in his pocket, but not nearly enough to keep him from thinking about what he could be making off of the game. After a while of fighting the urge to get back in the game, he was persuaded to get back in by one of his old girls, Julie. She was in love with him and wanted him back in the life with her. She had been talking to him about it for a few weeks and he had managed to tell her "no" at first. At some point, Donald had fallen into financial hardship due to child support garnishing his work wages. The financial stress had him considering entering the game. Donald had requested that Julie give him some money to help him out. She happily gave him some money, hoping that this would draw him back in. The entire time he inched more and more towards just quitting his job and jumping back in the game. He really needed the money. The last time she gave him some money he decided to invest into some illegal pharmaceuticals that he planned on selling for profit. He wanted to do anything to get money and avoid going back into the game. This idea worked for a couple weeks, until he was discovered, which led to his home being raided. Back in jail on a violation, he reconsidered all of his recent moves and finally knew that doing anything illegal for money had to be completely out of the question. Fast forward six years to today. Donald is now an electrician with a two-year-old daughter and lives with his child's mother and grandfather in a nice home that he pays for, with two cars of his own. He will hardly even entertain a conversation about how we were in the game, and stays far away from anybody that is still in the life.

Larry was one of the first people I knew of to enter the game here in San Diego. He was definitely one of the cool older kids when I was younger. Many young men looked up to him and followed in his footsteps. He lived in the Nutty's, which was right where the main track was located. Pimping was his career for over ten years. By the grace of God, he was able to see the possible destruction headed his way and chose to remove himself from the game. He quit and chose to use the drive and determination that he gained in the streets to get his car dealer's license and worked his way up over the past ten years. He currently owns and operates one of San Diego's largest luxury car dealerships.

Tre got his start in the street life as a gangster. His street credit made many respect him and made others want to kill him. We became friends as children. When the explosion of pimping and prostitution occurred in San Diego, he was right there with a lot of us that turned out to the game. Tre became one of the first to begin the new genre of pimp rap. He quickly became one of the biggest pimps and pimp rappers to come out of San Diego. He's toured all over this country, as both a rapper and a pimp. His music was the pimp and prostitute soundtrack for many people in the game. I was one of those people. Although he was a friend of mine, I was also a major fan of his music. He told me that at some point in his life he wanted to transition out of the game, but had no idea how. So he continued to stay in and thought that this was going to be the only thing his life would amount to. Then one night he was in his car outside of a hotel room, waiting on his bottom to finish a call that she was on, and something hit him. "I don't know what it was bro. It was like God had directly intervened in my life and told me to stop. I heard his voice clear, as if he was sitting right next to me. When my girl got back in the car from the date I told her that we were done." After that day, Tre has never looked back. He started a few businesses, realizing that it was actually the pursuit of money and handling business that he loved, and not necessarily the game. With his time now occupied with other money-driven productive activities, he now had no time to slip back into the game. Tre and his bottom decided to get married and have had a successful marriage for the past six years. They have a beautiful daughter and a new, legitimate life together. At times, the money is scarce and they struggle, but as he tells me, "It's better to struggle than to have to continuously look over your shoulder, afraid of the law or the bullet of your enemy." Tre now works as a real estate broker and his wife is in marketing.

William and I became great friends in high school. He was a basketball superstar in school and won national championships. In his mind (and ours) he was definitely going to the NBA. He was a member of my clique but kept his focus on sports, even the rest of us ventured into pimping. When he wasn't practicing or playing basketball, he was hanging out with us, smoking weed and chasing girls. He would ride the tracks with us and be around for all of the pimp activities, yet managed not to involve himself directly. Will got an opportunity to go to college in Florida, with his schooling paid for by San Diego MLB legend Tony Gwynn. For whatever reason, he was not able to maintain the college life and ended up back at home with us at the height of our pimp careers, but he still managed to stay away from the game. A year after his return, I was incarcerated for three years—only to return to Will and many other males from my neighborhood now fully engaged in pimping. Will, now known as "Charm," was pimping full throttle. It was weird seeing him as a pimp at that moment, and I figured that the murder of our other best friend and clique mate Richard "Fantastic" was the reason for his desire to get in now. For the next 10 years, Will pimped, but also became an occasional drug user. I slowly watched my friend crumble. He was eventually locked up in jail, serving almost a year. When he was released, he called me and told me how he was ready to change his life. He also asked me how he could get involved with the non profit that I had started called Paving Great Futures. I was excited and told him that his seat at the table was ready for him as soon as he came in. I couldn't wait for him to finally come back. I knew he would be a great addition to the team. I never expected to receive a call saying that he had overdosed only forty-eight hours later. It has now been a little over a year since his death. About three months after his funeral, another one of our clique mates Kenny, also on the verge of leaving the game behind, was murdered on the track in Houston. A few months after that, my twenty-year-old cousin Halifu Jr. was murdered in Sacramento, California. May God bless all of their souls.

Sunrise

February 10, 1981

Sunset

June 27, 2017

Forever In

Our Hearts

Memorial Service

Saturday July 15, 2017 11:00 a.m.

Greater Fellowship Missionary Baptist
Church

4351 Logan Avenue

San Diego, Ca 92113

William Waggoner III

209

JC was heavily involved in the pimp game in the mid 2000's. He was incarcerated (for unrelated reasons) and was sentenced to 7 years in the California State Prison. He was released about 3 years ago, and upon release immediately searched me and my organization out. He knew of us because we all grew up in the same neighborhood, and he turned out to the game from hanging around my brother Richard. When he got out of jail he was super motivated to do right and never to go back in. JC immediately connected with a female friend of his who was a part of the social justice movement here in San Diego. They started to date and life seemed promising for him. While JC was incarcerated he was able to pick up the welding trade. Welding only paid 50 cent an hour in prison, but paid well over $20 an hour in the normal world. JC approached me and the team and requested that we buy him his basic welding necessities so that he could start working. He had already applied and been hired at a great location. For the next three years he worked and was doing great with his girlfriend. About 6 months ago, I started to see certain negative verbiage in his posts on Facebook. His posts had more gang related remarks, which wasn't uncommon for others, but he had really moved away from talking like a gang member. I took it as him just trying to sound cool and relevant. Until those posts became live videos of him, laying up in hotel rooms, counting money with women that were obviously prostitutes. When I saw the first video my jaw dropped and all I could think about was how stupid he was. Why was he going backwards? He's too old and smart to be doing this—and on Facebook of all places. It was obvious that JC was trying to show his now ex-girlfriend and the world that he was back in the mix. A little over two weeks has passed since the first video aired, and I just heard that he was picked up by law enforcement on pimping charges. With his priors, and the fact that he was on parole at the time, he might not make it back out for a while.

Lani was a skinny, blonde, white girl from an upper-middle class, two-parent household. Lani and I met when we were about thirteen years old. We both used to skate at the same skating rink.

At the time I met her I was a major "wanna be" gangster and she was just a quiet little girl. By the age of sixteen, I had started my clique with my friends and we had already moved on to juicing girls for their money. When I caught wind of Lani liking my friend Richard, I quickly got word to him and told him that he needed to get with her. I knew she was not only willing to pay for anything that he wanted, but she liked to do that. He was reluctant to get with her at first because of the fact that she was a white girl. After a little more persuading, Richard ended up taking Lani on as his girlfriend. Just as I knew it would happen, she began giving him money, clothes, and anything else that he wanted. When she got her first car, it became his car. We called it the company car because everybody in our clique were able to use the car as if it were our own. Eventually, Lani and Richard turned out to the game together. Richard was the first of us to enter the game and Lani was the first girl that I knew personally that entered the game. I was on the blade watching Lani as she started working for the first time. Richard and Lani's pimp and prostitute relationship lasted for about a year before Lani left Richard for another pimp that we knew.

For the next seventeen years I didn't see or speak to Lani. Lani had remained in the game throughout that time, and I had heard continuously over the years about how great she was doing in the game. She had been with a couple of well-known pimps and had made them a lot of money. She had become known in the San Diego pimp and prostitute scene as some kind of magic money maker. A lot of pimps I knew wanted to have her. During the process of me writing this book, I also began creating a documentary that would coincide with it. The documentary was going to walk through the explosion of the pimp and prostitute explosion here in San Diego. The documentary is going to tell this story through the eyes of my friends Richard, Kenny, and Will who are now deceased. When it dawned on me that I would have to get Lani involved in this documentary, since she played such a crucial role in the start of my crew getting in the game, I knew that I had to find her. When I began my search for Lani I talked to a few people that knew her and they all had bad things to say about her.

Everyone that I spoke to said she was doing really poorly, lifestyle wise. One mutual friend of ours told me that she was addicted to drugs, and that the last time she saw Lani she looked as if she was about to die. I couldn't help but feel guilty in a way, for even introducing her to Richard as young teens. Although this may have happened to her even without my involvement, I still felt responsible. At this current stage in my life, with the survivor advocacy work that I've done, my mind became locked on finding her and seeing if I could help her get out of whatever situation that she was in.

Finally the day came when I made contact with Lani. It started with a friend of mine who was hanging out with her putting her on the phone with me. Two weeks later, I actually got to see Lani in person. She came by my office one night with a friend of hers. They had both just left Starbucks, using their Wi-Fi to post ads for themselves. When Lani came in she looked like the old Lani that I knew, just slightly aged. She sat down with me on my office couch and immediately broke down crying. She looked at me and said, "I want out of this." I hugged her and told her that I was going to help her get her life back. At this point, Lani had no idea what I did as far as my non profit or with my work in sex trafficking survivor advocacy. She didn't even know what a "survivor" was or anything about the current movement to end human sex trafficking.

Lani has always been shy, self-conscious, and reserved her entire life. After nearly two decades in the game, she had become that times ten. She had been around the game and street life for so long that she had no idea how to operate in normal settings. In some ways, I chose to use a little tough love with her. I would bring her out with me, in situations that she was extremely uncomfortable in, using a "sink or swim" mentality. I always asked her first if she would like to come and she would always decide yes. She would tell me how nervous and awkward she felt, but she liked coming. As she went to a few sex trafficking advocacy work group meetings with me, she began to fully understand the work that I was now into. When she heard the people in these groups speaking about trafficking, she would tell me after the meetings that she felt as if these people had no clue what they were talking about. At one point she told me, "These people would never reach me. For one, they could never find me, and two they would never connect with me." I agreed and told her that's exactly why our voices need to be at the table. Most of the people in this movement have great hearts and intentions, but without proper guidance from people with our experience they will never accomplish the mission of helping the masses of people that are trapped in the game.

For the past two months Lani has been with me going everywhere that I go and taking in all of the community work that I do. She is learning to be in a new environment and how to operate in the "square world." This transition has been hard at times. After leaving a human sex trafficking advocacy group meeting one day, she looked at me and said, "After hearing this stuff I can never turn a date again. I really can't. I don't care if I need money or not." For these two months she has actually stayed true to that. The only demon that has sporadically grabbed hold of her is her continued fight with drug addiction. Without placing any judgement on her, I remain there for her when she's ready to come back to shadow me and I continuously encourage her. Lately, she has been doing very well. She has recently moved back in with her parents and her two young daughters. She is enrolled in some community college courses, and began a paid internship at my non profit in early 2019. One of the main things I have also helped her with is setting up a daily routine and immediate goal achievement plan, in which I act as both her mentor and accountability partner. She will succeed.

My own personal process of exiting the game was patchy. When I came home from prison after serving a thirty-month bid, I came home and immediately started recruiting girls to work for me. Even though I had a decent job and a home, the desire to play catch up was overwhelming and I went hard trying to get money to replace the lost years. I also really felt like I had to keep up with all of my friends who were in the game. They all had nice cars, dressed in top-of-the-line gear, and had women. Even people who were not pimping before I went to jail were now pimping. I had to catch back up, even though the idea of being in the game was totally against all of the life goals and business plans that I created for myself when I was locked up. I went into the game again for only a few months until I ran into a girl I had known in high school. We fell in love and that put a halt on my player/pimp movements for almost six years. That is, until we broke up. I found myself heart broken, financially broke, and I had to move into a family member's house. Within a short period of time, I was right back in the game. I had been chosen by a well-known San Diego prostitute who really liked me and wanted me to be her pimp. She was hard to refuse. She came fully equipped with a new car that was already decked out with big custom rims, TVs, and a great sound system. She also had her own house in a nice area that I eventually moved into. Within two months I had two more girls on my team paying me. According to my pimp friends, I was doing great. They had no idea that my head and heart were in pain. I hated my current situation. Any one of them would have loved to trade places with me; meanwhile I was looking for any excuse to get out of this life. I don't know if the universe felt my internal cries for a way out, or if the fact that I wasn't giving the game enough attention made my current situation fall apart, but it did. The exact situations are more than I want to go into, and would probably warrant a book entirely on its own. The condensed version of the story is that each one of the girls that were with me began to go through personal, dramatic issues. Issues that I had neither the energy nor the desire to help with. Situations that in my younger years I would've worked out and had them all working together, but in my current state I let my stable implode. I was over living like this. Traveling with a constant headache, knowing that if I applied the same amount of energy into myself that it would take to get these girls operating right, I would be where I want to be in life. I walked away from the game drained and broke, but I knew things would be better in the long run because I could finally start living my life.

215

# Prevention and Intervention

## *Prevention*

In order to prevent anything from happening, especially something horrible, you must understand how, what, and why it came about it in the first place. Not only do we need to "understand," we need to do like the great Bob Marley said and "overstand." This means taking our thinking, feelings, and education to the next level.

How do we stop or prevent a young man from ever wanting to be a pimp, or a young woman from wanting to sell her body? Is there a simple answer to this question? I believe there is. In my opinion, the answer is simple, or better yet, the *answers* are simple. If left up to me, these solutions would be implemented and a massive change in the urban subculture of pimping and prostitution would begin, leading to its death. The problem is that I cannot implement my solutions without the backing of the government. That is the only complication.

In this book I explain what leads an individual into this lifestyle. The lack of opportunities and economic disparity are the key ingredients in a person's involvement in this subculture. Both pimp and prostitute are usually in this lifestyle in search of financial prosperity. Neither of them are truly involved because they like it. You will find people bragging about the lifestyle and glorifying it as if they love what they do, but the truth is they are psychologically justifying behavior they know is wrong to make themselves feel better about the behavior.

Creating more accessible opportunities for the inner cities of America can and should be done to prevent people from getting involved in the human trafficking lifestyle. Rather than the government and other organizations providing the usual handout system to impoverished communities, there should be a development of self-empowerment systems implemented. A "hand up" instead of a "handout." Entrepreneurial training, trade schools, and other life/career building programs need to be administered to youth in these communities at an early age. These programs would be the most effective during elementary and middle school.

I believe that middle school is the most important era in a kid's life for intervention and training. This time period is when a child is really beginning to figure out which direction they are about to go. This is usually when puberty hits and hormones start to race. As a young man growing up in the inner city, this was the time when myself and other peers were put in a position where we had to choose what gang we were going to be from or the gang would have chosen us. During this pre high school age, young girls start to feel the pressure of feeling like they have to be physically attractive. middle/junior high school students' minds are more developed than elementary aged children. This level of maturity gives them enough intellect to understand the depths of intervention conversations brought to them by older people. Although this may be the best time to reach the children, we should not leave it to this grade level alone. There should be intervention implemented at all three levels: Elementary, middle, and high school. Waiting primarily until high school is too late.

These programs should be taught by professionals from the communities that are willing to be personally involved in the child's development. If these professionals do not seem to exist in the city or region where the problem is needed, they should be created. It's hard for me to believe that there isn't one qualified person from that community that is interested in getting into this work for intervention. Often times these people exist and are already doing the work to some extent, but are being looked over and not connected to the people with the power and the resources to help manifest their work to its full potential. If attempts are being made to find these qualified individuals and there still is nobody to be found, then the next best thing would be to relocate these individuals from neighboring cities and towns and bring them in to do the work.

The youth must be taught how to transform their skills and interests into revenue-generating activities. The economic disparity in the inner city plays such a big role in the gang and human trafficking lifestyles that an extra emphasis must be placed on building the financial infrastructure in the community. For years the government believed that a system of welfare and free food would be the necessary help. In reality, it only further crippled the inner city, making it reliant on outside handouts instead of self-sufficiency. Its very important not to take my words to mean that the government should just suddenly cut off welfare, medical, and food stamps. That would be detrimental to millions of lives of all races. The problem must be gradually rectified. If our goal is to prevent people from going down the human trafficking path, there must be economic development in the communities that they come from. They must be exposed to the *legal* ways a person can make money in this world. The young people must see examples of people that look like them, that come from similar backgrounds create revenue-generating businesses or becoming successful professionals. Once they see these examples, they must be shown on a regular basis how they can follow in their footsteps.

## Developing the Person

Before teaching a person about owning a business, gaining a prosperous career, or any other move towards financial improvement, you must work on the person. From early childhood most people in the inner city have no sense of self-worth. Black youth in general are never taught they can achieve anything in this world unless they are in sports or entertainment. If they are not good in any of those areas they really don't see a future for themselves in this society. Compounded with multiple generations of poverty, gangs, drugs, and prostitution are left as the only viable options. Thanks to the media, those options are highlighted and broadcast to the point where it seems like those are the options kids are supposed to choose.

## Awareness

Teaching our youth about prostitution and human trafficking is a good thing. Yes, let's make them aware of the dangers that are out there. They need to know. However, to truly prevent them from entering into the lifestyle they must be given other options. Show them and teach them another way to get them out of what seems like an endless cycle of poverty. Let's teach our youth about their worth as individuals and as a community. Young boys and girls must be taught that they are worth more than what they see around them, or the conditions they might have already suffered through. This can be done through the mentorship of people from their same communities that have grown through similar circumstances that the children are currently living in. The people with these qualifications are out there. If resources are applied properly, and there is a budget for these individuals to work with these students, you will see more of them willing to come into the school system and become mentors. This work can be set up in many ways. One can be touring all at risk schools and holding mass assemblies, classroom speaking engagements, or just being present on the campus with one on one mentoring. There could be an actual life skills/personal development class that is implemented into the school curriculum. There is no one way to conduct this training. That can be up to the school. What this training does have to be is continual and intergenerational. There cannot be a one-time assembly that addresses the building of self-worth. For every one hour of assembly time the school gives society will be there waiting to give ten more hours of self-destruction.

Afterwards (if not simultaneously), as the person is being built up inside, they must be trained on how to be financially secure. Unless you grew up in the poor, urban community in America you might not realize how important an issue money becomes. I believe I was thirteen years old the first time I sold marijuana. At that time it wasn't just for lunch money and comic books. My family was homeless and sleeping on different friends' floors, barely surviving. My mom was on drugs and still took care of three young teens and a baby. No, that weed money was gas money to get to school, clothes money so I could have decent school attire. It was fast-food money so my siblings could eat. My situation growing up made me a hustler and trained me how to make illegal money to *survive*. This is the same with many other children in the inner city. No kid wakes up at ten years old and says, "I want to be a pimp or a hoe when I grow up." These ideas and thoughts are developed over time as it seems like the only logical option for survival and making it out of devastating poverty.

Awareness at an early age is good, but it is not the total answer. I was made aware of drugs, gangs, promiscuous sex, and crime as an elementary and junior high school student. None of that mattered when I got a little older. In fact, it was a joke to us. When you're trying to make it out, money is all that matters. We would rather take our chances. As I look back at the people that came into our classes to talk to us about crime and drugs, I remember thinking of them as jokes. People who came from a fairytale life to tell me what to do in the nightmare I lived in.

## *What Do We Do?*

To prevent youth from entering into a life of human sex trafficking, the following things must be done in the school systems:

1. Children must be continuously taught about self-worth. They must be shown until believed that they can be successful in life. Black youth in particular must know their true history as a people, before slavery in America. This will build their self-confidence. They must know that they are bigger than the environment that surrounds them. From entry level education and throughout this must be taught in the classroom.

2. Children must be made aware of what sex trafficking is. They need to know the effects it has on themselves, their community, and their future. They need to understand the devastating legal repercussions of being involved in the lifestyle.

3. Children must be taught how they can be financially prosperous at things other than crime, sports, or entertainment. Professionals must show the youth how their talents and ideas can be developed into avenues for income. I believe that these people do exist in every community, they are just not sought after and if they are found they are not seen as valuable enough to pay them for their time. In the event that they are not found in the immediate area then they must be brought in from neighboring areas.

This three-pronged process must be continuous throughout children's pre-college school career. The most effective and crucial part of these three steps is that they are facilitated by people who have been in their shoes and grown up like they have. People who truly understand what the children's lives are like. Traditional ways of teaching don't work with this population. New, innovative teaching methods must be introduced.

The hardest part of the prevention process is controlling a child's home life and community. Children can be built up all day with self-confidence and financial education, just to go home and be molested, abused, or neglected. The community they live in may promote prostitution, gangs, and pimping. To truly prevent future children getting involved in a destructive lifestyle, not only does this need to be done in schools, but similar methods must be used in the community as well. This is done through the support of true community based organizations that already have their boots on the ground doing the work. Often time through lack of financial support these groups die off or are unable to reach the masses of the people that they could if supported correctly.

We cannot wait for the people who are already involved in the game to die off or incarcerate everybody and wait for this new generation to emerge. The people in the community must be helped as well. We should never give up on people and say, "Well, they already messed up, why should we help them?" So many great people who have contributed greatly to this world have come from dark backgrounds. I believe it takes people who have made mistakes, survived the mud, and were able to clean themselves up to teach others on the path that they should not take. We need these people. They are and will be more effective than the people that have never seen the lifestyle that they are trying to prevent. However *all* of these people are necessary to accomplish this mission. This fight is like a football team striving to win a big game. All functions are needed no matter how small or big the roll may seem. Even the water boy is needed. Without him, the team may be dehydrated. The cheerleaders and fans are needed to boost morale and motivate. The coach is needed for direction. The team owners are needed to fund the team. They may not be on the field, putting their lives on the line like the players, but they are all needed. If one of these functions is missing, that could be the difference between them winning the game or suffering a detrimental loss. No matter if you grew up in a white middle or upper class two parent household, or in a impoverished ghetto—if your heart has lead you to genuinely put an end to human sex trafficking, you must find your lane and do everything within your power to be the best at that position.

## *So What Can I Do?*

Love, support, embrace, and let your loved ones know that your door is always open. Whether your loved one is a prostitute or a pimp, understand that they are a victim of an unbalanced world they did not create. As a loved one, your role is to be there for them and to teach with love. Give advice with love and respect. Listen to them when they speak to you. You must listen and wait for any indication of them wanting to leave the life. That could come in the form of them mentioning a dream job, idea, aspiration, or simply them expressing that they are tired of being in the game. At this pivotal point you must move in smartly and gently with whatever they need to transition out of the game.

The biggest thing that you need to reinforce with your loved one is that you are going to be there for them, and want what's best for them. Do this not just with words, but with genuine actions, always remembering that there is a fine line between being there for someone and letting them take advantage of you. Loving them does not mean letting them run over you and abuse your household or your love. You must know and realize that the more they are in the game and street life the better trained they are at manipulation. Being indoctrinated by the streets makes you as a student of fast talking and using your words to get what you want and need at any cost. If you don't learn fast, you can be on the other end of the manipulation and potentially lose your money, possessions, or your life. Some people get so deeply intertwined with the pimp subculture that they do not know how to turn it off even when dealing with family. So be there for them, love them, but be cautious of any signs of misuse.

You as a loved one may not be financially secure enough to aid in their transition. That's where outside advocates, organizations, and support groups come in. Have a list of services ready and if you really want to help you should have already established relationships with these organizations. In fact, volunteer for one of the sex trafficking advocacy groups in your town. This will help as a support base for you, and by you being there for others the energy you will create will help aid in saving your loved one.

## Outsiders Who Want to Help

If you are an independent person that wants to help end sex trafficking there are many different ways to get involved. Know that nothing you do is insignificant or too small. Every role is important, so discover your role and get involved.

Before you get involved I would suggest you do your research and become aware. You can't help the problem if you don't understand the problem. Find an organization that is already doing the work and ask what they need. So many times people want to give or help in one area when help is really needed in another area. Go to events, listen to panel discussions, read books, watch documentaries, and most importantly, keep an open mind. After you have an understanding of the issue then you can make an educated decision on where you want to place yourself in the cause. There is always more to learn about the issue and so many different angles to learn about. The sex trafficking problem is vast and it is going to require people on all levels to bring this to an end.

If you are going to get involved with an organization, make your decision based on researching as many as it takes, until there is one whose mission speaks to your heart. It's important that the one you choose aligns with what you believe in and want. That is the only way that you will truly get the best out of yourself and help get the mutual results you and the organization want.

If after researching organizations you find that none of them fit your desired method of outreach don't be discouraged. Create your own! This may be a community-based group, non-profit, faith-based, or you as a solo, independent soldier in the fight. Simply being an active supporter of the organizations and advocates on the field is important.

## "I'm Not Connected to the Streets"

Know your role in the advocacy team. Remember: not every position is meant for you to play and that's okay. Figure out where you can help the most in this large, diverse fight to end trafficking and work that position. Yes, there will more likely be overlap with multiple organizations working in different areas. Not every person is meant to go "rescue" girls off on the street. There are many other ways to help. The streets are not always safe for people who are not accustomed to their ways and you may cause more harm than good. The streets are barely safe for the people that do know how to navigate through them, let alone somebody who doesn't. We need you alive. Still, you must remember that all roles are equally vital. If we want to win the season games, the championship, and eventually the Super Bowl, we all must play our position to the best of our ability. There must not be fighting, bickering, and malice amongst each other. This sometimes becomes a problem when organizations or advocates don't like one another for some reason, or are competing for the same grant. Emotions must be left off of the field at all costs. Can you imagine if the quarterback of the team didn't throw the ball to another player who was open and could score the winning points for the game just because he didn't like him?

Yes, your heart and intentions may be in the right place—you truly want to help the victims caught in the street life, but in some areas of this fight it's better to not be the direct face or contact. Your role may be to supply information or resources to the ones with the direct street life contact. Far too often, the bigger organizations of the world will try to play every position in the game. Meanwhile the smaller grassroots organizations, who would have a greater effect on the target population, are left out. We must remember our mission as advocates.

# Chapter 8: Our Voices

Devon, the lack of visible options, opportunities, and most importantly the lack of having positive black male role models and mentors is what I believe led me down the wrong path. That same issue is what caused my dearest friends to lose their lives. This shit is not a game Devon. These streets can and will eat you alive. They don't care how old you are, how much talent or potential you have. There is a grave site and jail cell always open to receive your young body. Don't take the blessing of life for granted. Make every day count. If you were blessed to get up this morning and open your eyes, then you have just been granted another chance to work towards your goals. I've just laid a lot on you about this pimp life. Take your time and read through these pages as much as you can until you understand. The words that I write are not to brag and boost about the pimp and gang life. This is decades of pain, and loss of life. These are tears that will never stop running down my face. I would do anything to have my brothers back alive with me. Anything. Sometimes I don't know how I continue to move forward. I figure my life is here to serve a higher purpose. God is not ready for me to leave yet. As lonely as I am, I know that I have to keep helping others and put myself second to do the work. Honestly Devon, I don't even care about school that much. Yes, please get an education, but understand that an education can come in many forms. This school system is prehistoric and not designed to teach you properly for this new era of the world. So, yeah, I don't care about school. Not nearly as much as I care about two things for you nephew... Please try your hardest to avoid getting a long prison sentence or an early death. I pray that you can stay away from those things and get old enough to realize like I did, this is not the life or a game. This thing we call the game in reality is an illusion.

Love Always,
Your Uncle Armand King

After getting involved in the anti human sex trafficking movement in 2014, I was struck by how I continued to hear the same narratives about sex trafficking. However, so much regarding the pimping and prostitution subculture is not spoken about in its entirety. So many stories are untold, unspoken, and unheard.

The following are unedited pieces of work that were submitted to me by former pimp and prostitute friends of mine, better known as "Lived Experience Experts." All of the pieces are unique messages that the authors wanted to place in my book to express their feelings about the game.

# Secrets of the Streets
by Jaimee Johnson

That street you just drove past
I bet you have no idea the secrets it holds.
Did you know right there ...
at that spot ...
A trick decided he would rob me, rape me and punch me like a rag doll..
Right over there ...
where your tires just rolled ..
That trick hit me so hard
My nose broke.
And over there ...
Fragments of my skin might still be on the pavement...
From when he was done with me and shoved me out the moving car half naked.
Oh the secrets these streets hold.

Right down the street ....
Is the happiest place on earth ... during the day and early evening ...
Families laughing ...
eating good food and wearing mickey mouse hats...

Go figure,
Less than a mile away ... I stroll in my skimpy dress and 6 inch
heels...
Purse in hand ...
Contents include
lipstick .. condoms ... and mace ...
I longed for the days I went back to carrying things in my purse
"regular" girls did....
Oh the secrets these streets hold.

Right over there ...
My pimp dragged me by my hair for accidentally looking at another
pimp ..
In front of everyone ... cars slowed ... but no one stopped ...
Who wants to stop for a prostitute unless they are getting
something in return?

That building on the corner ...
It heard my cries as he punched the air from my lungs to discipline
me...
The baby wipe i used to clean my running makeup off ... is probably
blowing somewhere near still.
The walls have visions of me fixing my dress ... trying not to limp in
pain as I walk back to the busy street so I made sure I made my
quota for the night.

Oh the secrets these streets hold.

Time for work again no time to recover...
No time to cry
There's money to be made.
And you can bet that night I made sure I learned the concrete and
every crack in it...
I looked directly at it every step i took from that moment on ...
I refused to get in trouble again ...

That sidewalk holds so many tears ...
Tears that fell as I begged for it to just stop.
Tears it captured that flew away as I wiped them hastily so the car pulling over wouldn't see them...

Fake smiles .. fake conversation ... exchange of money as I tell this stranger where to park so he can pay for his pleasure.
Looking around his car just to make sure I have an escape plan ... in case he is like the last one ...

Gripping my mace .. ready to spray ...I wasn't getting raped twice in one night ...
Phew ...
He was normal ...for the most part I guess ...
He even was nice enough to drop me back off at the main street and tip me 60 bucks ...
One step closer to my 1000 I needed ...
to go back to my room and get something to eat
I day dreamed about a hot bath to wash away the dirtiness of this night ...
Oh how that hotel bed seemed like heaven ...
But then it hit me ... the only safe place for me was asleep ... in my dreams ...
Because even after this night was over ... after I washed away the nasty hands ..
iced the bruises
And enjoyed a couple precious hours of sleep ...
When my eyes cracked open ...
I would be right back here the next day ...
Giving more secrets to these streets

## Looking Glass
by Jaimee Johnson

Born into the world with a lens so beautiful
She saw the world as if there were no limits ..

232

Breathtaking...
No fears no questions .. just endless possibilities of good and
kindness
Her lens was vibrant and free
Until she reached the age of three ...
her lens was first shifted as she started to see
That maybe the world wasn't all she thought it could be ...
See her mama met a man ... and decided they were all going to
pick up and go ...
but her mama couldn't wait so three days her and her siblings were
left alone
Till her dad finally found out and came to the rescue ...
but he had no place for them to go so to mama they went once
more ..
a new life began ... and by age 5 the lens was getting even dimmer
...
watching her mama and that man fight every evening before dinner
...
She covered her ears hoping the yelling would stop ...
and it did ... because the rage went from his mouth to his fist ...
and mamas rage fought back ..
it was always a broken and bloody sight ...
the cops always came at the end of every fight....
By age 6 when the police kept taking mama to jail
Because her bruises hadn't surfaced yet but his blood always
prevailed ...
her lens got fogged as he put his fingers inside her ...
and showed her his manly parts she had only seen on her brother
when they innocently shared a bath together ...
but this wasn't innocent ... no this was a bit different ...
his parts were there to hurt her.
By 6 ... that lens turned into a mask ... she made sure to keep on at
all times ...
as time went on ..
she grew weary of her body ... her hair that was red and her,

what she thought were ugly, freckles ...
she did any and everything just to try to
Make friends ...
but by age 12 her lens to the world started to see evil.
She no longer tried to figure out ways to fit in ..
she just kinda... existed…
By age 14, she found that boys paid attention ...
but only to the girls that looked different than her ...
so when a football player came along and flirted a lil ...
she figured the way to show him her love was through sexual
pleasure ...
rumors stirred as people found out she was pregnant ...
15 and a child?
There's no way that can happen ...
so to the clinic she went .. her father by her side ...
as the doctor scraped out her first baby ...
from Deep inside .
Ashamed and confused she continued to seek acceptance
through what she could offer a man ...
so as you can imagine ... not even a year later
Growing inside her was baby #2...
16 years and you can see how experience changes her lens view
This one she kept ... with her boyfriend by her side ...
they stood hand in hand to
Buckle up for this ride ...
raising a baby ... well we know that's not cheap ...
so at 17 she dropped out of
School ...
Worked full time to make sure her and her family could eat ...
life seemed just fine ... the fog on the lens was clearing ...
as she approached 19 ... their second child was stirring ...
marriage was the sure solution ... to a happy ending ...
Oh if only she knew at 19 ... this was only the beginning ...
a year full of what seemed to be bliss ...

every morning started ... and every evening ended ... with a
meaningful kiss
Things started changing though ...
at 20 her and her husband grew apart ...
she couldn't figure out why it was so different than the start ...
an affair was in the air ... she could feel her husband going astray ...
and not far after she found out...
the father of her children and her supposed to be forever husband
...
was in fact gay.
Broken and betrayed ... she could
Barely tell
Left from right ... drowning but focus on her kids
was what she was gasping to try and keep
In
Sight ...
not too long after ... she wanted to go out ... have a little fun ...
since her and the kids had been at home struggling to even keep
The lights on ...
drunk and lonely ... she connected with a man ... little
Did she know ... about his life changing game plan ...
confiding in him ... even giving him her body ...
he knew just how to speak
To her properly ...
Promises of a happy ending ... and stability were back in view ...
but how she had to accomplish that ...
well that truly broke her view ...
As she approached her 21st birthday ...
she was no longer her own ... property of
Pimpin ... his name branded on her skin
Her gift for her birthday ... was her very first rape ...
police brushed it off as a trick who
Got a free "date"
22 and 23 ... her lens got bashed by his angry fists ...

at least she had been prepared for it early when she watched the abuse at age 5&6

The anger hurt less when she popped the pills and snorted coke ... the rapes got easier and the dates got manageable ...

as long as the drugs helped her escape ...

by her mid 20's the lens were so blurred ... she can't even recall a timeline ...

just events ... of the things that brought her to try to pop one pill too Many ...

seems there were other plans

Though ... because alive and back

On those streets ... she found herself till the late 20's

By 26 ... enough had been enough ...

One song on that stage, one private dance too many

One seizure from beatings

One random man's house

One pair of nasty hands

One rape

One abortion

One trauma

Too many

Too many days in jail

Too many hotels

Too many days without her children

Too many drugs

Too much pain

Death or change these were the only options

So she ran ... she ran to find a new lens and pray they were clear so she could

Figure out how to get her life back where it belonged ...

but how?

Would you guess at 26 she is pregnant all

Over again .. but this time was different she felt it in her soul ...

She would reconcile and step in to her most important role ...

a mother and mentor... all while

Healing along the way ...
surely making mistakes ... but never looking back unless
it's to see what she had overcome
Growing and fighting to heal from the cuts of the lens ...
she managed to create a life worth living once again
God told her clear at 27 years old ... your son ... your girls ... this life
is no mistake ...
I'm trusting in you .. as I have seen all you can take ...
Your second chance ... the time is now ... it's now time
Time for
You to show others how
How to overcome
How to live and love
How to forgive
How to break free and speak their truth
How to turn pain to power and how to
Touch another's soul
This my young queen is
Your true purpose and role
So as the fog lifted ... and the cracks in the lens faded ...
she started to see the world in a new light ... no
Longer jaded
This was a familiar place ... she recognized this view
And then she realized God had restored her lens back to
Their original View.

## You Really Wanna Help?
by Jaimee Johnson

I never needed a handout
Or sympathy from someone tryna be a savior
I never needed negativity
Or someone telling me everything I did wasn't in God's favor
I never needed to be judged
Or cast away because I slipped up

I never needed to go from him controlling me
To some program controlling me
I never needed to be bound by rules
Or have my life put in handcuffs
I never needed to be rescued
I never needed to be saved
I never needed pity
Or someone to look at me with shame

What I needed was empowerment
Someone to believe In my potential
I needed to hear that I was worthy
Of all the things they told me I wasn't
I needed freedom to make mistakes
And learn from them in my own time and pace
I needed a safe space to tell the truth
And understand how I had gotten where I had
I needed someone to help me up
When I got to knock on myself down
I needed someone to teach me
Through love and action
I needed someone to look me in the eyes
Without making me feel convicted
I needed a safe place to lay my head
Without worrying if I meet the criteria
I needed someone to hug me in a way that reassured me I was safe
I needed time to breathe, without someone having an expectation
I needed someone to hear me
Not to determine if it was truth
Or acceptable
Or to give me advice or answers
I just need to be heard
I needed to feel encouraged
Respected and included
I needed to be seen for my strength, my intelligence and my heart
I needed to be loved

# Remember?

by Jaimee Johnson

This isn't forever
One day you'll be Queen.
He promised you the world ...
Remember?
He cares...
He saw you struggling with those poor young babies ...
He's gonna make sure you guys are good.
Remember?
He feels your pain.. He listens to your words.
He would never hurt you.
He promised, remember?
He's gonna help...
Help you reach your dreams ...
Help you forget the pain of the past...
Help you accomplish your dreams.
He's gonna be your one and only.
Your only friend.
Your only love.
The only one you see.
He's gonna be your King.
Remember?
He's gonna make you guys a family ...
Even though the kids aren't his ...
he loves you enough to love them too.
Remember?
He's gonna treat you better than any other ever has.
He's gonna show you love you have never seen before ...
He would never hurt you.
Remember?

I guess I forgot ... the first time he beat me.
But he reminded me of his original promises...
with a fresh set of nails and a meal at red lobster.

I was In heaven ...
the pain from
His fists faded Away quickly when He gave me all his attention.
Especially when he helped me remember why he HAD to hit me…
"I just want you to be the best ... you are different than the others ..I
need you on point ... don't MAKE me do it again , okay? I love you."
That's right ... He did it because he cares.
Now I remember.


I understood when he couldn't keep all his initial promises ...
like clothes for my kids..
Or money for our rent.
It's okay ... I understood. He needed that Cadillac ... he had
important things to do.
And you can't have a Cadillac without rims and bangin system...
right??
He needed the drugs ... so he could stay up and protect me while I
walked the streets to make money for "us"
Right?
He must have just been doing something really important that time
that date went bad and the trick raped me and stabbed me and took
all my money ...
And he only beat me right after to remind me not to be so stupid
because I had to care as much as Him about "our money"....
"Never get robbed again. By any means"
Good lesson he taught me ..
Because he cares ...
Right?
Our money.
Our dreams.
Our money.

Wait. It's getting real hard to remember.
When did our money turn to his money?

Why was I sleeping with 10 nasty men a day just to be told we can't afford a "number whatever" when we finally hit the drive through at mcdonalds after 14 hours of "working"?
Why was I in fear of not making my quota everyday ...
Just to be told I can't buy my kids a $10 toy?

Something wasn't right.
Something's a bit off.

My bruises won't fade because he keeps making new ones.
My family is gone because he said they were no good.
My insides are sore, my jaw is swollen shut from all the dates that I've turned,
My days have no end ... they are all just a huge blur.
My home is a hotel room ...
My only conversation is about a financial exchange

He's growing greater while I deteriorate to nothing.

My minds gone.
My spirit is weak.
My flesh is sick.
My body hurts.
My soul is gone.

The promises he made when we first met ... I try to hold on to them
...
I swear to do.
Why can't I remember??
They are so far gone I Just can't remember.
When did it become this ...
When did it all change?
The promises he made.
Does HE even remember??

Why didn't anyone tell me this was the outcome of the game?

## Truth #1: If I felt I could have, I would have done something else.
by Jaimee Johnson

—

A reason I'm so big on breaking stigmas is because I remember trying to leave the life at least 7 times - Over the course of 6 years. The first time was about 7 months into the game ... I remember already being so lost In who I was and hating my daily routine. I tried to leave. I even went home and told my family what had been going on. Unfortunately I didn't know there was much more to it then just leaving. I didn't realize how difficult it would be to function every day with the PTSD I had developed along with ongoing depression that had already existed and only gotten worse with my experience in the game. I didn't realize how hard it would be to find a steady job with prostitution on my record to mention forgetting how to be disciplined enough to get up and go to work every day when I had just spent every day the last 7 months up all night and hustling all day. I didn't realize how difficult it would be to deal with my family criticizing or not understanding my experiences. I didn't realize how difficult it would be to break the bond I had with my ex pimp. I didn't realize how diminished my self worth had become and how unworthy I felt. I didn't realize how out of place I would feel walking among who used to be my peers and dealing with breaking the habits and normalities I had formed (like not making eye contact with people, not talking to a certain race of men, lack of social skills that my friends didn't really understand). As much as I didn't love doing what I did in the game , I felt comfortable there. I felt accepted. I felt like I was finally good for something.

—

No one was really offering me any options at that time. I felt like my self worth had completely diminished and I had no drive to  or even idea what I would do outside of hoin. I had taken on the persona of a prostitute and I wasn't able to easily break that. At this point i was not really aware there were alternate options after what I had allowed myself to become.

—

I was not engaged in any support services or systems to try to transition or understand what I had just dealt with. I was just kinda stumbling in the dark trying to find my way which led me to feeling frustrated and triggered which ultimately led me right back to the game.

—

Sometimes the most helpful thing we can do for those entrapped In the Streets — is offer hope. Offer options. Offer opportunities. Empower the dreams and passions buried deep down in those living the hustle and reignite a flame in them to want different. Defining them by who they are not what they have done. Breaking down the stigmas that lie in your own heart and mind about those impacted by the game. Reminding them that they are valuable, loved and powerful beyond measure is a huge step in how we end this issue.

## Truth #2: Just Leave
by Jaimee Johnson

People used to always tell me — JUST LEAVE.  Everyone always was trying to tell me how horrible my pimp was —- how he needed to rot in hell. How he needed to die. And I won't lie — there was a point in my experience — actually a few — that I agreed. I hated him — but loved him at the same time. I condemned him ... I talked badly about him and the horrible things he did or was he treated me — and I allowed myself to justify the fact that I had done almost the exact same thing to other women and girls on the fact I was traumatized or being "forced" when in actuality ... I was not Much different than him.

As obvious as it may seem that he didn't love me  ... in my eyes I knew different. It may have not been loved based on what other normal view of love was ... but for someone who has a twisted and misconstrued view of love from a very young age ... In my world ... we were in love. I would do anything for him ... I had loyalty to him. I had trust in him. I had a friend in him. I laughed with him. I fought with him but I also fought for him. I had his back. I have him everything in me I possibly had. I had faith in him, in our future. To me — it felt like love. And although we had our bad times .. although there was abuse and it wasn't a traditional relationship — he protected me. He gave me advice. He listened to me. He took care of me. He taught me things. He cared about me to the best of his ability in my

Mind. To me — it was love. From the outside it seems crazy ... but in our lifestyle , in our world — it made sense. So when people said , JUST LEAVE. They weren't only not thinking of all the obstacles I would face when trying to transition my life —- they also didn't realize they were asking me to leave a man I depended on greatly, a man I had become co dependent on, a man I had given so much that I couldn't see myself living without him. They didn't understand the trauma bond I had developed, they didn't understand even a small inkling of the many aspects this life contained.

On top of that, I felt I was damaged goods. Who would love a ho besides a pimp. Who would want me after all the things I had done? Who would understand, who would care about my well being? Who would love me? Why would I wanna start over with anyone who would judge me or leave me once they found out who I was?

People have to think ... often times people who get into the game .. do it because they are seeking something. There's a vulnerability that exists .. there's some type of void they need filled whether it be physical, emotional, financial or mental. So when someone comes into your life, especially in a vulnerable time, and offers to fill those voids...most normal human beings would easily fall into a relationship with that person and become attached.

Not to mention , often times those who get into the game have already experienced many traumas already so when a new

244

opportunity comes along as well as someone to make them feel loved and accepted ... the act of sex for money doesn't seem like the worst option when it's in exchange for needs being met, a relationship,love, protection, companionship and loyalty.

We can't expect others minds or perspectives to be the same as ours. We can't expect people to think about what we think is acceptable is acceptable to them and what's unacceptable to us is unacceptable to them. We are unique individuals all with a diverse spectrum of experience, needs, perspectives, traumas and desires. For us to tell someone what they should be doing or shouldn't be doing without ever stepping a moment in their shoes, is a huge reason issues like exploitation continue.

Nothing or no one could have convinced me to leave a person I felt loyalty and love too. I had to get to a place that I wasn't happy within myself, I had to understand that what was going on wasn't the love I desired. I had to want to be in a different situation for myself, not for anyone else.

My point being, talking badly about someone's partner ... boyfriend, husband, pimp, wife, abuser, trafficker, whatever you wanna call it .. won't ever get you anywhere. The focus should never be on how bad the other person is. The focus should always be on the individual you are trying to support and opening up hope for other opportunities.

## Truth #3
by Jaimee Johnson

To be honest, i don't identify as a survivor of human trafficking for many reasons. But a huge one is that when I first got into the "anti trafficking" world ... I was basically being fed and forced a narrative that someone else wanted me to embrace. Certain narratives and certain ways of sharing my experience were "encouraged" to me .. and it wasn't my full truth. At least not the way I would have shared it. When i started to realize this and speak out and share my actual truth .. I started getting a lot of backlash but equally the same amount of respect as well.

When I got in the game, it didn't take long for me to find my identity in my hoin. It didn't take me long to find out I was good at what I was doing. It didn't take long for me to want my pimp to be proud of me. It didn't take me long to realize I could use my words and body to touch as much money as I desired. It didn't take me long to conform into a ho, a prostitute.

The thing people fail to realize is the reason a lot of people can't grasp the concept of "force, fraud and coercion" is because we often seem we are enjoying the life we are living and the truth is, often times we do. At least in that moment, in that mind frame — or at least we convince ourselves we do. The very first date I turned on El Cajon Blvd, changed me forever. Something inside me wasn't the same. I wasn't innocent and could never be again. I had no idea at that time but every date I turned — which was a lot— added a new layer of ice to my heart. I wasn't me anymore.

I was no longer Jaimee. I was Chanel Love. A bad ass white bitch that could break a trick quick and get my folks a rack in a few hours. I started taking pride in this. I started flaunting my sexiness. I started embracing my hoin. I started to love my pimp bragging about me and how much i could make. I started loving sitting in the front seat of the car next to my folks because I had made him proud. I loved when he called me his snow bunny. I started loving the attention, no one had ever paid attention this way. I started finding my value in the amount of money I could make every day. And I started believing myself when I shouted out to the world "Down for my Daddy." "All on a bitch" and "daddys bottom" I was all about it. So of course it looked like I enjoyed it. Because In that moment, in those times, looking back. In order to survive I had to learn to love what my life had become. And if I was gonna do anything, why not be the best. At least I was finally good at something. At least the people around me finally accepted me. At least I felt like I finally had a place.

## Truth #4: I Was a Pimp
by Jaimee Johnson

You read that right. I was a pimp. I get a lot of backlash and hate for my opinion and outlook on wanting to Be all Inclusive in the work I do (meaning involving the sex buyer and the pimp) I get a lot of disrespect behind the fact that I value their voices and believe they need to be treated as humans who Need rehabilitation and support and are victims of vulnerabilities just as much as a woman or man who is exploited. Unpopular opinion ... I have many of those ... but let me break it down to you.

I pimped on girl. I turned girls out. I beat girls up. I robbed girls. I tricked girls. I even watched a girl get raped in front of me and didn't stop it. I did almost everything my pimps did to me at some point or another to someone else. Most people will give me a free pass because I was "being forced" and "just surviving" so let's talk about about that. I was abused and became an abuser. Period. Whether that was because I was in survival mode or not —- doesn't take away the pain I caused. I live with that every single day. I hold guilt and shame for that. I get pained thinking of the women I introduced into this game.

But for a minute let's say it was strictly because I was in survival mode. If we pay attention to a huge percentage of those that pimp ... at least in domestic sex trafficking culture ... we will find that when you break it down ... many of them were in survival mode themselves. Many have been given a short list of options (we have to be realistic in what our country is built on and how segregated and oppressed many populations are) ... minorities and lovers stricken areas aren't given the same opportunities or even education on opportunities that others are ... often times many young people are being fed this normalizing imagery of pimps hos,

247

blowing money, slangin drugs and gangbangin. Many young people aren't even presented with options or opportunities until they get into trouble or are considered "troubled youth" many kids are raising themselves, or being raised by the streets or their peers who are also being raised under the same means. On top of the fact that humanity has died and so many people from such a young age are being abused, brought up on addiction and living in a community of crime, violence and poverty. It's easy for us to say "everyone has the same opportunity" but let's be real — marginalization, racism and oppression exists and thrive in our country. So do people REALLY have the same opportunities? We perpetuate this violent glamorization, pimp culture glamorization, boys will be boys/ rape culture and prom culture normalization, as well as lack of love support and resources and then act surprised when people become the things we perpetuate in our every day lives.

So if a young man, has all these odds stacked against him by the age of 14,15,16. Racism, poverty, addiction, legal issues, lack of education, homelessness, lack of support, lack of parenting, constant cycles of normalizing drugs, violence,money and sex — topping it off with abuse of any kind and a toxic masculinity culture... What route do we honestly expect a person to take. Now this isn't to JUSTIFY anyone's abuse or actions in wrong. This is to wake up and open our eyes to the fact that all of the things that drive violence .. pain... crime ... abuse ... etc —- all have something in common. ROOT ISSUES. And similar root issues at that.

If that same young man, was actually looked at as a human with all his outside circumstances he lives daily with ... would he not be considered in survival mode? Is he not just finding a route that works for him to get out of his current situation or make the burden and difficulty less than it is? Is he not truly a victim of our toxic nation and everything that holds us in captivity?

If you break it down ... does it really differ much from the things I did in survival mode? Does it differ from me doing any and everything to make it though my day? Does it differ from me feeling like I had no other choices?

In my mind ... it's all very similar. In my mind it reassures my perspective that we all need and deserve healing. It reassures my perspective that we MUST pay attention and take it all the way back to hold ourselves accountable in our parts in where our nation and world and communities are at this point. It reassures that we MUST give those who abuse and violate a chance to heal and understand how they got to where they are. It reassures me that we MUST stop labeling and start humanizing.

Because if I deserve forgiveness, resources, love, grace, opportunity, healing, understanding ... so does every single person that exists next to me, in front of me, behind me and around me.

## Voice of Britney C.

To my knowledge, my mom and my brother don't know. I've never opened up to them or anything like that. My godparents have caught me on the track, but never have I talked to them about it. Not with my blood brother or my pink booty mother. The only stories my brother has heard was when the hater phony Kim felt like she wanted to call and tell him. When he heard he cut me off and for a long ass time.

Ooook, you (Armand) say pick a story, any story. Well bro this is one big ass story with so many chapters in it. So hard to just pick. You got my mind racing but I'm going to tell. I'm going to tell the story the first time I hit the triznac, aka the blade!!! Yeah I grew up for the longest on Whitman Street. We'd catch the bus to Lemon Grove Middle School . I seen them stomping down early mornings getting on the bus sometimes but had no idea and knew nothing about these bitches on the other side of the street walking down the street to holla for a dollar. I was introduced to this man cuz that's what he is first and foremost, but I had no idea what really was going on. All I knew was my homegirls took me to meet this guy. He wasn't balling. Matter of fact I met him in his cousins bucket of a car when he pulled up on us in North Park but I couldn't get him out my mind cuz his personality. Shit the friendship that we begin to acquire was something totally different and just hella cool. I called him one night. He was like "What you doing? Pull up." He said he was thinking about me earlier but had to get to his business and then he was like "My nigga I need you to get me a room for this bitch." My ass was like "Oh sure no problem. I'm in El Cajon bitty at my mom house". He said "Meet me at the Travelodge, naw nevermind I'm coming to get you. I'm down the street." He pulls up to go get this bitch a room. A girl who is still my friend to this day. She's my day one. I started inquiring about the game. I was intrigued and it wasn't long before I stepped out there. It was not that night we hung out but two nights later though, I started walking. I never thought I would ever in life but there I was ten toes down and ready to go full fledge on a track. Damn I'm lying that was the second time I hit the track. The first time I hit the track it was the first real experience of walking a track cuz I started out with somebody I knew. The first time I was sat down the police stopped me and told me I'm going to end up on drugs. They told me I look too clean to be on the streets get out of there. This was El Cajon Boulevard on a back street somewhere. Damn. To think that I only did this because I wanted to be with the person I went to El Cajon City High School with.

El Cajon City! My mom lives out there. For some reason I didn't think nothing of it. Not really because I didn't care but more because me and my mom were never close like that and she was in the streets her damn self. So I started walking El Cajon City. I was nervous as hell didn't know what to do or what to say but I did it and it damn near felt good. Now that I think about it, why did it feel good? I don't know. It was just weird. It just felt really good to go get this money. For him, for us, for the cause, right? That's what He told me anyways. Reality super kicked in when I hopped out of at tricks car to go in the 7-Eleven to buy some more condoms and sneak me a beer to chug down. That's when I say that my pink booty mother was coming in 7-Eleven. I ducked my head and did everything I could to run up out the store with the condoms and my beer. I passed the trick like oh well, he don't have to find me again. That night I was ducking on Corners cuz I just knew my mom saw me and I already had the tricks money. In my mind, I'm like fuck it. I already got his money and got me some condoms. Let me call p to come pick me up cuz I got to go. It wasn't an issue but when I saw his face for some reason when he came to pick me up, I said nevermind. I don't want to go. I want to stay on the track. I got to get this bread. Mind you, I wouldn't go around having sex like that at all. I might have had sex a total of maybe 10 times. Damn I was a fresh 18 when I started in this here game. Walking the track. I used to think if a bitch ain't walking on the track she wasn't shit! She was a faggot! In reality on the track I was always nervous until I caught my first trick and then it was like stompdown! If I could take it all back… The experiences, the drama, the track life. Would I? Yes and no.

## Outcall
by Erikka Thorpe

Here I go once more
blindfolded, not knowing what's in store
I close my eyes and breathe deep
I gain my composure so that I can leave
sometimes I drive in silence so that I can think
other times I blast the stereo to drown this misery
if you look at the whole picture, it's not as bad as it seems
It's just a job and the money will help me achieve my dreams
I try not to think of the roads I've chosen to take
but better the destination to which one day I will awake
this is what keeps me striving everyday
the thought that when I have children they will have food in their tummies,
a clean place to lay

# Pricetag
by Erikka Thorpe

There's a price on my body, A price on my mind
Selling myself and selling my time
Self-propertization, self-exploitation, it all takes its toll
It hurts to know there's a small fee to pay for a piece of my soul!

## "Healing Hands: A Sex Surrogate Helps Men Get Over Their Sexual Dysfunction by Getting Into Bed with Them. Is This Medicine or Just Plain Old-fashioned Prostitution Served with a Spoonful of Love?"
by Amy Sohn  and Erikka Thorpe

Rita Bell is a sex surrogate; men pay her to have sex with them. It's a form of therapy to help them with various sexual problems. Some men come to her with erectile dysfunction, premature ejaculation or fetishes they feel uncomfortable discussing with their partners. Mrs. Bell says, "There is a difference between her work and that of a prostitute." She talks with her clients extensively about their dysfunctions. Although she advertises the same places as prostitutes do, she finds it important that people do not mistake her for s sex-worker. She "is a doctor" she says, "Surrogacy is much more cerebral than prostitution. I have to figure out what the underlying issues are." She continues, "These people don't want to sit and talk, they want to get busy in the bedroom. If you're good at this and you are successful - which are not necessarily related - you have to be pretty smart." When asked how a typical session with her goes, she begins: "The patient comes in and we begin talking in the living room. I ask about his relationships, his attitudes towards sex when he was a child, his first sexual experience, whether he is on antidepressants."

Mrs. Bell then describes how she "sets the mood by lighting candles, turning on some smooth music and takes it slow, being sure to highlight the sensuality of foreplay often running her fingers, a feather, or a piece of silk across the man's body." She explains that her first session with a particular client tends to be less intense, but after that, she allows the client to set the pace. Some things that stood out to me in this article were Mrs. Bell saying that she enjoyed the intimacy and the feeling of being helpful in a profound way. "Sex was fun," she said. She didn't want to discuss her rates with Amy Sohn but she did mention that it compares to "that of a therapist." When asked if she had ever had an orgasm during a session, she hesitated then said, "Occasionally, most men like it, they feel more competent when she orgasms."

In class we discussed "sex and money." I felt awkward because I felt the lecture and the comments made by students in class were biased. There is very little information about sex workers that is not second (if not third) hand. Many sex workers are seen to do what they do because they are forced into it, or because they are addicted to drugs. Few are seen as respectable, intellectual beings. I feel that in researching a topic, especially one so controversial, the researcher should seek out sources to present both sides of the argument. I don't believe Amy Sohn, the author of this article, intended for this article to be biased and discriminatory, as it is an interview. However, I do believe Mrs. Bell's opinions regarding sex work was biased and elitist. She held very negative views and spoke harshly of sex workers, otherizing them in order to differentiate her work from theirs.

I decided to do some extensive research into the sex industry, from exotic dancing, porn, and escorting. I interviewed a close friend for this class assignment. She began by telling me "providers offer different types of services, some are full service, some are fetish-specific." Most of her sessions began with her getting to know her clients. She continues, "We talk about what he does for a living, how he likes his job, whether or not he is married, what he likes to do for fun, sometimes we talk about politics, sports, education, music, books, stressors and more." She explains that her first session is more about getting to understand the client's specific needs and so therefore is a little "less intense." I asked what the other sessions would typically look like and she continued, "at some point once we have established boundaries and a mutual understanding, much of the session, I leave up to the client's discretion with the exception of a few "hard limits," some clients want to simply cuddle and talk, some need to be caressed and wooed, others just want to relieve their stress or supplement intimacy lacking at home." I was curious about the type of client that she sees so I asked her what a typical client does, she responded with, "I have seen doctors, lawyers, teachers, students, yoga instructors, police officers, fire fighters, hockey coaches, military, pizza delivery guys, IT analysts, dentists, Dope Boy's, pimps, business consultants and many more… some have sexual problems like getting it up, coming too fast, or fetishes, others experience a fear of rejection, fear of commitment, or just from a need for attention or appreciation, some men's wives neglect their sexual needs, some have no time for relationships because they work themselves to death, some just enjoy the occasional escape from reality." After hearing her describe the services she provides in that way, I felt compelled to read her the article by Amy Sohn.

After reading her article about sexual surrogacy, my friend laughed and said that she should change her title to sexual surrogate. She also mentioned that she was offended by Mrs. Bell's statements about sex workers lacking the cerebral capacity. "Many sex workers," she says in rebuttal, "myself included, are students, we pay our way through college or start our own businesses or invest our money, and contrary to Mrs. Bell's beliefs, I help most of my clients with different problems, it really matters to me that the client see some relief or progress regarding their dis-ease." In concluding the interview, and to contrast the remarks made by Mrs. Bell, I asked whether or not my friend had ever orgasmed during a session, she paused, then replied, "occasionally, and sometimes I fake it, it makes most men feel more competent, more confident."

There is virtually no difference between what a sexual surrogate does and what a prostitute does, other than a few years of education, and a degree, if that. Something I feel is important to mention is that many women of color are arrested and charged with various prostitution charges, while predominantly white women continue to find ways to maneuver the system working in brothels and cat-houses, porn actresses, strippers, sexual surrogates and sex therapists that use cognitive-behavioral therapy methods such as the start and stop method (a form of therapy that works by orgasm or semen retention for men suffering from premature ejaculation) and exposure therapy (which works by gradually exposing the client to specific stimuli in order to reduce anxiety associated with that stimuli). Aside from the ability to prescribe psychoactive stimulants or vasocongestion medications, aside from using specific medical terminology and the level of education received, what factors determine which form of sex work to privilege and which to criminalized?

# Bibliography

Alk, Howard, director. *The Murder of Fred Hampton*. Facets Multi-Media Chicago Film Group, MGA Inc., 1971.

Grant, Melissa. *Playing the Whore*. Verso, 2014.

Hendricks, LaVelle, and Angie Wilson. "The Impact of Crack Cocaine on Black America." *National Forum Journal of Counseling and Addiction*, vol. 2, no. 1, 2013.

Jackson, Kenneth T., editor. *The Encyclopedia of New York City: Second Edition*. Yale University Press, 201"Life as a Hooker." *Ken Magazine*, 1938.

"Life as a Hooker." *Ken Magazine*, 1938.

Nelson, Stanley, director. *The Black Panthers: Vanguard of the Revolution*. Firelight Films, 2015.

Rosen, Ruth. *The Lost Sisterhood: Prostitution in America, 1900-1918*. Johns Hopkins University Press, 1982.

"The XY Factor/Sex in the City." Season 1, episode 2, The History Channel, 2001.

Wright, George C. *A History of Blacks in Kentucky. Vol. 2: In Pursuit of Equality, 1890-1980* . Kentucky Historical Society, 1992.

# Glossary of Terms

**Blade** – The name of the outside street area where prostitution is conducted (also known as a **Track** or **Hoe Stroll**).

**Bloods** – Primarily, though not exclusively, an African-American street gang founded in Los Angeles, California. They are identified by the red color worn by their members and by particular gang symbols, including distinctive hand signs.

**Blow up** – When a prostitute leaves a pimp to work for another pimp, to work independently, or has left the lifestyle completely.

**Bottom Bitch** – The main or lead prostitute in a pimp's crew or stable.

**Brothel** – A house where men can buy sex from prostitutes.

**Buyer** – The person who purchases services from a prostitute or other form of sex worker (also known as a **John** or a **Trick**).

**Choose** – When a woman decides to be with and work with a certain pimp.

**Choosing fee** – The amount of money that a pimp requires for a woman to work with him.

**Clique/Click** – A small group of people with shared interests or other features in common, who spend time together and do not readily allow others to join them. They can be a direct split from the gang or totally independent. Often a clique can be mistaken for a gang due to their extremely similar mannerisms and behaviors.

**Commercial sex** – Using sexual behavior for making (or intending to make) a profit.

**Crips** – A primarily African-American gang. They were founded in Los Angeles, California in 1969. These members traditionally wear blue clothing.

**Cuz** – A name used by the Crip gang and affiliates to address one another

**Dog** – A name used by the Crip gang and affiliates to address one another.

**Domestic human sex trafficking** – The subculture of pimping and prostitution here in the U.S. This form of sex trafficking is usually birthed out of many impoverished communities throughout the U.S. This form usually pertains to minority men that facilitate, and woman (of varying demographics) that become prostitutes.

**Escort** – a woman who may be hired to accompany a Buyer to a social event, private meetup, hotel room or other location. An escort can provide anything from a conversation to sexual intercourse for a Buyer.

**Exotic dancer** – Also known as a "stripper." A woman who performs erotic dances, usually in an adult strip club.

**Folks** – Another word for Pimp used by those involved in the pimp and prostitution subculture.

**Gang** – A small group of people with shared interests or other features in common, who spend time together and do not readily allow others to join them.

**Gang banger** – Also referred to as an "active" gang member. A person that is on the streets representing the gang. Typically involved in activities such as shootings, robberies, holding weapons, drug dealing, and fighting opposing gang members on the streets for the gang.

**Gangbanging** – The activity of an urban street gang member participating in a gang.

**Gangster rap** – A sub-genre of hip hop music that is based on lyrics describing gang activity. Usually extremely violent in content.

**Gangsterism** – A distinctive practice, system, or philosophy of a gang member.

**Gang documentation** – A system set up by the California state organization Cal Gangs to track and prosecute impoverished men of color.

**Gang injunctions** – A type of restraining order issued by U.S. courts that prohibit assumed gang members from participating in certain activities. This includes being around other assumed gang members.

**Gentleman of Leisure** – Another name for a pimp.

**Grooming** – The action by an individual in preparing another for a pimping, exploitation, or prostitution lifestyle.

**Hoe** – A street slang term for a prostitute

**Hoe stroll** – The name of the street area where prostitution is conducted (also known as the **Track** or **Blade**).

**Hood** – An impoverished inner-city neighborhood.

**Hound** – A name used by the Blood gang and affiliates to address one another.

**Human sex trafficking** – the use of force, fraud, or coercion to get someone to sell sex in exchange for something of value.

**Hungry** – A word describing desires turned into action in the pursuit of financial gain. For example, someone can be "money hungry."

**Hustle** – The manner in which an individual earns their money, whether legally or illegally.

**Inner-city** – The impoverished neighborhoods within a larger city. Usually inhabited by people of color.

**John** – A person who purchases services from a prostitute or other form of sex worker.

**Lady of Leisure** – Another term for a sex worker or prostitute.

**Loc** – A name used by the Crip gang and affiliates to address one another.

**Mac** – Sometimes used generally as another word for a pimp, but it can also be used to describe a certain type of pimp. Mac's typically make their money off of prostitution, but will entertain other methods of gaining finances.

**Madam** – A female pimp usually operating brothels.

**Nutty's** – The San Diego, California community of North Park (before it was gentrified).

**Pandering** – To gratify or indulge an immoral or distasteful desire, need, or habit, or a person with such a desire.

**Pimp** – A man who utilizes prostitutes as a means to make money. A pimp takes 100% of the profits earned by his women.

**Pimp God** – A superhuman being or spirit worshiped as having power over the pimping and prostitution subculture; a deity.

**Pimping** – The act of a man making money off the sexual exploitation of a prostitute.

**Pimp rap** – A Hip Hop music sub-genre focusing almost exclusively on pimping and prostitution. Emerged widely in the late 1990's.

**Pimptress** – A woman who utilizes prostitution as a means to make money. A pimp takes 100% of the profits earned by her women.

**Prostitute** – A person, typically a woman, who engages in sexual activity for payment.

**Real pimp** – A "real" pimp makes his entire living off of the earnings of a prostitute. They tend to follow all of the unwritten rules and regulations of the pimp game that have been passed down for decades.

**Renegade** – A prostitute who is involved in sex work without a pimp.

**Ru** – A name used by the Piru Blood gang to address one another.

**Sentencing enhancements** – Additional time added to a court sentence. Usually enhancements come from being a documented gang member or for prior convictions.

**Set** – Another word for a gang-controlled area.

**Sexual exploitation** – The action or fact of treating someone unfairly in order to benefit from their sex work. Making use of a situation to gain unfair advantage for oneself.

**Square** – Anybody not involved in the pimp and prostitution subculture is viewed as a "square."

**Survivor** – A woman that has been prostituted and has transitioned out of the pimp and prostitution subculture.

**The Game** – The pimp and prostitution subculture.

**The Life/Lifestyle** – The pimp and prostitution subculture.

**Tools** – People, businesses, nice cars, fancy clothes, jewelry, and money, or anything used by a pimp to impress and recruit prostitutes.

**Track** – The name of the outside street area where prostitution is conducted (also known as the **Blade** or **Hoe Stroll**).

**Trap** – The earnings of a pimp or prostitute from work.

**Trick** – A person who purchases services from a prostitute or other form of sex worker (also known as a **Buyer** or **John**).

**Turnout** – A male or female entering into the pimp and prostitution subculture for the first time.

**Webcam girl** – A woman who engages in sexual activity on the internet for payment.

**Working girl** – A woman who engages in sexual activity for payment.

**Order this book in bulk!**
100+ copies · $25
500+ copies · $20
1,000+ copies · $15
5,000+ copies · $10

**Speaking engagements, trainings, and consultations**
Armand King has conducted speaking engagements and trainings for universities, medical professionals, law enforcement, survivor advocates and many more. Educating thousands on many topics surrounding the complexities of human sex trafficking. He has also consulted on both State and Federal Court cases for attorneys. His perspective and lived experience is not readily available and is truly needed in the fight to understand and combat human sex trafficking issues. If you would like to book him for any upcoming event please contact his management today.

**Ask questions or follow Armand King online:**
Facebook: Armand King
Instagram: mr.armand_king
Twitter: @MrArmandKing
LinkedIn: Armand King

**For bulk book orders, speaking engagements, or training use the following contact information:**
Email: info@armandking
Phone: 858.997.7690

Made in the USA
San Bernardino,
CA